Cancún & the Yucatán For Dummies, 1st Edition

D1531802

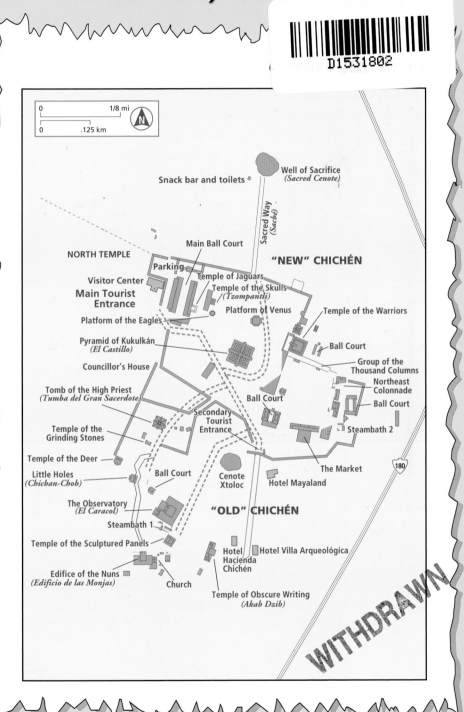

| 0 | | 1/8 mi |
| 0 | | .125 km |

N

Well of Sacrifice
(Sacred Cenote)

Snack bar and toilets

Sacred Way
(Sacbé)

NORTH TEMPLE

Main Ball Court

Parking

"NEW" CHICHÉN

Visitor Center
Main Tourist Entrance

Temple of Jaguars
Temple of the Skulls
(Tzompantli)

Platform of Venus

Temple of the Warriors

Platform of the Eagles

Pyramid of Kukulkán
(El Castillo)

Ball Court

Councillor's House

Group of the Thousand Columns

Tomb of the High Priest
(Tumba del Gran Sacerdote)

Ball Court

Northeast Colonnade

Ball Court

Temple of the Grinding Stones

Secondary Tourist Entrance

Steambath 2

Temple of the Deer

Little Holes
(Chichan-Chob)

Ball Court

Cenote Xtoloc

Hotel Mayaland

The Market

180

The Observatory
(El Caracol)

"OLD" CHICHÉN

Steambath 1

Temple of the Sculptured Panels

Hotel Hacienda Chichén

Hotel Villa Arqueológica

Edifice of the Nuns
(Edificio de las Monjas)

Church

Temple of Obscure Writing
(Akab Dzib)

For Dummies: Bestselling Book Series for Beginners

Cancún & the Yucatán For Dummies, 1st Edition

Cheat Sheet

Mileage Chart: Distances in the Yucatán[1]

	Akumal	Cancún	Chichén-Itzá	Cobá	Cozumel[2]	Isla Mujeres[2]	Playa del Carmen	Puerto Morelos	Puerto Aventuras	Tulum	Xcaret	Xel-ha	Xpu-ha
Akumal	*												
Cancún	105km/65mi	*											
Chichén-Itzá	175km/109mi (via Cobá)	178km/110mi	*										
Cobá	70km/44mi	143km/89mi (via Nuevo Xcán)	110km/68mi	*									
Cozumel[2]	55km/34mi	72km/45mi	238km/148mi	123km/76mi	*								
Isla Mujeres[2]	115km/71mi	5km/3mi	188km/117mi	153km/95mi (via Nuevo Xcán)	58km/36mi	*							
Playa del Carmen	37km/23mi	68km/42mi	220km/136mi	105km/65mi	18km/11mi	78km/48mi	*						
Puerto Morelos	69km/43mi	36km/22mi	194km/120mi	137km/85mi	30km/19mi	46km/29mi	32km/20mi	*					
Puerto Aventuras	7km/4mi	87km/54mi	245km/152mi	88km/55mi	37km/23mi	97km/60mi	25km/16mi	58km/36mi	*				
Tulum	26km/16mi	131km/81mi	154km/95mi (via Cobá)	44km/27mi	81km/50mi	141km/87mi	63km/39mi	95km/59mi	44km/27mi	*			
Xcaret	33km/21mi	74km/46mi	225km/140mi	101km/63mi	24km/15mi	84km/52mi	6km/3.7mi	38km/24mi	22km/14mi	59km/37mi	*		
Xel-ha	17km/11mi	122km/76mi	162km/100mi (via Cobá)	51km/32mi	72km/45mi	132km/82mi	54km/33mi	87km/54mi	35km/22mi	9km/5.6mi	50km/31mi	*	
Xpu-ha	4km/2.5mi	101km/63mi	179km/111mi (via Cobá)	72km/45mi	51km/32mi	106km/66mi	33km/21mi	65km/40mi	3km/1.9mi	30km/19mi	18km/11mi	21km/13mi	*

[1] Distances given in kilometers/miles
[2] Both Cozumel and Isla Mujeres are islands; travel by boat is required.

For Dummies: Bestselling Book Series for Beginners

Cancún & the Yucatán

FOR

DUMMIES®

1ST EDITION

by Lynne Bairstow and
David Baird

WILEY

Wiley Publishing, Inc.

Cancún & the Yucatán For Dummies®, 1st Edition

Published by
Wiley Publishing, Inc.
909 Third Avenue
New York, NY 10022
www.wiley.com

Copyright © 2003 by Wiley Publishing, Inc., Indianapolis, Indiana

Published simultaneously in Canada

For general information on our other products and services or to obtain technical support, please contact our Customer Care Department within the U.S. at 800-762-2974, outside the U.S. at 317-572-3993, or fax 317-572-4002.

Wiley also publishes its books in a variety of electronic formats. Some content that appears in print may not be available in electronic books.

Library of Congress Control Number: 2003101840

ISBN: 0-7645-2437-2

ISSN: 1541-6348

Manufactured in the United States of America

10 9 8 7 6 5 4 3

WILEY   is a trademark of Wiley Publishing, Inc.

About the Authors

For **Lynne Bairstow** (who wrote Chapters 1 through 12, 16 through 18, and Appendixes A and B), Mexico has become more home to her than her native United States. After exploring the country and living in Puerto Vallarta for most of the past 12 years, she's developed a true love of Mexico and its complex, colorful culture. Her travel articles on Mexico have been published in *The New York Times, San Francisco Chronicle, Los Angeles Times, Arthur Frommer's Budget Travel*, and *Alaska Airlines Magazine*. In 2000, Lynne was awarded the Pluma de Plata, an honor granted by the Mexican Government to foreign writers, for her work with the Frommer's guide to Mexico.

David Baird (who wrote Chapters 13, 14, and 15) is a writer, editor, and translator who feels uncomfortable writing about himself in the third person (too much like writing his own obituary). Now based in Austin, Texas, he spent years living in various parts of Mexico, Brazil, Peru, and Puerto Rico. But, whenever possible, he manages to get back to the turquoise-blue waters of the Yucatán because he thinks he looks good in that color, and because he's excessively fond of the local cooking.

Dedication

This book is dedicated to my many friends in Mexico who, through sharing their insights, anecdotes, knowledge, and explorations of Mexico, have shared their love of this country. In particular, Carlos, Claudia, and Ricardo have shared with me and have shown me what a magical place Mexico is, and how much more I have to discover and enjoy. — *Lynne Bairstow*

To my brother John, whose sheer willpower overcame my objections and forced me to take that vacation many, many years ago that first brought me to these shores. — *David Baird*

Authors' Acknowledgments

Many thanks to the people who helped me gather the information, tips, and treasures that have made their way into this book. I am especially grateful for the assistance of Claudia Velo, whose tireless work ensured that the information in this book is correct, and for her valuable ideas and contributions. — *Lynne Bairstow*

I would like to acknowledge my indebtedness to the irrepressible Desiré Sanromán, a Cozumeleña who knows her island and befriended me for reasons that are not quite clear (sympathy? pity? concern for the readers I might mislead?). I would also thank that most capable of guides, Claudia Hurtado Valenzuela, who opened the doors of the Riviera Maya to me, and whose views on all matters touristic were well worth hearing. — *David Baird*

Publisher's Acknowledgments

We're proud of this book; please send us your comments through our Dummies online registration form located at *www.dummies.com/register/*.

Some of the people who helped bring this book to market include the following:

Editorial

Editors: Kelly Ewing, Kelly Regan

Cartographer: Nicholas Trotter

Editorial Manager: Michelle Hacker

Senior Photo Editor: Richard Fox

Cover Photos: Front Cover: Grant V. Saint/Getty Images; Back Cover: Cosmo Condina/Getty Images

Cartoons: Rich Tennant, www.the5thwave.com

Production

Project Coordinator: Maridee Ennis

Layout and Graphics: Amanda Carter, Carrie Foster, LeAndra Johnson, Stephanie D. Jumper, Michael Kruzil, Tiffany Muth, Shelley Norris, Barry Offringa, Jacque Schneider, Julie Trippetti

Proofreaders: Dave Faust, Carl Pierce, Angel Perez, TECHBOOKS Production Services

Indexer: TECHBOOKS Production Services

Publishing and Editorial for Consumer Dummies

Diane Graves Steele, Vice President and Publisher, Consumer Dummies

Joyce Pepple, Acquisitions Director, Consumer Dummies

Kristin A. Cocks, Product Development Director, Consumer Dummies

Michael Spring, Vice President and Publisher, Travel

Brice Gosnell, Publishing Director, Travel

Suzanne Jannetta, Editorial Director, Travel

Publishing for Technology Dummies

Andy Cummings, Vice President and Publisher, Dummies Technology/General User

Composition Services

Gerry Fahey, Vice President of Production Services

Debbie Stailey, Director of Composition Services

Contents at a Glance

Maps at a Glance

Table of Contents

Introduction

Mexico's Yucatán peninsula not only offers travelers some of the best beaches in the world, but it also presents a rich, thousand-year-old culture and amazing natural wonders to explore. Whether it's the ancient Mayan pyramids or the Caribbean reef off Cancún and Cozumel, this spectacular coastline is a virtual playground for travelers. In addition to the many natural attractions, the Yucatán's beach resorts have added golf, tennis, diving, and abundant watersports to their lures. But can the rest of your knowledge about this area fit inside a mango seed? For many people, Mexico is both familiar and a mystery, and some opinions of this land are influenced by inaccurate or outdated stereotypes.

How do you sift through the destination choices — and then all the hotel options — without throwing in the beach towel in a daze of confusion? How do you plan a vacation that's perfect for you — not one that simply follows the recommendations of a friend or travel agent? You've come to the right place. This guide rescues you from both information overload and detail deficit — those annoying syndromes that afflict far too many would-be travelers. We give you enough specifics to help you figure out and plan the type of trip you want and steer clear of the type of trip you don't want.

Sure, plenty of other guidebooks cover Mexico and the beach resorts of its popular Yucatán peninsula, but many of them may as well be encyclopedias: They include practically everything you can possibly see and do. When the time comes to decide upon accommodations, attractions, activities, and meals, you have a tough time finding the best options because they're buried in with other mediocre to not-so-hot suggestions.

Cancún & the Yucatán For Dummies, 1st Edition, is a whole new enchilada. In the following pages, we streamline the options, focusing on the high points (and warning you about the low points) of each vacation spot. Because this book covers a specific area and the most traveled-to region among Mexico's beach resorts, it's able to focus in on the most popular (and most exciting) destinations. With the straightforward tips that we offer — how to get there, what to expect when you arrive, where to stay, where to eat, and where to have big fun — arranging your dream vacation can't be easier.

About This Book

You can use this book in three ways:

- **As a trip planner:** Whether you've already decided on Cancún or are still considering your options along the Riviera Maya, this book helps you zero in on the ideal beach resort for you. It guides you through all the necessary steps of making your travel arrangements, from finding the cheapest airfare and considering travel insurance to figuring out a budget and packing like a pro. Chapters are self-contained, so you don't have to read them in order. Just flip to the chapters as you need them.

- **As a beach-resort guide:** Pack this book along with your sunscreen — it will come in just as handy while you're away. Turn to the appropriate destination chapters whenever you need to find the best beaches, a good place to eat, a worthwhile boat cruise, a challenging golf course, the lowdown on a hot nightspot, or tips on any other diversions.

- **For an enjoyable overview:** If you want a feel for Cancún and the other popular beach resorts in Mexico's Yucatán peninsula, read this book from start to finish to get a taste of all the highlights.

Travel information is subject to change at any time — call ahead for confirmation when making your travel plans. Your safety is important to us (and to the publisher), so we encourage you to stay alert and be aware of your surroundings. Keep a close eye on cameras, purses, and wallets — all favorite targets of thieves and pickpockets.

Conventions Used in This Book

Two of us collaborated on this book, but we each cover different destinations in the Yucatán. That's why although we call ourselves "we" in this introduction, in each chapter the "we" turns into "I" — so you get the benefit of our individual opinions. (To find out who wrote which chapters, see our "About the Author" information at the front of the book.)

In this book, we use the Mexican method for providing street addresses. Using this style, the building number comes after the street name, not before it. For example, if a hotel has a building number of 22 and is located on Calle Atocha (Atocha Street), the address is written as Calle Atocha 22. Likewise, in many towns, you often come across an address in which the building has no number. In these cases, the address is written Calle Atocha s/n, where s/n stands for sin número (without number).

In this book, we include reviews of our favorite hotels and restaurants, as well as information about the best attractions within the Yucatán. As we describe each listing, we use abbreviations for commonly accepted credit cards. Here's what those abbreviations stand for:

> **AE** (American Express)
>
> **DC** (Diners Club)
>
> **MC** (MasterCard)
>
> **V** (Visa)

We also include some general pricing information to help you as you decide where to unpack your bags or where to dine on the local cuisine. We use a system of dollar signs (U.S. dollars) to show a range of costs so that you can make quick comparisons.

Prices in this book are quoted only in U.S. dollars. Most hotels in Mexico quote prices in U.S. dollars. So, although the value of the peso continues to fluctuate, such currency fluctuations are unlikely to affect the hotel rates.

Unless we say otherwise, the lodging rates given are for two people spending one night in a standard double room. At the end of each listing, we give prices for both high season — the most popular travel time that runs roughly from Christmas to Easter — and the generally lower-priced summer season (or low season). At the top of the listing, the dollar sign pricing system indicates the high-season rates. Some hotel rates are much higher than others no matter what time of year it is. Don't be too quick to skip an accommodation that seems out of your price range, though. Some rates include breakfast, both breakfast and dinner, or even three meals per day. Other resorts are *all-inclusive*, which means that after you pay for your room, you never have to dip into your pocket again for meals, beverages, tips, taxes, most activities, or transportation to and from the airport. So, although a price tag may seem sky-high at first, you may actually find it affordable upon second glance. The dining rates are for main courses only.

Check out the following table to decipher the dollar signs:

Cost	*Hotel*	*Restaurant*
$	Less than $75	Less than $15
$$	$75–$125	$15–$30
$$$	$125–$175	$30–$50
$$$$	$175–$250	$50 and up
$$$$$	More than $250 per night	

Foolish Assumptions

As we wrote this book, we made some assumptions about you and what your needs may be as a traveler. Here's what we assumed about you:

- ✔ You may be an inexperienced traveler looking for guidance when determining whether to take a trip to Cancún, or one of the other beach resorts of the Yucatán, and how to plan for it.

- ✔ You may be an experienced traveler who hasn't had much time to explore the Yucatán or its beaches and wants expert advice when you finally do get a chance to enjoy some time in the sun.

- ✔ You're not looking for a book that provides all the information available about Mexico or that lists every hotel, restaurant, or attraction available to you. Instead, you're looking for a book that focuses on the places that offer the best or most unique experiences in the beach resorts of the Yucatán.

How This Book Is Organized

We have divided this book into six parts. The chapters within each part cover specific subjects in detail. Skip around as much as you like. You don't have to read this book in any particular order. In fact, think of these pages as a buffet. You can consume whatever you want — and no one cares if you eat the flan for dessert before you have the enchiladas.

For each beach resort, we include a section called Fast Facts. These sections give you handy information that you may need when traveling in Mexico, including phone numbers and addresses to use in an emergency, area hospitals and pharmacies, names of local newspapers and magazines, locations for maps, and more.

Part 1: Getting Started

In this part, we compare and contrast the Yucatán's most popular beach resorts so that you can decide which place best suits your tastes and needs. Sure, they all have gorgeous beaches, but that's where the similarities end. To help you plan a vacation that's tailored to your preferences, this part guides you through the process of figuring out which resort or resorts are best for you.

We also give you a brief overview of local customs, cuisines, and fiestas and celebrations. We take you through the best — and worst — times of year to travel and explain the differences between high season and low season. We also tell you about special holidays that may help you decide when to visit this part of Mexico. We offer some budget-planning tips, and finally, special trip-planning advice for families, singles, gay and lesbian travelers, seniors, and travelers who are physically challenged.

Part II: Ironing Out the Details

This part is where we lay out everything you need to know about making all the arrangements for your trip. We help you decide whether to use a travel agent, a packager, or the Internet. We offer advice on finding the best airfare — and airline — for your destination. Likewise, we explain how to estimate the total cost of your vacation and how to stay within your budget. Finally, we take you through all the ins and outs of other vacation essentials, from getting a passport and considering travel insurance to staying safe and packing like a pro.

Part III: Cancún

Welcome to Mexico's most popular beach resort. This area is a great destination for first-time travelers to Mexico. Why? Because it has all the comforts of home (familiar restaurant and hotel chains along with great shopping) plus easy access to diverse cultural and geographical activities (excursions to the ancient ruins of Tulum, covered in Chapter 15), world-class scuba diving, and plenty of Mexican fiestas. We provide all the details for getting to, eating at, staying in, and playing at all of Cancún's hot spots.

Part IV: Isla Mujeres and Cozumel

Staying on a tropical island is a dream for many, and these two island getaways, not far from Cancún, offer a distinctive, relaxed vacation experience. Though it's actually an older tourist town than its sister across the channel, Isla Mujeres is a decidedly laid-back anecdote to the nonstop activity of Cancún. Cozumel's calling card has always been its myriad water activities, most centered around the famous reef that outlines the southwest coast. If you're looking for a diver's paradise, you can stop and get off the boat at Cozumel!

Part V: Exploring the Yucatán

This region has more to it than the well-known names of Cancún and Cozumel. Further south along the mainland from Cancún, the Riviera Maya provides a stunning stretch of pristine beaches, unique towns, and mega-resorts down to Tulum, in the south. Check out the up-and-coming town of Playa del Carmen, visit one of the ecoparks, or visit some nearby ancient ruins. The area offers plenty for everyone. In this part, we cover all the information you need to travel to and around these areas.

Part VI: The Part of Tens

Every *For Dummies* book has a Part of Tens. In this part, we take a look at the ten most common myths about Mexico, and we share with you our ten favorite uniquely Yucatecan moments.

In the back of the book, we also include two appendixes. One is a Quick Concierge, which contains lots of handy information you may need when traveling in Mexico's Yucatán, like phone numbers and addresses of emergency personnel or area hospitals and pharmacies, contact information for baby sitters, lists of local newspapers and magazines, protocol for sending mail or finding taxis, and more. Check it out when searching for answers to lots of little questions that may come up as you travel. Also included in this appendix is a list of useful toll-free numbers and Web sites, as well as a guide to other sources of information. The second appendix is a helpful table of Spanish words and phrases, along with a section that defines the Yucatán's most popular dishes and drinks.

You also can find worksheets to help make your travel planning easier at the very back of the book. You can locate them easily because they're printed on yellow paper.

Icons Used in This Book

Throughout this book, helpful icons highlight particularly useful information. Here's a look at what each symbol means:

Keep an eye out for the Bargain Alert icon as you look for money-saving tips and great deals.

Watch for the Heads Up icon to identify annoying or potentially dangerous situations such as tourist traps, unsafe neighborhoods, budgetary rip-offs, and other things to avoid.

Look to the Kid Friendly icon for attractions, hotels, restaurants, and activities that are particularly hospitable to children or people traveling with kids.

The Tip icon alerts you to practical advice and hints to make your trip run more smoothly.

Note the Viva Mexico icon for food, places, or experiences that offer a true taste of the spirit of Mexico.

Where to Go from Here

Nothing quite compares to a beach vacation — whether you spend it lazing in the sun or pursuing active, water-bound activities — and it's even better when planned with the right advice and insider tips. Whether you're a veteran traveler or new to the game, *Cancún & the Yucatán For Dummies* helps you put together just the kind of trip you have in mind. So, start turning these pages, and before you know it, you'll feel those balmy beach breezes on your face!

Part I
Getting Started

"Of all the stuff we came back from Mexico with,
I think these adobe bathrobes were the least
well thought out."

In this part . . .

*P*lanning a trip can be daunting — so I'm here to give you a sense of the place you're visiting. Mexico's Yucatán is a vast part of a varied country with a bevy of unique beach resorts — plus some amazing archeological sites. I introduce you to the highlights of the most popular places, so you can pick the destination that best matches your idea of the perfect seaside getaway.

In Part I, I cover the basics: Each of the beach resorts along Mexico's Yucatán peninsula has an appeal all its own, and Chapter 1 gives you the lowdown. Deciding which area best suits your preferences is the first step in planning your ideal vacation. Next come the details — like when to go and which local festivals you shouldn't miss. (Check out Chapter 2 for advice.) I also give tips and tricks for accurately planning your vacation budget. Nothing will take away the pleasure of lazy days faster than worries about spending too much money, so spend some time reading through Chapter 3 to ward away those stressful thoughts and stay in the green. Finally, in Chapter 4, I offer some tips for travelers with special needs — whether you're a solo traveler or a family — in order to help ensure that you pick exactly the right place that fulfills both your personal requirements and your expectations.

Chapter 1

Discovering the Yucatán

· ·

In This Chapter

▶ Introducing the Yucatán's beach resorts

▶ Deciding which area you'd like to visit

▶ Examining the pros and cons of each destination

· ·

The Yucatán should be the beach vacation of your dreams. All those glossy images of long stretches of pure, powdery, white-sand beaches and tranquil turquoise waters do exist — and they're found along the eastern coast of Mexico's Yucatán peninsula.

Not only does this vacation destination boast possibly the most perfect beaches in the world, but it has the added attraction of nearby ruins of ancient cultures, nature-oriented diversions that make avid adventurers drool, and enough shopping, dining, spa services, and nightlife to entertain the most demanding of consumers. We're here to help you plan your ideal escape to the magical shores of Mexico's Yucatán.

The Yucatán has a lot going for it in terms of attracting travelers — warm weather, miles and miles of coastline, and a location so close to the United States that sometimes it almost seems like a part of it. Although the official language is Spanish, the use of English is almost as common as Spanish in all the resort areas covered in this book. A visit to Mexico's Yucatán can offer the experience of visiting a foreign country accompanied by many of the familiarities of home.

Understanding the Lay of the Land

The beaches of Cancún and the Yucatán are, in a word, spectacular — and the main reason most people travel here. But the two areas also have differences. Whereas Cancún is a full-blown resort, known as much for its sizzling nightlife as its tropical tanning opportunities, the resorts further south along the coast are custom-made for pure relaxation and lazy days of napping under a palm tree.

You can also explore a couple of laid-back islands, along with unique, ecologically oriented enclaves. Deciding which one is right for you depends a lot on what you're looking for in a vacation. As you read this chapter, think about what you really want in a destination. Romantic? Family fun? Lively singles scene? And consider how you want to travel. Budget? Luxury? Somewhere in between? These considerations can help narrow down your planning. One thing's for certain — no matter what you're seeking, at least one Yucatán beach resort fits the bill perfectly.

If you don't know where to begin in choosing between Cancún or a rustic costal retreat, don't worry. In this book, I tell you everything you need to know about each of the destinations that I cover in order to help decide which one is right for you. In this chapter, I give you a rundown of the highlights and drawbacks of each of the region's most popular beach resorts. Because the type of accommodations you want may determine where you go — or don't go — I also explain the different types of lodging available at each destination.

Picking the Right Beach Resort

The resorts along Mexico's Yucatán peninsula are known for their crystalline waters, which border the coral reefs of the Caribbean, and flat, scrubby landscapes. This area was the land of the ancient Maya, and their impressive remains are close enough to the popular beach destinations to explore.

A total of 26,000 hotel rooms to choose from and a full complement of attractions in Cancún make it the most popular choice for travelers to Mexico today — more than 7 million visitors come here each year. But Cancún's popularity has also given rise to a whole range of more relaxed options further down the coast to the south, appealing to those who love many aspects of Cancún, but who want a little heavier dose of the natural. Cozumel island, actually an older and more traditional vacation destination, offers a laid-back retreat beneath palm fronds and sunny skies — with the added allure of world-class diving. And, all along the Yucatán coast — now known as the *Riviera Maya* — you can find everything from palapa-topped huts to extravagant, all-inclusive resorts, bordering stunning beaches and a tropical jungle. In a nutshell, each resort has its own look, character, and special something. The following sections are snapshots to help you focus on the resort that's right for you.

Also see Table 1-1 at the end of this chapter for a concise rating of each aspect of the resort areas covered in this book.

Choosing Cancún

Cancún is Mexico's most popular beach resort — and the reason most people travel to Mexico. Simply stated, it perfectly showcases both the country's breathtaking natural beauty and the depth of its thousand-year-old history. Cancún is also especially comforting for first-time visitors to Mexico, as it offers a familiarity of life back home that makes foreigners feel instantly at ease in this beach resort.

Cancún offers an unrivaled combination of high-quality accommodations, dreamy beaches, and diverse, nearby shopping, dining, and nightlife. The added lure of ancient culture is also evident in all directions. And the best part? Cancún is also a modern mega-resort. Even if you're a bit apprehensive about visiting foreign soil, you'll feel completely at home and at ease in Cancún. English is spoken, dollars are accepted, roads are well paved, and lawns are manicured. Malls are the place for shopping and dining, and you'll quickly spot recognizable names for dining, shopping, nightclubbing, and sleeping.

Two principal parts comprise Cancún: **Isla Cancún** (Cancún Island), with a 14-mile-long strip of beachfront hotels reminiscent of Miami Beach, and **Ciudad Cancún** (Cancún City), on the mainland, with hotels as well as the functional elements of any community.

Cancún, located on the Yucatán peninsula, is also the departure point for wonderful day-trips to the nearby islands of Cozumel and Isla Mujeres (meaning Island of Women), where you can enjoy first-class diving, as well as the inland remains of ancient cultures.

If you're looking for an incredible introduction to Mexico's beaches and want to experience a Mexican-lite vacation while enjoying world-class shopping in a pampered environment, Cancún is your beach. (Check out the chapters in Part III for more detailed information on this area.)

Top aspects of a vacation in Cancún include

- Great beaches of powdery, white sand and turquoise-blue water.
- First-class facilities, modern accommodations, and tons of shopping and dining options.
- Numerous outdoor activities including jungle tours, visits to Mayan ruins, and eco-oriented theme parks.
- No need to worry about communication — an English language-friendly destination.

Mexico's Yucatán Peninsula

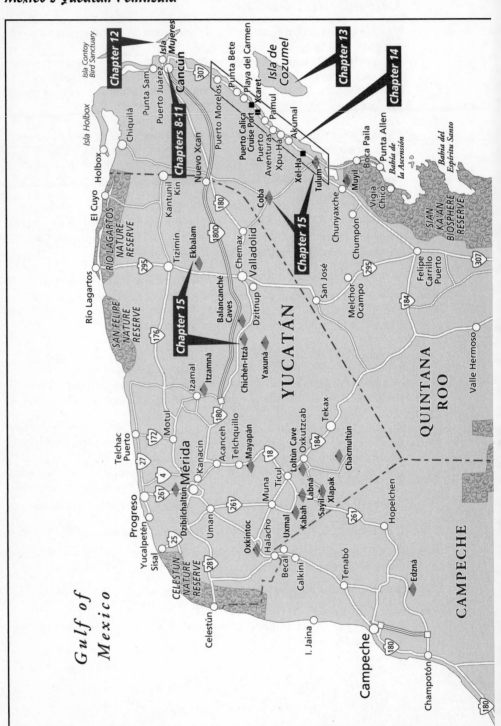

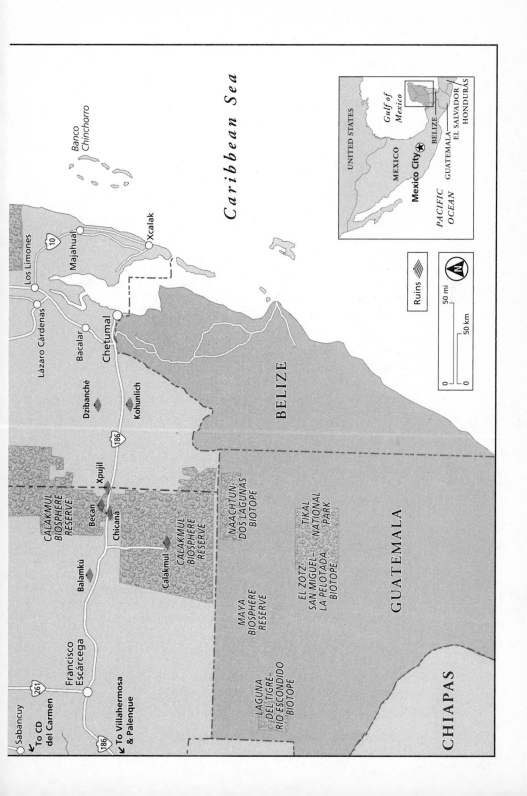

But also consider the following:

- ✔ You can easily forget that you're in Mexico and may miss the Mexican experience altogether.

- ✔ Built for tourism, the prices in Cancún are higher than in most other Mexican beach resorts.

- ✔ Cancún's popularity means you'll have lots of company here!

Contemplating Isla Mujeres

Isla Mujeres is a perfect island escape, offering travelers an idyllic Mexican beach experience complete with a wide stretch of palm-fringed beach, abundant opportunities for diving, snorkeling, and fishing, a tiny but lively town, intriguing guest houses and small hotels, and an ample dose of culture that's *muy Mexicana*. Where Mexico's only other true island — Cozumel — has become a bustling cruise ship port of call, Isla Mujeres remains a laid-back island, the kind where you can string a hammock between two palms and simply doze away a week in perfect sea breezes and sunshine.

Isla's proximity to Cancún and its active international airport (just 3 miles off Cancún's shore) makes the island easily accessible. Once there, you'll feel a million miles away from the bustle of civilization. Restaurants are the family-owned variety, and accommodations are in small, independently-owned hotels and guest houses, with a few deluxe options in the mix.

If you're looking for a true laid-back vacation, and you prefer the simplistic to the superlative, Isla Mujeres is your spot. (Check out Chapter 12 for more detailed information.)

Top aspects of a vacation in Isla Mujeres include

- ✔ Excellent value for money, with numerous inexpensive hotel and dining options.

- ✔ A relaxed pace and simple lifestyle.

- ✔ Abundant options to enjoy the surrounding Caribbean waters — snorkeling, diving, deep-sea fishing, and explorations to nearby ecological preserves. There's even a small Mayan ruin.

But also consider the following:

- ✔ The island may be *too* small and relaxed for those who prefer constant activity.

- ✔ During the day, the island crowds up with day-trippers from Cancún.

- ✔ Nightlife is quiet and the dining scene simple — this isn't the place for those who prefer a little glitz.

Diving into Cozumel

If underwater beauty is your most important criteria for choosing a beach, then Cozumel will dazzle you. Considered by many to be one of the top-five diving spots in the world, few places can top the aquatic splendor of the waters surrounding this island, about 45 miles south of Cancún.

And when you come up for air or if you're a nondiver, Cozumel has several inland attractions, a variety of watersports, a brand-new golf course, and ample choices for dining and libations. As Mexico's most important port of call for cruise ships, Cozumel also has the best duty-free shopping and one of the largest selections of fine-jewelry shops in the country. The island's one town, San Miguel, has a charming old-Mexico feel to it.

Cozumel has more budget-friendly accommodations and places to dine than newer, nearby Cancún. However, while the island is really active during the day, it's generally a quiet place at night.

Just a short ferry ride away from mainland Mexico, Cozumel makes for a great jumping-off point for explorations along the Yucatán's coastline. Just across the channel from Cozumel is captivating Playa del Carmen, quickly growing in popularity due to its central location and funky-sophisticated charms.

In addition to being a diver's dream destination, staying in Cozumel can be like enjoying multiple beach resorts in one vacation! On the ocean-side of the island, you find a deserted coast that you can have practically all to yourself. While on the protected mainland side (where the town and all the hotels are), you find perfectly calm waters — just right for swimming or snorkeling without seagrass or any surf that can wreak havoc with those string bathing suits. (Take a look at Chapter 13 for more on Cozumel.)

Top aspects of a vacation in Cozumel include

- ✔ World-class diving.
- ✔ Secluded beaches on one side, calm water on the other.
- ✔ Relaxed island atmosphere.
- ✔ A short ferry trip away from the mainland's cultural and historical attractions.

But also consider the following:

- ✔ The nightlife is low-key.
- ✔ Cozumel is super-casual; there's not a dress-up place on the island.

✔ Stores tend to be more expensive than elsewhere because they cater to cruise-ship visitors.

✔ When the cruise ships arrive, crowds descend on the town and nature park.

Considering Playa del Carmen

The hottest spot along the Riviera Maya is Playa del Carmen, which lies 40 miles south of Cancún. Playa — as locals refer to it — is a small town that's both funky and sophisticated. In the early '80s, it was nothing more than the ferry landing for Cozumel, but it has since developed into an engaging resort town, with powdery-sand beaches and an eclectic mix of lodging, dining, and shopping.

Playa attracts visitors who are looking for a combination of simplicity and variety. Recently, though, Playa has also attracted developers. As they rapidly change the beachscape to the north and south with the addition of mega-resorts, they're also changing Playa's previously playful, laid-back vibe. But Playa still has enough of its original flavor to make it different from any other resort in the area.

Top aspects of a vacation in Playa include

✔ Great beaches and great water.

✔ Friendly crowds (emphasis on the friendly).

✔ Good dining scene and an active street life.

✔ Excellent location for day-trippers.

But also consider the following:

✔ The boomtown feel that impinges on the zen of total relaxation.

✔ Friendly crowds (emphasis on the crowds).

✔ A rental car is necessary if you want to snorkel or dive.

✔ Parking problems.

Exploring the Riviera Maya

Cancún's popularity has given rise to a growing curiosity and desire to explore other parts of the Yucatán's Caribbean coastline. The 81-mile stretch of coast called the Riviera Maya is now a mix of small resort towns, nature parks, all-inclusive resorts, and roadside attractions extending all the way from Cancún south to the town and ruins of Tulum. This area is ideal for either more adventurous travelers or those who simply want to get to their all-inclusive hotel and stay there.

If you love getting away from it all, the Riviera Maya is a natural choice for exploration and relaxation. (See the chapters in Part V for more details.)

Top aspects of a vacation in the Riviera Maya include

- Beautiful beaches and an array of ecoparks ideal for nature lovers.
- Favored by more adventurous travelers, some of whom have settled here to offer eclectic accommodations, shopping, and dining options.
- Smaller crowds and lower prices.
- All-inclusive heaven with great savings for travelers with children.

But also consider the following:

- Limited shopping and dining exist outside of Playa del Carmen.
- You want nightlife? What nightlife — unless you consider stargazing an aspect of nightlife.
- Without a rental car, you'll be stuck where you stay.

Table 1-1	The Yucatán's Resorts: The Score Card (3 points indicate the highest rating)				
Points for:	*Cancún*	*Cozumel*	*Isla Mujeres*	*Playa del Carmen*	*Riviera Maya*
Luxury	3	2	1	2	1
Nightlife	3	2	1	3	1
Great Food	2	2	1	3	1
Beaches	3	2	2	3	3
Bargain	1	2	3	2	2
Local Color	1	2	3	2	2
Mexican Culture	2	2	1	1	2
Golf	1	2	0	2	1
Senior Appeal	2	1	2	1	1
Hiking	1	1	1	1	2
Natural Beauty	2	3	3	2	3

(continued)

Table 1-1 *(continued)*

Points for:	Cancún	Cozumel	Isla Mujeres	Playa del Carmen	Riviera Maya
Sightseeing	3	1	1	2	3
Diving/ Snorkeling	3	3	3	2	3
Watersports	3	2	2	2	2
Peace & Quiet	1	2	3	1	3
Family Friendly	3	2	2	2	3
Easy Access	3	3	1	1	1

Chapter 2

Deciding When to Go

. . . .

. . . .

Mexico's Yucatán beach resorts enjoy sun-drenched and moderate winters, and they logically attract the most visitors when the weather at home is cold and dreary. However, almost any time of the year has its pros and cons for travel. In this chapter, I review what you can expect from the weather during different months of the year. I also highlight some of the Yucatán's most festive celebrations that you may want to plan your trip around.

Forecasting the Weather

Mexico's Yucatán peninsula has two main climatic seasons: a **rainy season** (May to mid-October) and a **dry season** (mid-October through April). The rainy season can be of little consequence in the dry, interior part of this region, but the coastal region typically receives regular tropical showers, which begin around 4 or 5 p.m. and last a few hours, as well as an occasional tropical storm that passes up the coast. Though the daily rains can come on suddenly and be quite strong, they usually end just as quickly as they began, and they cool the air for the evening. During peak hurricane season (September and October), take a look at the weather reports just before traveling to see whether you might run into any particularly foul weather and pack a rain slicker just in case.

Hurricane season runs from June through October and particularly affects the Yucatán peninsula.

June, July, and August are very hot and humid on the Yucatán peninsula, with temperatures rising into the mid-80s (30° C) and 90s (33° C). Most of the coastal part of this region experiences temperatures in the 80s in the hottest months. During winter months, temperatures average 70 to 75 (22° to 25° C) during the days, and about 55 to 65 (12° to 18° C) in the evenings.

Unlocking the Secret of the Seasons

Mexico — and its Yucatán peninsula — has two principal travel seasons: high and low. The **high season** begins around December 20 and continues through Easter, although in some places the high season can begin as early as mid-November. The **low season** begins the day after Easter and continues to mid-December; during the low season, prices may drop between 20% and 50%. At beach destinations popular with Mexican travelers, such as Cancún, the prices jump up to high-season levels during July and August, the traditional, national summer vacation period. Prices may rise dramatically during the weeks of **Easter** and **Christmas,** which are the two peak travel weeks in Mexico. In Isla Mujeres and Playa del Carmen, both on the Yucatán coast, the high season starts in mid-November as well, but a "second" high season occurs in August, when many European visitors arrive. I mention all these exceptions and others in the relevant chapters later in this book.

I find **November** to be the best month to travel to Mexico: The scenery is still green from the recently ended rainy season, and temperatures are just beginning to turn a bit cooler, which can produce crystal-clear skies. Crowds are also at a minimum, and you're likely to find some good deals.

One time you may want to avoid is **spring break** (usually from March through early April). The highest concentration of high-octane party crowds is found in Cancún. Frankly, why travel to see college kids behaving badly? Other times you may want to avoid are the weeks of Christmas and Easter. During these traditional Mexican holiday periods, both crowds and prices are at their highest, but the crowds consist more of families and couples than young and rowdy revelers.

Yucatán's Calendar of Events

Mexicans are known for throwing a great party — *fiesta!* — and their love of fireworks is legendary. You may choose to plan your visit around a colorful national or religious celebration. Watersports enthusiasts may consider visiting during one of the numerous regattas and sport-fishing festivals held at many of the resorts. Remember, however, that during national holidays, Mexican banks and government offices — including immigration — are closed.

Christmas and Easter are celebrated similarly to the way they're celebrated in the United States, but Christmas is much more religiously oriented, and less emphasis is placed on Santa and the exchange of gifts.

January/February/March

Día de Reyes (Three Kings Day) commemorates the three kings bringing gifts to the Christ child. On this day, children receive gifts, much like the traditional exchange of gifts that accompanies Christmas in the United States. Friends and families gather to share the *Rosca de Reyes,* a special cake. A small doll representing the Christ child is placed within the cake; whoever receives the doll in his or her piece must host a party the next month that features *tamales* (meat or sweet filling wrapped in a corn husk) and *atole* (a thick, slightly sweet hot drink). January 6.

Music, dances, processions, food, and other festivities are features of **Día de la Candelaria (Candlemass)** and lead up to a blessing of seed and candles in a celebration that mixes pre-Hispanic and European traditions marking the end of winter. All those who attended the Three Kings celebration reunite to share *atole* and *tamales* at a party hosted by the recipient of the doll found in the *rosca.* February 2.

Día de la Constitución (Constitution Day) is a celebration in honor of the current Mexican constitution that was signed in 1917 as a result of the Mexican Revolution of 1910. If you're in Mexico on this day, you'll see a parade wherever you are. February 5.

Carnaval (Carnival) is the last celebration before Lent, and it's celebrated with special gusto in Cozumel. Here, the celebration resembles New Orleans's Mardi Gras with a festive atmosphere and parades. You're best off making reservations in advance and arriving a couple of days before the beginning of celebrations. Three days preceding Ash Wednesday and the beginning of Lent.

Benito Juárez was a reformist leader and president of Mexico who became a national hero. The national holiday honoring **Benito Juárez's Birthday** is the same date of the **spring equinox,** an important celebration of the ancient Mexicans. In Chichén-Itzá (chee-*chin* eat-*zah*), the ancient Mayan city located 112 miles/179km from Cancún, the celebration of the first day of spring is particularly interesting. The Temple of Kukulkán — Chichén-Itzá's main pyramid — aligns with the sun, and the shadow of the body of its plumed serpent moves slowly from the top of the building downward. When the shadow reaches the bottom, the body joins the carved-stone snake's head at the base of the pyramid. According to ancient legend, at the moment that the serpent is whole, the earth is fertilized to assure a bountiful growing season. Visitors come from around the world to marvel at this sight, so advance arrangements are advisable. In the custom of the ancient Mexicans, dances are performed, and prayers to the elements and the four cardinal points (north, south, east, and west) are said in order to renew their energy for the upcoming year. It's customary to wear white with a red ribbon. March 21. (You can see the serpent's shadow at Chichén-Itzá from March 19 to 23.)

April/May/June

Semana Santa (Holy Week) celebrates the last week in the life of Christ from Palm Sunday through Easter Sunday with somber religious processions, spoofs of Judas, and reenactments of specific biblical events, plus food and craft fairs. Businesses close during this traditional week of Mexican national vacations. If you plan on traveling to Mexico or around the Yucatán during Holy Week, make your reservations early. Airline seats on flights into and out of the country are reserved months in advance. Buses to almost anywhere in Mexico are always full, so try arriving on the Wednesday or Thursday prior to the start of Holy Week. Easter Sunday is quiet. The week following is a traditional vacation period. Week before Easter.

Labor Day is a national holiday celebrating workers. It features countrywide parades and fiestas. May 1.

Cinco de Mayo is a national holiday that celebrates the defeat of the French at the Battle of Puebla in 1862. May 5.

The **International Jazz Festival of Cancún** takes place in late May each year, featuring renowned jazz artists from North America and Europe. Locations are generally in the heart of Cancún, at the *parque de las Palapas* and at the Cancún Convention Center, over several days and nights. Visit www.cancunjazz.com or www.cancuncvb.org for details and schedules.

July/August/September

During the traditionally slower month of September, the Cancún Tourism Board hosts a series of special events throughout the month, celebrating Mexico's kaleidoscope of culture, art, food, and fun. **En Septiembre ¡Viva Mexico en Cancún!** Events include tequila festivals, Mexican-Caribbean cuisine tastings, traditional dance performances, and Mexican film showings. For event listings and details, visit the Web site www.vivamexicoencancun.com or the Cancún Tourism Board, at www.cancuncvb.org.

Mexico begins **Día de Independencia (Independence Day)** — the holiday that marks Mexico's independence from Spain — at 11 p.m. on September 15, with the president of Mexico's famous independence *grito* (shout) from the National Palace in Mexico City. The rest of the country watches the event on TV or participates in local celebrations, which mirror the festivities at the national level. September 16 is actually Independence Day and is celebrated with parades, picnics, and family reunions throughout the country. September 15 and 16.

During the **fall equinox,** Chichén-Itzá once again takes center stage as the same shadow play that occurs during the spring equinox repeats itself for the fall equinox. September 21 and 22.

October/November/December

What's commonly called the **Día de los Muertos (Day of the Dead)** is actually two days: All Saints Day, honoring saints and deceased children, and All Souls Day, honoring deceased adults. Relatives gather at cemeteries countrywide, carrying candles and food and often spending the night beside the graves of loved ones. Weeks before, bakers begin producing bread formed in the shape of mummies and round loaves decorated with bread "bones." Decorated sugar skulls emblazoned with glittery names are sold everywhere. Many days ahead, homes and churches erect special altars laden with bread, fruit, flowers, candles, photographs of saints and of the deceased, and favorite foods. On these two nights, children walk through the streets dressed in costumes and masks, often carrying mock coffins and pumpkin lanterns, into which they expect money to be dropped. November 1 and 2.

Día de Revolución (Revolution Day) is a national holiday commemorating the start of the Mexican Revolution in 1910 with parades, speeches, rodeos, and patriotic events. November 20.

During the **Día de Nuestra Señora de Guadalupe (Feast of the Virgin of Guadalupe),** the patroness of Mexico is honored throughout the country with religious processions, street fairs, dancing, fireworks, and masses. It's one of Mexico's most moving and beautiful displays of traditional culture. In December 1531, the Virgin of Guadalupe appeared to a young man, Juan Diego, on a hill near Mexico City. He convinced the bishop that he had seen the apparition by revealing his cloak, upon which the Virgin was emblazoned. December 12.

Christmas Posadas celebrates the Holy Family's trek to Bethlehem. On each of the nine nights before Christmas, door-to-door candlelit processions in cities and villages nationwide reenact the Holy Family's search for an inn. December 15 to 24.

Chapter 3

Planning Your Budget

● ●

● ●

*T*he brochures are in front of you, and visions of lazy, sunny days fill your thoughts — so who wants to think about money? Trust me — take a few minutes to figure out your expected expenses now, so you can enjoy a worry-free vacation later.

Your budget is greatly affected by your choice of beach resort. An all-inclusive resort on the Riviera Maya costs more than a modest beach-side hotel in Cozumel. Within Cancún itself, a room on the beach of Isla Cancún is considerably more expensive than one in Cancún City (Ciudad Cancún), and ditto for all the other expenses down the line. After you decide where you want to go, and you have your hotel and airfare down, it's a good idea to calculate the other estimated costs associated with your trip to plan a proper budget.

You can use the worksheets at the back of this book to jot down antici-pated costs so that you can easily see whether you need to trim any of your expenses. Or even better, you may discover that you can afford to slip into that oceanfront room or plan that sunset sail you've been dreaming of.

To make certain that you don't forget any expenses, try taking a mental stroll through your entire trip. Start with the costs of transportation from your home to the airport, your airline tickets, and transfers to your hotel. Add your daily hotel rate (don't forget taxes!), meals, activities, entertainment, taxis, tips, your return to the airport, and finally, your return trip home from the airport and any parking fees you may have incurred. Just to be safe, add an extra 15% to 20% for extra, unexpected costs that may pop up.

Calculating Your Hotel Cost

The biggest part of your vacation budget will go toward your hotel and airfare, so I suggest getting those expenses down to as low as possible. In the various destination chapters, I use dollar signs ($–$$$$) to indicate the price category of each hotel. (Check out the Introduction of this book for a rundown on the price categories and their corresponding dollar signs.) You can get a room for $30 a night, or you can get a room for $700 a night!

Keep in mind that some room rates include breakfast — or all meals, beverages, and entertainment — so be sure to compare mangos with mangos. Also, when finalizing your reservations, be sure to check whether the total cost includes taxes and tips. Even within a resort, the price of rooms can vary widely.

Room location — oceanfront versus a view of a dumpster — is one differential. Ask yourself how much your room location matters. Do you view your room as simply a place to sleep, shower, and dress? Or will you not feel officially "on vacation" unless you can fall asleep to the sound of the surf? If so, a pricier room may well be worth it. However, remember that many "garden view" rooms in my recommendations are only steps away from the beach and possibly even more tranquil than their oceanfront counterparts.

When it comes to rates, the most common term is **rack rate.** The rack rate is the maximum rate that a resort or hotel charges for a room. It's the rate you get if you walk in off the street and ask for a room on a night that the place is close to being full.

The rack rate is the first rate a hotel offers, but you usually don't have to pay it. Always ask whether a lower rate or special package is available — it can't hurt, and you may at least end up with a free breakfast or spa service.

In this book, I use rack rates as a guidepost, not expecting that you'll have to pay them. Minimum night stays, special promotions, and seasonal discounts can all go a long way in bringing the rack rate down. Also, be sure to mention your frequent-flier or corporate-rewards programs if you book with one of the larger hotel chains. Please note that rates change very often, so the prices quoted in this book may be different from the prices you're quoted when you make your reservation.

Room rates also rise and fall with occupancy rates. If your choice of hotels is close to empty, it pays to negotiate. Resorts tend to be much more crowded during weekends.

Feeling romantic? Special packages for **honeymooners** are really popular in Mexican beach resorts. Even if you've been hitched for a while, it could be a second honeymoon, right? If you ask, you may end up with a complimentary bottle of champagne and flower petals on your bed.

Mexico couldn't be more accommodating to travelers with children. Many of the larger chains don't charge extra for children staying in the same room as their parents, and some offer special meal programs and other amenities for younger travelers. While rollaway beds are common, you may have a challenge finding a crib. Ask about this contingency when making your reservation.

Totaling Transportation Costs

After taking care of your airfare (for tips on keeping airfare costs down see Chapter 5), your transportation costs vary depending upon your choice of Yucatán beach resorts. While some areas — like Cancún — offer economical shuttles and great public transportation options, others along the Riviera Maya are more expensive to get to and have little in the way of local transportation once you've arrived at your resort, making a rental car desirable if you're the type of traveler who likes to explore. These extra charges, however, can make getting around cost even more than getting there.

One advantage of a **package** tour (when you make one payment that covers airfare, hotel, round-trip transportation to and from your accommodations, and occasionally meals or tours) is that the round-trip ground transportation between the airport and your hotel is usually included. If you're not sure whether your package covers ground transportation, ask. Note that the taxi union inside Mexico is strong, so you're unlikely to find any shuttle transportation provided by your hotel.

Generally, renting a car doesn't make sense, unless you're planning on exploring the Yucatán on your own (and possibly Cozumel, if you're looking to explore the far side of the island there). Renting a small car runs about $70 a day on average, including insurance, so you may want to squeeze your car-dependent explorations into a day or two at the most. You should also try to time your rental-car excursions to coincide with your arrival or departure so that you can use your wheels for either leg of your airport-hotel transportation needs.

As a rule, taxis tend to be the most economical and efficient transportation for getting around Cancún, Cozumel, and Isla. In each of the chapters detailing these resorts, I provide taxi rates for getting around town.

Estimating Dining Dollars

In each resort's dining section, I describe my favorite restaurants, all of which include dollar signs ($–$$$$$) to give you an idea of the prices you can expect to pay. Refer to the Introduction of this book for a detailed explanation of these price categories.

The prices quoted refer to main courses at dinner, unless otherwise specified. I eliminated the most expensive shrimp and lobster dishes from my estimates to avoid pre-trip sticker shock. In most cases, you can find additional entrees above and below the quoted price range. To estimate your total dining expenses, add in estimated costs for beverages, appetizers, desserts, and tips as well.

Hotels increasingly are offering dining plans. To help you wade through the terminology, here's a review of the basics:

✔ **Continental plan (CP):** Includes a light breakfast — usually juices, fruits, pastries or breads, and coffee.

✔ **Breakfast plan (BP):** Includes a full, traditional American-style breakfast of eggs, bacon, French toast, hash browns, and so on.

✔ **Modified American plan (MAP):** Includes breakfast (usually a full one) and dinner.

✔ **Full American plan (FAP):** Includes three meals a day.

✔ **All-inclusive:** Includes three all-you-can-eat meals a day, plus snacks, soft drinks, and alcoholic beverages. Sometimes, additional charges apply for premium liquors or wines.

✔ **European Plan (EP):** No meals are included.

Mexican beach-resort hotels are known for their expansive breakfast buffets. But the buffets can also be expensive, averaging about $20, even for small children. If breakfast is your main meal or only meal of the day, these all-you-can-eat extravaganzas may be worthwhile; otherwise, you're probably better off sleeping in or finding breakfast elsewhere.

Be sure to explore restaurants away from your hotel. You're likely to get a much better dining value, and you can truly savor the diverse flavors of Mexico. For eateries that best represent the flavorful (and I don't mean spicy) cuisine of Mexico, look for the Viva Mexico icon that accompanies some of the restaurant reviews throughout this book.

While you're in Mexico, be sure to try the local beers. Corona is the best-known brew, but other excellent choices are Bohemia, Modelo Especial, Pacifico, Indio, and Dos Equis Negro. Beer in Mexico is often cheaper than soft drinks! Your vacation is looking better and better, isn't it?

Tipping Tips

Many travelers skimp on tips in Mexico, but please don't. Most of the employees in this country's hospitality industry receive the majority of their income from tips. For bellmen or porters, the equivalent of $1 per bag is appropriate. For hotel housekeeping, tip between $1 and $2 per night, depending upon the type of hotel you're staying in. For restaurant service, 15% is standard, but consider 20% if the service is particularly noteworthy. Oddly enough, the one area you don't need to consider tips for is taxis — it's not customary to tip taxi drivers here unless they help with baggage, or you've hired them on an hourly basis and they double as a tour guide.

You'll no doubt run into all sorts of enterprising young boys looking for a tip to point you in the direction of your restaurant, help you into a parking spot, or do some other sort of unnecessary favor. In cases like these, tip as you see fit, or as the spirit moves you.

Spending Wisely on Activities, Attractions, and Shopping

You're going to a beach resort, so regardless of your budget, you always have the option of simply soaking up the tropical sun during the day and then taking in the moonlit nights. It's the most economical plan and a relaxing and enjoyable option for many. Still, with so much to do and see, you're likely to want to spend some time and money getting out and enjoying the many treasures of Mexico.

Pricing for **sightseeing tours** varies by the destination, the length of time of the excursion, whether a meal and beverages are included, and other extras. However, I can give you some pretty typical ranges that you can use as a guideline. A city tour generally runs from $12 to $20; half-day boat cruises that include lunch can cost between $40 and $60; and full-day excursions to neighboring ruins run between $60 and $150.

If you plan to take part in any **sports-related activities** like golf, diving, or sport fishing, you may find the prices to be higher than back home. Dives range from around $50 to $70 for a two-tank dive, but here, you tend to really get what you pay for in terms of quality of equipment and dive guides, so it's best to pay up. Cozumel has the greatest selection of expert dive shops, and the competition makes Cozumel's prices the most reasonable for the quality of experience. Going fishing? You have to decide variables beyond your point of departure, including size of boat, charter options, and type of gear and refreshments, but count on between $50 and $75 per person for a half-day charter.

As for **nightlife,** the cost depends more on your personal tastes. The "hot" nightlife is concentrated in Cancún, so if that's important to you, this is "the" spot in the Yucatán, although Playa del Carmen has some notable options as well. In Cancún, $20 cover charges are common during busier times. When you're out on the town, beer is the best bargain and costs about $1 to $3 per beer. National-branded drinks can run you around $3 to $5 each. Ladies can easily find bargains like "two-for-one" or "all-you-can-drink" specials.

If **shopping** is your call, you can plan to spend or save here. Besides silver jewelry and other souvenirs, the best excuse for shopping in Mexico are the great prices on duty-free perfumes, watches, and other goods in Cancún and along the Riviera Maya. I discuss shopping specialties in greater detail within the respective destination chapters.

Cutting Costs

While planning your trip, you need to keep in mind certain things that may help you save some money. Before you leave for vacation, don't forget to consider the incidentals that can really add up — hotel taxes, tips, and telephone surcharges.

Here are a few other suggestions to help keep a lid on expenses so that they don't run amuck and blow your vacation budget:

- ✔ **Travel in the off-season.** If you can travel at nonpeak times (September through November, for example), you can usually find better hotel bargains.

- ✔ **Travel on off days of the week.** If you can travel on a Tuesday, Wednesday, or Thursday, you may find cheaper flights to your destination. When you inquire about airfares, ask whether flying on a different day is cheaper.

- ✔ **Try a package tour.** With one call to a travel agent or packager, you can book airfare, hotel, ground transportation, and even some sightseeing for many of these destinations for a lot less than if you tried to put the trip together yourself. (See Chapter 5 for specific suggestions of package tour companies to contact.)

- ✔ **Always ask for discount rates.** Membership in AAA, frequent-flier plans, AARP, or other groups may qualify you for a discount on plane tickets and hotel rooms if you book them in the United States. In Mexico, you can generally get a discount based on how full the hotel is at the time you show up; however, you're also taking a chance on a vacancy not being available.

- ✔ **Get a room off the beach.** Accommodations within walking distance of the shore can be much cheaper than those right on the beach. Beaches in Mexico are public, so you don't need to stay in a hotel that's on the sand to spend most of your vacation at the beach.

✔ **Share your room with your kids.** In Mexico, this setup is usually the norm rather than the exception, so book a room with two double beds. Most hotels won't charge extra for up to two children staying in their parent's room.

✔ **Use public transportation whenever practical.** Not only will you save taxi fare, but simply getting to where you're going can be like a mini-excursion as you enjoy the local scene. In Cancún, you're apt to run into mostly tourists on the clean, public buses of the hotel zone.

✔ **Cut down on the souvenirs.** I don't expect you to return home without any local treasures, but think hard about whether that oversized sombrero will be as charming back home. Your photographs and memories are likely to be your best momentos.

✔ **Use public phones and prepaid phone cards to call home.** Avoid using the phone in your hotel room to call outside the hotel. Charges can be astronomical, even for local calls. Rather than placing the call yourself, ask the concierge to make a reservation for you — they do it as a service.

You'll even be charged a surcharge for using your own calling card and its 800 number. Remember: Most 800 numbers are not toll-free when dialed from Mexico.

Also avoid using the public phones that urge you, in English, to call home using their 800 number. This ploy is the absolute most expensive way to call home, and the service charges the call to your home phone. The best option? Buy a Ladatel (brand name for Mexico's public phones) phone card, available at most pharmacies, and dial direct using the instructions in Appendix A of this book.

✔ **Steer clear of the minibar and room service.** Those little bottles can really add up! Consider buying your own supplies and bringing them to your room, and you'll save a bundle. Likewise, room service is the most expensive way to dine — a service charge and tip are added on top of generally inflated prices. Also, some hotels provide complimentary bottled water, but others can charge as much as $5 per bottle, so be sure you know what you're drinking.

✔ **Drink local.** Imported labels can be twice the price as the locally popular brands, which often are also imported but just different brands than the ones you may be accustomed to seeing. At least ask what's being served as the house brand — you may be pleasantly surprised.

✔ **Follow Mexican custom and have lunch as your main meal.** If the restaurant of your dreams is open only for dinner, save that one for your one "splurge" evening and try out the others for your midday meal. Lunch tabs are usually a fraction of their dinner counterparts, and they frequently feature many of the same specialties.

✔ **Skimp on shrimp and lobster.** Sure, I know — you're sitting seaside and dreaming of that tasty lobster. Just understand that they're the priciest items on the menu, and the less expensive, local, fresh fish is often just as good or better.

✔ **Buy Mexican bottled water.** Forget the water labels that you know — Mexico's bottled waters are just as good as the imports and about half the price. Look for such brands as Santa María, Ciel, and Bonafont.

Chapter 4

Planning Ahead for Special Travel Needs

. . . .

In This Chapter
▶ Bringing the kids along
▶ Traveling tips for folks with special needs
▶ Getting hitched in Mexico

. . . .

*M*ost individuals consider themselves unique and as having special needs, but some types of travelers really do warrant a little extra advice. In this chapter, I cover information that's helpful to know if you're traveling with children. If you're a senior traveler or you're traveling solo, I have plenty of tips for you, too. Individuals with disabilities can also mine this chapter for useful info. Gay and lesbian travelers can find a section devoted to them as well. And for those of you planning a wedding, I include a section on tying the knot in Mexico. Throughout the chapter, I clue you in on what to expect, offer useful tips, and whenever possible, steer you to experts concerning your particular circumstances.

Vacationing with Children

Children are considered the national treasure of Mexico, and Mexicans warmly welcome and cater to your children. Although many parents were reluctant to bring young children to Mexico in the past, primarily due to health concerns, I can't think of a better place to introduce children to the exciting adventure of exploring a different culture. One of the best destinations for children in Mexico is Cancún. Hotels can often arrange for a baby sitter. Some hotels in the moderate-to-luxury range have small playgrounds and pools for children and hire caretakers who offer special-activity programs during the day, but few budget hotels offer these amenities. All-inclusive resorts make great options for family travel because, as a rule, they offer exhaustive activities programs. They also make mealtime easy by offering buffet-style meal services almost around the clock.

Before leaving for your trip, check with your pediatrician or family doctor to get advice on medications to take along. Mexican-brand disposable diapers cost about the same as diapers in the United States, but the quality is poorer. You can purchase U.S.-brand diapers, but you'll pay a higher price. Familiar, brand-name baby foods are sold in many stores. Dry cereals, powdered formulas, baby bottles, and purified water are all easily available in midsize and large cities or resorts.

Cribs, however, may present a problem; only the largest and most luxurious hotels provide them. However, rollaway beds to accommodate children staying in a room with their parents are often available. Child seats or highchairs at restaurants are common, and most restaurants go out of their way to accommodate the comfort of your children. You may want to seriously consider bringing your own car seat along because they're not readily available to rent in Mexico.

I recommend you take coloring books, puzzles, and small games with you to keep your children entertained during the flight or whenever you're traveling from one destination to the next. Another good idea is to take a blank notebook, in which you and your children can paste souvenirs from your trip — perhaps the label from the beer daddy drank on the beach, or small shells and flowers that they collect. And don't forget to carry small scissors and a glue stick with you, or the blank notebook may remain blank.

The following is a list of Web sites where you can find helpful advice on traveling with children:

- **Family Travel Network** (www.familytravelnetwork.com) offers travel tips and reviews of family-friendly destinations, vacation deals, and thoughtful features such as "What to Do When Your Kids Are Afraid to Travel" and "Kid-Style Camping."

- **Travel with Your Children** (www.travelwithyourkids.com) is a comprehensive site offering sound advice for traveling with children.

- **The Busy Person's Guide to Traveling with Children** (http://wz.com/travel/TravelingWithChildren.html) offers a "45-second newsletter" where experts weigh in on the best Web sites and resources for tips on traveling with children.

Seeking Specials for Seniors

People over the age of 60 are traveling more than ever before. And why not? Being a senior citizen entitles you to some terrific travel bargains. If you're not a member of **AARP** (601 E St. NW, Washington, DC 20049; ☎ **800-424-3410** or 202-434-AARP; Internet: www.aarp.org), formerly the American Association of Retired Persons, do yourself a favor and join. AARP offers members a wide range of benefits, including *Modern Maturity* magazine and a monthly newsletter. Anyone over 50 can join.

Mature Outlook (P.O. Box 9390, Des Moines, IA 50322; ☎ **800-336-6330**) is a similar organization, offering discounts on car rentals and hotel stays. The $19.95 annual membership fee also gets you $200 in Sears coupons and a bimonthly magazine. Membership is open to all Sears customers 18 and over, but the organization's primary focus is on the 50-and-over market.

In addition, most of the major domestic airlines, including American Airlines, United, Continental Airlines, and US Airways, offer discount fares for senior travelers — be sure to ask whenever you book a flight. *The Mature Traveler,* a monthly newsletter on senior citizen travel, is a valuable resource. It's available by subscription ($30 a year). For a free sample, send a postcard with your name and address to GEM Publishing Group, P.O. Box 50400, Reno, NV 89513, or you can e-mail the folks at *The Mature Traveler* at maturetrav@aol.com.

Another helpful publication is ***101 Tips for the Mature Traveler,*** available from **Grand Circle Travel** (347 Congress St., Suite 3A, Boston, MA 02210; ☎ **800-221-2610;** Internet: www.gct.com). Grand Circle Travel is also one of the hundreds of travel agencies that specialize in vacations for seniors. But beware: Many agencies are of the tour-bus variety, with free trips thrown in for those who organize groups of 20 or more. Seniors seeking more independent travel should probably consult a regular travel agent. **SAGA International Holidays** (222 Berkeley St., Boston, MA 02116; ☎ **800-343-0273**) offers inclusive tours and cruises for those 50 and older.

Mexico is a popular country for retirees and for senior travelers. For decades, North Americans have been living indefinitely in Mexico by returning to the border and re-crossing with a new tourist permit every six months. Mexican immigration officials have caught on, and they now limit the maximum time you can spend in the country to six months in any given year. This measure is meant to encourage even partial residents to comply with the proper documentation procedures.

AIM (Apdo. Postal 31–70, 45050 Guadalajara, Jalisco, Mexico) is a well-written, candid, and very informative newsletter for prospective retirees. Subscriptions are $18 to the United States and $21 to Canada. Back issues are three for $5.

Sanborn Tours (2015 S. 10th St., Post Office Drawer 519, McAllen, TX 78505-0519; ☎ **800-395-8482**) offers a "Retire in Mexico" orientation tour.

Ensuring Access for Travelers with Disabilities

A disability needn't stop anybody from traveling. More options and resources are out there than ever before. *A World of Options,* a 658-page book of resources for travelers with disabilities, covers everything from biking trips to scuba outfitters. It costs $35 and is available from **Mobility International USA** (P.O. Box 10767, Eugene, OR 97440; ☎ 541-343-1284 voice and TTY; Internet: www.miusa.org).

Another source to check out is **Access-Able Travel Source** (Internet: www.access-able.com), a comprehensive database of travel agents who specialize in arrangements for travelers with disabilities; it's also a clearinghouse for information about accessible destinations around the world.

However, I need to honestly say that Mexico does fall far behind other countries when it comes to accessible travel. In fact, the area may seem like one giant obstacle course to travelers in wheelchairs or on crutches. At airports, you may encounter steep stairs before finding a well-hidden elevator or escalator — if one exists. Airlines often arrange wheelchair assistance for passengers to the baggage area. Porters are generally available to help with luggage at airports and large bus stations after you clear baggage claim.

In addition, escalators (and you won't find many in the beach resorts) are often non-operational. Stairs without handrails abound. Few restrooms are equipped for travelers with disabilities, and when one is available, access to it may be via a narrow passage that won't accommodate a wheelchair or a person on crutches. Many deluxe hotels (the most expensive) now have rooms with baths for people with disabilities. Budget travelers may be best off looking for single-story motels, although accessing showers and bathrooms may still pose a problem outside of specially equipped deluxe hotels. Generally speaking, no matter where you are, someone will lend a hand, although you may have to ask for it.

Few airports offer the luxury of boarding an airplane from the waiting room. You either descend stairs to a bus that ferries you to a waiting plane that you board by climbing stairs, or you walk across the airport tarmac to your plane and climb up the stairs. Deplaning presents the same problems in reverse.

In my opinion, the wide, modern streets and sidewalks of Cancún make it the most "accessible" resort. In addition to the superior public facilities, you can find numerous accommodation options for travelers with disabilities.

Travelers with disabilities may also want to consider joining a tour that caters specifically to them. One of the best operators is **Flying Wheels Travel** (P.O. Box 382, Owatonna, MN 55060; ☎ **507-451-5005;** Internet: www.flyingwheelstravel.com). The company offers various escorted tours and cruises, as well as private tours in minivans with lifts. Another good company is **FEDCAP Rehabilitation Services** (211 W. 14th St., New York, NY 10011). Call ☎ **212-727-4200** or fax 212-727-4373 for information about membership and summer tours.

Accessible Journeys (☎ **800-846-4537** or 610-521-0339; Internet: www.disabilitytravel.com) caters specifically to slow walkers and wheelchair travelers and their families and friends. **Access Adventures** (☎ **716-889-9096**), a Rochester, New York-based agency, offers customized itineraries for a variety of travelers with disabilities. **The Moss Rehab Hospital** (☎ **215-456-9603;** Internet: www.mossresourcenet.org) provides friendly, helpful phone assistance through its **Travel Information Service. The Society for Accessible Travel and Hospitality** (☎ **212-447-7284;** Fax: 212-725-8253; Internet: www.sath.org) offers a wealth of travel resources for people with all types of disabilities and informed recommendations on destinations, access guides, travel agents, tour operators, vehicle rentals, and companion services. Annual membership costs $45 for adults; $30 for seniors and students.

Vision-impaired travelers should contact the **American Foundation for the Blind** (11 Penn Plaza, Suite 300, New York, NY 10001; ☎ **800-232-5463;** Internet: www.afb.org) for information on traveling with Seeing Eye dogs.

Gathering Advice for Gays and Lesbians

Mexico is a conservative country with deeply rooted Catholic religious traditions. Public displays of same-sex affection are rare, and two men displaying such behavior is still considered shocking, especially outside the major resort areas. Women in Mexico frequently walk hand in hand, but anything more would cross the boundary of acceptability. However, gay and lesbian travelers are generally treated with respect and shouldn't experience any harassment, assuming that the appropriate regard is given to local culture and customs.

The International Gay & Lesbian Travel Association (IGLTA) (☎ **800-448-8550** or 954-776-2626; Fax: 954-776-3303; Internet: www.iglta.org) can provide helpful information and additional tips. The **Travel Alternatives Group (TAG)** maintains a database and a gay-friendly accommodations guide. For details, call ☎ **415-437-3800** or e-mail the group at info@mark8ing.com. **Arco Iris** is a gay-owned, full-service travel agency and tour operator specializing in Mexico packages and special group travel. Contact the agency by phone (☎ 800-765-4370 or 619-297-0897; Fax: 619-297-6419) or through its Web site at www.arcoiristours.com. **Now, Voyager** (☎ 800-255-6951; Internet: www.nowvoyager.com) is a San Francisco-based, gay-owned and operated travel service. **Olivia Cruises & Resorts** (☎ 800-631-6277 or 510-655-0364; Internet: http://oliviatravel.com) charters entire resorts and ships for exclusive lesbian vacations all over the world.

Traveling Solo

Mexico is a great place to travel on your own without really being or feeling alone. Although identical room rates for single and double occupancy are slowly becoming a trend in Mexico, many of the hotels mentioned in this book still offer singles at lower rates.

Mexicans are very friendly, and meeting other foreigners is easy. But if you don't like the idea of traveling alone, try **Travel Companion Exchange (TCE)** (P.O. Box 833, Amityville, NY 11701; ☎ 800-392-1256 or 631-454-0880; Fax: 631-454-0170; Internet: www.whytravelalone.com), which brings prospective travelers together. Members complete a profile and then place an anonymous listing of their travel interests in the newsletter. Prospective traveling companions then make contact through the exchange. Membership costs $99 for six months or $159 for a year. TCE also offers an excellent booklet, for $3.95, on avoiding theft and scams while traveling abroad.

As a female traveling alone, I can tell you firsthand that I generally feel safer traveling in Mexico than in the United States. But I use the same commonsense precautions I use when traveling anywhere else in the world, and I stay alert to what's going on around me.

Mexicans, in general, and men, in particular, are nosy about single travelers, especially women. If taxi drivers or anyone else with whom you don't want to become friendly ask about your marital status, family, and so on, my advice is to make up a set of answers (regardless of the truth): "I'm married, traveling with friends, and I have three children."

Saying you're single and traveling alone may send the wrong message about availability. Face it — whether you like it or not, Mexico is still a macho country with the double standards that a macho attitude implies. Movies and television shows exported from the United States have created an image of sexually aggressive North American women. If someone bothers you, don't try to be polite — just leave or head into a public place.

You may even consider wearing a ring that resembles a wedding band. Most Mexican men stay away at the sight of a ring, and it also deters many uncomfortable questions.

For specific tips and travel packages for single women traveling to Mexico, check out the following online resources:

- ✔ Journeywoman: www.journeywomen.com
- ✔ BudgetTravel Women's Guide: www.budgettravel.com/women.htm
- ✔ Women's Travel Club: www.womenstravelclub.com

Planning a Wedding in Mexico

Mexico's beaches may be old favorites for romantic honeymoons, but have you ever considered taking the plunge in Mexico? A destination wedding saves money and can be less hassle compared with marrying back home. Many hotels and attractions offer wedding packages, which can include everything from booking the officiant to hiring the videographer. Pick the plan you want and, presto, your wedding decisions are done! Several properties also provide the services of a wedding coordinator (either for free or at a reasonable cost) who not only scouts out sweetheart pink roses but can also handle marriage licenses and other formalities. A destination wedding can be as informal or as traditional as you like. After returning from their honeymoon, many couples hold a reception for people who couldn't join them. At these parties, couples sometimes continue the theme of their wedding locale (decorate with piñatas or hire a mariachi band, for example) and show a video of their ceremony so that everyone can share in their happiness.

If you invite guests to your destination wedding, find out about group rates for hotels and airfare, which can save 20% or more off regular prices. Plan as far ahead as possible so that people can arrange their schedules and join you.

Under a treaty between the United States and Mexico, Mexican civil marriages are automatically valid in the United States. You need certified copies of birth certificates, driver's licenses, or passports; certified proof of divorce or the death certificate of any former spouses (if applicable); tourist cards (provided when you enter Mexico); and results of blood tests performed in Mexico within 15 days before the ceremony.

Check with a local, on-site wedding planner through your hotel to verify all the necessary requirements and obtain an application well in advance of your desired wedding date. Contact the **Mexican Tourism Board** (☎ **800-446-3942;** Internet: www.visitmexico.com) for information.

For more information, see *Honeymoon Vacations For Dummies* (Wiley Publishing, Inc.).

Part II
Ironing Out the Details

The 5th Wave   By Rich Tennant

THE MEXICAN EXPERIENCE

Your glass of water...

In this part . . .

Ready to travel to Mexico's Yucatán? Well then, it's probably time to do a little planning. In the next three chapters, I help you with all the things you need to consider when booking your ideal trip to one of Mexico's Yucatán beach destinations. Chapter 5 helps you decide whether to use a travel agent or take care of the arrangements on your own and covers the pros and cons of package deals. In Chapter 6, I tell you all you need to know about Mexican currency and taxes. Finally, Chapter 7 covers all the final details — from getting your passport to packing your bags — you need to enjoy a hassle-free vacation.

Chapter 5

Making Your Travel Arrangements

*M*exico is known for its simplicity of life and easygoing ways, so why should getting there be any more complicated? Whether you're a do-it-yourselfer or a person who prefers to let someone else take care of all the details, reading this chapter can save you time, money, and confusion. I point you in the direction of travel agents — and Internet tools — and explain the benefits and limitations of traveling on a package tour. I offer tips on getting the best airfares and choosing the best airline to whisk you away to your dreamy beach along Mexico's Yucatán peninsula.

Using a Travel Agent versus Planning on Your Own

Deciding whether to use the services of a travel agent or do your own planning comes down to basically one component: time. If you don't have a lot of time, seeking a travel agent may be the way to go. If you've got some time to spare, you may enjoy planning your own trip. Either way, both options have their benefits.

Going with a travel agent

The best way to find a good travel agent is the same way you find a good plumber, mechanic, or doctor — through word of mouth. The similarities don't end there. Travel agents can be as valuable as these other pros in your life, especially if you're a frequent traveler.

In fact, today, one of the main benefits of using a travel agent is that he or she can save you time. If a travel agent specializes in Mexico, it's even better. He or she is likely to have personal insights or be able to tell you things about a destination or hotel that simply can't come through in a brochure.

Any travel agent can help you find a bargain airfare, hotel, or rental car. A good travel agent stops you from ruining your vacation by trying too hard to save a few dollars at the expense of a good experience. The best travel agents can tell you how much time you should budget for a destination, find a cheap flight that doesn't require you to change planes multiple times, get you a better hotel room for about the same price, arrange for a competitively priced rental car, and even give recommendations on restaurants.

Using a travel agent is the right choice if:

✔ You're not too Internet savvy.

✔ You prefer discussing your options with a live person.

✔ You may need to make changes in your itinerary.

✔ You're traveling with a group, with members coming together from several parts of the country.

✔ You're departing from one city, but returning to a different city.

Opting to plan on your own

The Internet has given mere mortals many of the same tools that used to be the exclusive domain of travel agents. Now you can find as good a deal — or perhaps an even better deal — on travel as an agent can usually find. The key to this self-guided, money-saving process? You must be willing to invest the time and patience required to uncover the best deals.

Don't underestimate the value of a first-hand recommendation from a friend or coworker. Talk to whoever you know who has been to the place you're thinking of visiting for a fresh assessment and a first-hand opinion. Then, after taking all your "research" into consideration, make your decisions and plans based on your own experiences and preferences.

Getting the Most from Your Travel Agent

To get the most out of your travel agent, do a little homework. Read up on your destination (you've already made a sound decision by buying this book) and pick out some accommodations and attractions you think you may like.

If you have access to the Internet, check prices on the Web before meeting with an agent to get a sense of ballpark prices. (See the "Finding the Best Airline and Airfare" section later in this chapter.) Then take your guidebook and Web information to the travel agent and ask him or her to make the arrangements for you. Because travel agents have access to more resources than even the most complete Web travel site, they may be able to get you a better price than you could get by yourself. And they can issue your tickets and vouchers right there at the office. If they can't get you into the hotel of your choice, they can recommend an alternative, and you can look for an objective review in the guidebook that you conveniently brought with you.

Try to find a travel agent who has been to Cancún and the Riviera Maya — recently. Even if the agent has traveled there, be aware that it's likely he or she stayed at only one or two hotels, probably one of the larger hotels that may have provided the agent with a complimentary room.

Before you call or meet with your travel agent, you should have one or two places in mind to compare. *Cancún & the Yucatán For Dummies* is a useful tool in narrowing down your choices. I've done the preliminary research to help you choose a place that has the features you're most interested in, and I've weeded out the mediocre hotels and restaurants from my selections to give you a head start. Jot down your preferences and maybe check the Web for some ideas of seasonal promotions and prices so that you have a ballpark idea of what to expect.

Keep in mind that travel agents work on commission. The good news is that *you* don't pay the commission; the airlines, accommodations, and tour companies do. The bad news is that unprincipled travel agents often try to persuade you to book the vacations that provide them with the most money in commissions. Over the past few years, some airlines and resorts have begun to limit or eliminate travel-agent commissions altogether. The immediate result has been that travel agents don't even bother booking certain services unless the customer specifically requests them. And some travel agents have started charging customers for their services. Don't be too put off by this system — if you're working with a pro with real, hands-on knowledge of your resort, it may be well worth the extra fee to truly enjoy your vacation.

Understanding Escorted and Package Tours

First, bear in mind that there's a big difference between an escorted tour and a package tour. With an *escorted tour,* the tour company takes care of all the details and tells you what to expect at each attraction. You know your costs up front, and an escorted tour can take you to the maximum number of sights in the minimum amount of time with the least amount of hassle. However, escorted tours are extremely rare in Cancún and elsewhere in the Yucatán; most travelers, once they arrive at their destination, simply book tours and excursions with local travel agents.

Package tours generally consist of round-trip airfare, ground transportation to and from your hotel, and your hotel room price, including taxes. Some packages also include all food and beverages and most entertainment and sports, when booked at an all-inclusive resort. You may find that a package tour can save you big bucks and is an ideal vacation option.

For popular destinations like Cancún, package tours are the smart way to go. In many cases, a package that includes airfare, hotel, and transportation to and from the airport costs less than just the hotel alone if you booked it yourself. That's because packages are sold in bulk to tour operators who resell them to the public. It's kind of like buying your vacation at one of those large, members-only warehouse clubs — except the tour operator is the one who buys the 1,000-count box of garbage bags and resells them 10 at a time at a cost that undercuts what you'd pay at your average, neighborhood supermarket.

Package tours can vary as much as those garbage bags, too. Some offer a better class of hotels than others. Some offer the same hotels for lower prices. Some offer flights on scheduled airlines; others book charter planes (which are known for having miniscule amounts of legroom). In some packages, your choice of accommodations and travel days may be limited. Some tours let you choose between escorted vacations and independent vacations; others allow you to add on just a few excursions or escorted day-trips (also at discounted prices) without booking an entirely escorted tour.

Each destination usually has one or two packagers that are better than the rest because they buy in even bigger bulk. The time you spend shopping around will be well rewarded.

The best place to start looking is the travel section of your local Sunday newspaper. Also check the ads in the back of national travel magazines like *Travel + Leisure, National Geographic Traveler,* and *Condé Nast Traveler.* **Liberty Travel** (☎ **888-271-1584** to find the store nearest you; Internet: www.libertytravel.com) is one of the biggest packagers in the Northeast and usually boasts a full-page ad in Sunday papers. **American Express Vacations** (☎ **800-346-3607;** Internet: http://travel.americanexpress.com/travel/) is another option.

When comparing packages, here are a few tips:

✔ **Read the fine print.** Make sure you know *exactly* what's included in the price you're being quoted, and what's not.

✔ **Don't compare Mayas and Aztecs.** When you look at different packagers, compare the deals that they offer on similar properties. Most packagers can offer bigger savings on some hotels than others.

✔ **Know what you're getting yourself into — and if you can get yourself out of it.** Before you commit to a package, make sure that you know how much flexibility you have. Often, packagers offer trip-cancellation insurance for around $25 to $30, which guarantees return of your payment if you need to change your plans.

✔ **Use your best judgment.** Stay away from fly-by-night and shady packagers. Go with a reputable firm with a proven track record. This area is one where your travel agent can come in handy.

You can even shop for these packages online — try these sites for a start:

✔ For one-stop shopping on the Web, go to www.vacationpackager.com, an extensive search engine that links you to more than 30 packagers offering Mexican beach vacations and even lets you custom design your own package.

✔ Check out www.2travel.com and find a page with links to a number of the big-name Mexico packagers, including several of the ones listed in this chapter.

✔ For last-minute, air-only packages or package bargains, check out **Vacation Hotline** at www.vacationhotline.net. After you find your "deal," you need to call them to make final booking arrangements, but they offer packages from both the popular Apple and Funjet vacation wholesalers.

✔ So-called "opaque-fare" services like **Priceline.com** (Internet: www.priceline.com) now allow you to bid on vacation packages. This feature means if you do a little homework to see what the average pacakge rates are, you may reap substantial savings with a lower bid. For a discussion of Priceline and other opaque-fare services, see "Using an 'opaque-fare' service," later in this chapter.

Another good resource is the airlines themselves, which often package their flights with accommodations. When you pick the airline, you can choose one that has frequent service to your hometown and the one on which you accumulate frequent-flier miles. Among the airline packagers, your options include

✔ **Aeromexico Vacations** (☎ 800-245-8585; Internet: www.aero mexico.com) offers year-round packages to almost every destination it flies to, including Cancún and Cozumel. Aeromexico has a large selection of resorts in these destinations and others in a variety of price ranges. The best deals are from Houston, Dallas, San Diego, Los Angeles, Miami, and New York, in that order.

✔ **American Airlines Vacations** (☎ 800-321-2121; Internet: www.aavacations.com) has year-round deals to Cancún and the Riviera Maya. You don't have to fly with American if you can get a better deal on another airline; land-only packages include hotel, airport transfers, and hotel room tax. American's hubs to Mexico are Dallas/Fort Worth, Chicago, and Miami, so you're likely to get the best prices — and the most direct flights — if you live near those cities. Its Web site offers unpublished discounts that are not available through the phone operators.

✔ **Continental Vacations** (☎ 800-634-5555 and 888-989-9255; Internet: www.continental.com) has year-round packages available to Cancún and Cozumel, with the best deals from Houston; Newark, New Jersey; and Cleveland. You have to fly Continental. The Internet deals offer savings not available elsewhere.

✔ **Delta Vacations** (☎ 800-872-7786; Internet: www.deltavacations. com) has year-round packages to Cozumel and Cancún. Atlanta is the hub, so expect the best prices from there.

✔ **Mexicana Vacations** (☎ 800-531-9321; Internet: www.mexicana. com) offers getaways to all the resorts buttressed by Mexicana's daily direct flights from Los Angeles to Cancún.

✔ **US Airways Vacations** (☎ 800-455-0123; Internet: www.usairwaysvacations.com) offers packages to Cancún, Cozumel, and the Riviera Maya. Charlotte, N.C., is the hub and will likely offer the best deals.

Several companies specialize in packages to Mexico's beaches; they usually fly in their own, chartered airplanes, so they can offer greatly discounted rates. Here are some of the packagers I prefer:

✔ **Apple Vacations** (☎ 800-365-2775; Internet: www.applevacations. com) offers inclusive packages to all the beach resorts and has the largest choice of hotels in Cancún, Cozumel, and the Riviera Maya. Apple perks include special baggage handling (company representatives take your bags from the airport directly to the hotel room, saving you the hassle) and the services of an Apple representative at the major hotels.

✔ **Funjet Vacations** (bookable through any travel agent, with general information available on its Web site at www.funjet.com) is one of the largest vacation packagers in the United States. Funjet has packages to Cancún, Cozumel, and the Riviera Maya.

✔ **GOGO Worldwide Vacations** (☎ **888-636-3942;** Internet: www. gogowwv.com) has trips to all the major beach destinations, including Cancún, offering several exclusive deals from higher-end hotels. These trips are bookable through any travel agent.

✔ **Pleasant Mexico Holidays** (☎ **800-448-3333;** Internet: www. pleasantholidays.com) is another of the largest vacation packagers in the United States with hotels in Cancún and Cozumel.

The biggest hotel chains and resorts also offer packages. If you already know where you want to stay, call the hotel or resort and ask whether it offers land/air packages.

Coping with Airport Security Measures

In the wake of the terrorist attacks of September 11, 2001, the airline industry began implementing stricter security measures in airports. Delays have mostly eased by now, but during busy travel times you may have to get to the airport earlier than usual. Regulations vary from airline to airline; you can make the process smoother by taking the following steps:

✔ **Arrive early.** Arrive at the airport at least two hours before your flight is scheduled to depart.

✔ **Don't count on curbside check-in.** Some airlines and airports have stopped curbside check-in altogether, while others offer it on a limited basis. For up-to-date information about specific regulations and implementations, check with the individual airline.

✔ **Be sure to carry the proper documentation.** On any trip to Mexico, your best ID is a passport. For information on the documentation needed to travel to Mexico, see Chapter 7. You will need to show your ID at various checkpoints. With an electronic ticket, you also may be required to have with you printed confirmation of purchase, and perhaps even the credit card with which you bought your ticket. This policy varies from airline to airline, so call ahead to make sure that you have the proper documentation. And *be sure that your ID is up-to-date:* An expired passport, for example, may keep you from boarding the plane.

✔ **Know what you can carry on — and what you can't.** Travelers in the United States are now limited to one carry-on bag plus one personal item (such as a purse or briefcase). The Transportation Security Administration (TSA) also has issued a list of newly restricted carry-on items, but the list changes frequently. Consult the TSA Web site at www.tsa.gov for the latest information.

✔ **Prepare to be searched.** Expect spot-checks. Remove electronic items, such as laptops and cell phones, from your carry-on bags and hand them over for additional screening. Limit the metal items you wear on your person so that you're less likely to set off the metal detector.

✔ **Don't joke around.** When a check-in agent asks whether someone other than you packed your bag, don't decide that it's a good time to be funny. The agent will not hesitate to sound an alarm.

✔ **Don't try to get to the gate unless you have a ticket.** Only ticketed passengers are allowed beyond the screener checkpoints, except for those people with specific medical or parental needs.

Finding the Best Airline and Airfare

The first step for the independent travel planner is finding the airlines that fly to Cancún or Cozumel, the two major airport gateways for the Yucatán's beach resorts. Mexico is becoming more easily accessible by plane. Many new regional carriers offer scheduled service to areas previously not served. In addition to regularly scheduled service, direct charter services from U.S. cities to Cancún and Cozumel are making it possible to fly direct from the largest airports in the United States. However, if you find that no direct flights are available, you can always reach your destination through an almost painless connection in Mexico City.

If you're booked on a flight through Mexico City, always try to check your luggage to your final destination. This arrangement is possible if you're flying with affiliated or code-share airlines — separate airlines that work closely together to help travelers reach final destinations via connecting flights. This way, you don't have to lug your bags through the Mexico City airport, and it saves some time during the connecting process.

For information about saving money on airfares using the Internet, see "Researching and Booking Your Trip Online," later in this chapter.

The main airlines operating direct or nonstop flights to Cancún and the Yucatán peninsula include

✔ **Aeromexico** (☎ 800-237-6639; Internet: www.aeromexico.com). Flights to Cancún and Cozumel.

✔ **American Airlines** (☎ 800-433-7300; Internet: www.aa.com). Flights to Cancún and Cozumel.

✔ **ATA** (☎ 800-225-2995; Internet: www.ata.com). Flights to Cancún.

✔ **British Airways** (☎ 800-247-9297, 0345-222-111 or 0845-77-333-77 in Britain; Internet: www.british-airways.com). Flights from London to Cancún.

- ✓ **Continental Airlines** (☎ 800-525-0280; Internet: www.continental. com). Flights to Cancún and Cozumel.

- ✓ **Delta** (☎ 800-221-1212; Internet: www.delta.com). Flights to Cancún and Cozumel (serviced through Aeromexico).

- ✓ **Mexicana** (☎ 800-531-7921; Internet: www.mexicana.com). Flights to Cancún and Cozumel.

- ✓ **Northwest Airlines** (☎ 800-225-2525; Internet: www.nwa.com). Seasonal flights to Cancún and Cozumel.

- ✓ **US Airways** (☎ 800-428-4322; Internet: www.usairways.com). Flights to Cancún and Cozumel.

Competition among the major U.S. airlines is unlike that of any other industry. A coach seat is virtually the same from one carrier to another, yet the difference in price may run as high as $1,000 for a product with the same intrinsic value.

Business travelers, who need flexibility to purchase their tickets at the last minute, change their itinerary at a moment's notice, or want to get home before the weekend, pay the premium rate, known as the *full fare.* Passengers who can book their ticket long in advance, who don't mind staying over Saturday night, or who are willing to travel on a Tuesday, Wednesday, or Thursday pay the least — usually a fraction of the full fare. On most flights, even the shortest hops, the full fare is close to $1,000 or more, but a 7- or 14-day advance purchase ticket is closer to $200 to $300. Obviously, it pays to plan.

The airlines also periodically hold sales, in which they lower the prices on their most popular routes. These fares have advance purchase requirements and date-of-travel restrictions, but you can't beat the price: usually no more than $400 for a cross-country flight. Keep your eyes open for these sales as you're planning your vacation. The sales tend to take place in seasons of low travel volume. You almost never see a sale around the peak summer vacation months of July and August or around Thanksgiving or Christmas, when people have to fly, regardless of what the fare is.

Consolidators, also known as bucket shops, are a good place to check for the lowest fares. Their prices are much better than the fares you can get yourself and are often even lower than what your travel agent can get you. You can find their ads in the small boxes at the bottom of the page in your newspaper's Sunday travel section. Some of the most reliable consolidators include **Cheap Tickets** (☎ 800-377-1000; Internet: www.cheaptickets.com), **1-800-FLY-CHEAP** (Internet: www.flycheap. com), and **Travac Tours & Charters** (☎ 800-872-8800; Internet: www. thetravelsite.com). Another good choice, **Council Travel** (☎ 800-226-8624; Internet: www.counciltravel.com), now owned by STA, especially caters to young travelers, but its bargain-basement prices are available to people of all ages.

Here are some travel tips — tested and true — for getting the lowest possible fare:

✔ **Timing is everything.** If you can, avoid peak travel times. In Mexico, the weeks surrounding the Christmas/New Year holidays and Easter are so jam-packed that I find it unenjoyable to be at a beach resort anyway. Airfares are relatively expensive anytime between January and May, with September through mid-November offering the best deals. Specials pop up throughout the year, however, based on current demand, and last-minute specials on package tours are an increasingly popular way to travel.

✔ **Book in advance for great deals.** Forgetting what I said in the previous sentence, you can also save big by booking early — with excellent fares available for 30-, 60-, or even 90-day advance bookings. Note that if you need to change your schedule, a penalty charge of $75 to $150 is common.

✔ **Choose an off-peak travel day.** Traveling on a Tuesday, Wednesday, or even Thursday can also save you money. Even if you can't travel both ways on these lower-fare days, you can still save by flying off-peak at least one way.

✔ **The midnight hour.** In the middle of the week, just after midnight, many airlines download cancelled low-priced airfares into their computers, so shortly after midnight is a great time to buy newly discounted seats. Midnight is the cutoff time for holding reservations. You may benefit by snagging cheap tickets that were just released by those who reserved — but never purchased — their tickets.

Researching and Booking Your Trip Online

More and more savvy travelers turn to the Internet when planning the perfect vacation to find out where the good deals are. Sites such as **Travelocity** (www.travelocity.com), **Microsoft Expedia** (www.expedia.com), and **Orbitz** (www.orbitz.com) allow consumers to comparison shop for airfares, book flights, learn of last-minute bargains, and reserve hotel rooms and rental cars. **Qixo** (www.qixo.com) allows you to search for flights and hotel rooms on 20 other travel-planning sites (such as Travelocity) at once. Qixo sorts results by price, after which you can book your travel directly through the site.

Knowing the benefits

With most sites requiring you to complete some sort of one-time registration form, Internet research can be a rather time-consuming task, but the benefits of researching your trip online can be well worth the effort:

✔ Airlines offer **last-minute specials,** such as weekend deals or Internet-only fares, to fill empty seats. Most of these E-savers are announced on Tuesday or Wednesday and must be purchased online. Check mega-sites that compile comprehensive lists of E-savers, such as Smarter Living (www.smarterliving.com) or WebFlyer (www.webflyer.com).

✔ Some sites send you **e-mail notification** when a cheap fare to your favorite destination becomes available, and some let you know when fares to a particular destination are at their lowest. Sign up for weekly e-mail alerts at airline Web sites to keep up with the latest deals.

✔ All major airlines offer **incentives** — bonus frequent-flier miles, Internet-only discounts, or sometimes free cell phone rentals — when you purchase online or buy an E-ticket.

✔ Advances in mobile technology provide travelers with **the ability to check flight statuses, change plans, or get specific directions** from handheld computing devices, mobile phones, and pagers. Some sites e-mail or page a passenger if a flight is delayed.

The good news is that you don't even have to book your trip online to reap the research benefits of the Web. The Internet can be a valuable tool for comparison shopping, for approaching a travel agent with a base of knowledge, and even for chatting with other travelers to truly rate the quality of the buffets at that all-inclusive you're considering.

One caution as you start to hunt for online deals: **Avoid online auctions.** Sites that auction airline tickets and frequent-flier miles are the No. 1 perpetrators of Internet fraud, according to the National Consumers League.

Using an "opaque-fare" service

Another category of online travel agent is the *opaque-fare* service, so called because some details of your flight remain hidden until you purchase your ticket. When you book an opaque fare, you give up control of your flight times and your choice of airline (although you're guaranteed to fly a full-service, large-scale carrier). You give up frequent-flier miles and lock yourself into a nonchangeable, nonrefundable ticket. You *can* specify the days you travel, whether you're willing to take *off-peak* flights (those that leave before 6 a.m. or after 10 p.m.), and how many connections you will accept (with a minimum of one). You also get to pick the airports you fly into and out of. Only after you pay for your ticket do you get the full details of your flight.

The most popular opaque-fare sites are Priceline (www.priceline.com) and Hotwire (www.hotwire.com), although Expedia and Travelocity now offer similar services as well. Priceline allows you to "name your price" for airline tickets, hotel rooms, vacation packages, and rental cars, while

Hotwire, Expedia, and Travelocity offer fixed-price deals on unnamed airlines (at least, unnamed until you purchase the ticket).

Opaque-fare sites are undoubtedly the source of some rock-bottom fares to Mexico (as well as some great deals on package trips to Cancún). But you need to be flexible. Opaque fares are a *bad choice* for these types of people:

- ✔ Those who can't stomach 6 a.m. departures.
- ✔ Those who may need to change their tickets.
- ✔ Those who demand nonstop flights.
- ✔ Those who are planning a quick, two-day trip — you might land in town at 10 p.m. on Saturday and be forced to leave at 6 a.m. on Sunday, eight hours later!

Choosing a Room That's Right for You

Whether you've chosen a package deal or you're planning your trip on your own, getting a room is a crucial part of your vacation planning. In this section, I help you decipher the various rates and provide some tips on how to get the best one. I also compare the pros and cons of different types of places to stay.

From small inns to large all-inclusives, the beach resorts along Mexico's Yucatán peninsula offer every type of vacation accommodation. And the prices can vary even more! Recommendations for specific places to stay are in the chapters devoted to the individual beach towns. I try to provide the widest range of options — both in types of hotels as well as budgets — but I always keep comfort in mind. What you find in this book is what I believe to be the best value for the money. Here are the major types of accommodations:

- ✔ **Resorts:** These accommodations tend to be the most popular option — especially with package tours — because they offer the most modern amenities, including cable TV, hairdryers, in-room safes, and generally, a selection of places to dine or have a drink. Large by definition, they may also boast various types of sporting facilities, spa services, shopping arcades, and tour-desk services. These places also tend to be the most expensive type of accommodation, but they can be heavily discounted if your timing is right.

- ✔ **Hotels:** These quarters tend to be smaller than resorts, with fewer facilities. In terms of style, look for anything from hacienda-style villas to all-suite hotels or sleek, modern structures. Most hotels at

Mexican beach resorts have at least a small swimming pool, and if they're not located directly on a beach, hotels frequently offer shuttle service to a beach club or an affiliate beachfront hotel.

✔ **All-inclusives:** In Mexico, all-inclusives are gaining rapidly in popularity, and they seem to be getting larger and larger in size. As the name implies, all-inclusives tie everything together in one price — your room, meals, libations, entertainment, sports activities, and sometimes, off-site excursions. The advantage that many travelers find with this option is an expected fixed price for their vacation — helpful if you need to stay within a strict budget. Many all-inclusives have their own nightclubs or, at least, offer evening shows and entertainment, such as theme nights, talent contests, or costume parties. As for the food, you may never go hungry, but you're unlikely to go gourmet either. Food quality can be an important variable, about which it helps to have talked to someone who's recently been to the particular all-inclusive.

✔ **Condos, apartments, and villas:** One of these accomodations can be a good option, especially if you're considering a stay longer than a week, and the reach of the Internet has made these lodging options extremely viable. Many condos, apartments, and villas come with housekeepers or even cooks. It's hard to know exactly what you're getting — and often it's futile to complain after you arrive — so again, word of mouth can be helpful here. At the very least, ask for references or search on the Internet to see whether anyone can offer an experience. In addition to the Internet, select options are always advertised in the major metropolitan newspapers, such as the *Los Angeles Times, Chicago Tribune,* and *The New York Times.* My recommendation? Save this option for your second visit when you have a better idea about the various parts of town and the area in general.

Finding Hotel Deals Online

When it comes to looking for great deals on **hotel rooms,** you're better off using a Web site devoted primarily to lodging because you may find properties that aren't listed on more general online travel sites. Some lodging sites specialize in a particular type of accommodations, such as bed-and-breakfasts, which you won't find on the more mainstream booking services. Others, such as TravelWeb, offer weekend deals on major chain properties, as discussed later in this section.

✔ Although the name **All Hotels on the Web** (www.all-hotels.com) is something of a misnomer, the site *does* have tens of thousands of listings throughout the world. Bear in mind that each hotel has paid a small fee ($25 and up) to be listed, so it's less of an objective list and more like a book of online brochures.

✔ **hoteldiscount!com** (www.180096hotel.com) lists bargain room rates at hotels in more than 50 U.S. and international cities. The cool thing is that hoteldiscount!com prebooks blocks of rooms in advance, so sometimes it has rooms — at discount rates — at hotels that are "sold out." Select a city and input your dates, and you get a list of the best prices for a selection of hotels. This site is notable for delivering deep discounts in cities where hotel rooms are expensive. The toll-free number is printed all over this site (☎ **800-96-HOTEL**); call it if you want more options than are listed online.

✔ **InnSite** (www.innsite.com) has B&B listings in all 50 U.S. states and more than 50 countries around the globe. Find an inn at your destination, see pictures of the rooms, and check prices and availability. This extensive directory of bed-and-breakfasts only includes listings if the proprietor submitted one. (It's free to get an inn listed.) Innkeepers write the descriptions, and many listings link to the inns' own Web sites. Also check out the **Bed and Breakfast Channel** (www.bedandbreakfast.com).

✔ **Places to Stay** (www.placestostay.com) lists one-of-a-kind places, with a focus on resort accommodations, in the United States and abroad that you may not find in other directories. Again, listing is selective: This directory isn't comprehensive, but it can give you a sense of what's available at different destinations.

✔ **TravelWeb** (www.travelweb.com) lists more than 26,000 hotels in 170 countries, focusing on chains such as Hyatt and Hilton, and you can book almost 90 percent of these listings online. The site's Click-It Weekends, updated each Monday, offers weekend deals at many leading hotel chains.

✔ Specific to Mexico, **Mexico Boutique Hotels** (http://mexicoboutiquehotels.com) has listings of small, unique properties that are unlikely to show up on the radar screens of most travel agents or large Web travel sites. In addition to very complete descriptions, the site also offers an online booking service.

✔ Another site specializing in Mexico accommodations is www.mexicohotels.com.

✔ Check the Web sites of Mexico's top hotel chains for special deals. These include www.caminoreal.com, www.hyatt.com, www.starwood.com, and www.fiestaamericana.com.

Chapter 6

Money Matters

*M*ost people save all year to be able to enjoy a wonderful vacation, so in this chapter, I share with you the finer points of stretching your dollars into pesos. I tell you about the nuances of changing currency to get more for your money and present the pros and cons of traveler's checks, credit cards, and cash. Finally, I tell you how to regroup after your wallet is lost or stolen.

Making Sense of the Peso

The currency in Mexico is the **Mexican peso,** and in recent years, economists have been talking about its amazing recovery and resiliency against the U.S. dollar. At this book's time of print, each peso is worth close to 10 U.S. cents, which means that an item costing 10 pesos would be equivalent to US$1. Like most things in Mexico, the paper currency is colorful, and it comes in denominations of 20 (blue), 50 (pink), 100 (red), 200 (green), and 500 (burgundy) pesos. Coins come in denominations of 1, 2, 5, 10, and 20 pesos and 50 **centavos** (100 centavos equals 1 peso).

New 50- and 500-peso bills look very similar, but 50-peso bills have a slightly pinkish hue and are smaller in size. However, always double-check how much you're paying and your change to avoid unpleasant surprises. The same applies to 10- and 20-peso coins. Twenty-peso coins are slightly larger than the 10-peso coins, but they look very similar.

Getting change continues to be a problem in Mexico. Small-denomination bills and coins are hard to come by, so start collecting them early in your trip and continue as you travel. Shopkeepers — and especially taxi drivers — always seem to be out of change and small bills; that's doubly true in a market. In other words, don't try to pay with a 500-peso bill when buying a 20-peso trinket.

Before you leave your hotel, it's a good idea to get a hundred pesos — about US$10 — in change so that you're sure to have change for cab and bus fares.

In this book, I use the universal currency sign ($) to indicate both U.S. dollars and pesos in Mexico. When you're in Mexico, you'll notice the common use of the currency symbol ($), generally indicating the price in pesos. Go ahead and ask if you're not sure because some higher-end places do tend to price their goods in U.S. dollars. Often, if a price is quoted in U.S. dollars, the letters "USD" follow the price.

The rate of exchange fluctuates a tiny bit daily, so you're probably better off not exchanging too much currency at once. Don't forget, however, to have enough pesos to carry you over a weekend or Mexican holiday, when banks are closed. In general, avoid carrying the U.S. $100 bill, the bill most commonly counterfeited in Mexico, and therefore, the most difficult to exchange, especially in smaller towns. Because small bills and coins in pesos are hard to come by in Mexico, the U.S. $1 bill is very useful for tipping. A tip of U.S. coins is of no value to the service provider because they can't be exchanged into Mexican currency.

To make your dollars go further, remember that ATMs offer the best exchange rate; however, you need to consider any service fees. Mexican banks offer the next-best fare, and they don't charge commission, unless you're cashing traveler's checks, in which case they usually charge a small commission. After banks, *casas de cambio* (houses of exchange) are your next best option, and they usually charge a commission. You can almost always get a lower exchange rate when you exchange your money at a hotel front desk.

Choosing Traveler's Checks, Credit Cards, or Cash

You need to think about *what kind* of money you're going to spend on your vacation before you leave home.

ATMs and cash

These days, almost all the Mexico beach resorts detailed in this book have 24-hour ATMs linked to a national network that almost always includes your bank at home. **Cirrus** (☎ 800-424-7787; Internet: www.mastercard.com/cardholderservices/atm/) and **Plus** (☎ 800-843-7587; Internet: www.visa.com/atms) are the two most popular networks; check the back of your ATM card to see which network your bank belongs to. The 800-numbers and Web sites will give you specific locations of ATMs where you can withdraw money while on vacation.

Using ATMs permits you to withdraw only as much cash as you need for a few days, which eliminates the insecurity (and the pick-pocketing threat) of carrying around a wad of cash. Note, however, that a daily maximum of about US$1,000 is common, though this amount does depend on your particular bank and type of account.

One important reminder: Many banks now charge a fee ranging from 50 cents to $3 when a non-account-holder uses their ATMs. Your own bank may also assess a fee for using an ATM that's not one of its branch locations. These fees mean that, in some cases, you get charged *twice* just for using your bankcard when you're on vacation. Although an ATM card can be an amazing convenience when traveling in another country (put your card in the machine and out comes foreign currency at an extremely advantageous exchange rate), banks are also likely to slap you with a "foreign currency transaction fee" just for making them do the pesos-to-dollars-to-pesos conversion math.

Credit cards

Credit cards are invaluable when traveling. They're a safe way to carry "money," and they provide a convenient record of all your travel expenses when you arrive home.

Travel with at least two different credit cards if you can. Depending on where you go, you may find MasterCard accepted more frequently than Visa (or vice versa), American Express honored or refused, and so on.

You can get **cash advances** from your credit card at any bank, and you don't even need to go to a teller — you can get a cash advance at the ATM if you know your **PIN number.** If you've forgotten your PIN number or didn't even know you had one, call the phone number on the back of your credit card and ask the bank to send it to you. It usually takes five to seven business days, though some banks will do it over the phone if you tell them your mother's maiden name or some other security clearance.

Remember the hidden expense to contend with when borrowing cash from a credit card: Interest rates for cash advances are often significantly higher than rates for credit-card purchases. More importantly, you start paying interest on the advance *the moment you receive the cash*. On an airline-affiliated credit card, a cash advance does not earn frequent-flier miles.

Traveler's checks

Traveler's checks are something of an anachronism from the days when people wrote personal checks instead of going to an ATM. Because you could replace traveler's checks if lost or stolen, they were a sound alternative to filling your wallet with cash at the beginning of a trip.

Still, if you prefer the security of traveler's checks, you can get them at almost any bank. **American Express** offers checks in denominations of $20, $50, $100, $500, and $1,000. You pay a service charge ranging from 1 to 4%, though AAA members can obtain checks without a fee at most AAA offices. You can also get American Express traveler's checks over the phone by calling ☎ **800-221-7282.**

Visa (☎ **800-227-6811**) also offers traveler's checks, available at Citibank locations across the country and at several other banks. The service charge ranges between 1.5 and 2%; checks come in denominations of $50, $100, $500, and $1,000. **MasterCard** also offers traveler's checks; call ☎ **800-223-9920** for a location near you.

Although traveler's checks are very safe, you should consider that:

✔ You usually get charged a commission to cash your traveler's checks, and when you add that to the exchange-rate loss, you end up getting fewer pesos for your money.

✔ Many smaller shops don't take traveler's checks, so if you plan to shop, cash the traveler's checks before you embark on your shopping expedition.

Knowing What to Do If Your Wallet Gets Stolen

Odds are that if your wallet is gone, you've seen the last of it, and the police aren't likely to recover it for you. However, after you realize it's gone and you cancel your credit cards, you need to inform the police. You may need the police-report number for credit-card or insurance purposes later. After you've covered all the formalities and before you head to the nearest bar to drown your sorrows, retrace your steps — you may be surprised at how many honest people are in Mexico, and you're likely to discover someone trying to find you to return your wallet.

Almost every credit-card company has an emergency toll-free number you can call if your wallet or purse is stolen. They may be able to wire you a cash advance off your credit card immediately; in many places, they can get you an emergency credit card within a day or two. The issuing bank's toll-free number is usually on the back of the credit card, but that doesn't help you much if the card was stolen. Write down the number on the back of your card before you leave and keep it in a safe place just in case.

If your credit card is stolen, major credit-card companies have emergency 800 numbers. Here's a list of numbers to call in the United States as well as internationally:

> ✔ **American Express** cardholders and traveler's check holders should call ☎ **800-327-2177** (U.S. toll free); ☎ **336-393-1111** (international direct-dial) for gold and green cards.
>
> ✔ The toll-free, U.S. emergency number for **Visa** is ☎ **800-336-8472**; from other countries, call ☎ **410-902-8012.** Your card issuer can also provide you with the toll-free, lost-/stolen-card number for the country or countries you plan to visit.
>
> ✔ **MasterCard** holders need to dial ☎ **800-826-2181** in the United States or 800-307-7309 from anywhere in the world; or ☎ **314-542-7111.** Also check with your card issuer for the toll-free, lost-/stolen-card number for the country or countries you want to visit.

To dial a U.S. toll-free number from inside Mexico, you must dial 001-880 and then the last seven digits of the toll-free number.

If you opt to carry **traveler's checks,** be sure to keep a record of their serial numbers so that you can handle this type of emergency.

Taxing Matters

There's a 15% **value-added tax (IVA)** on goods and services in most of Mexico, and it's supposed to be included in the posted price. This tax is 10% in Cancún and Cozumel. Unlike other countries (Canada and Spain, for example), Mexico doesn't refund this tax when visitors leave the country, so you don't need to hang on to those receipts for tax purposes.

All published prices you encounter in your travels around Mexico's beaches are likely to include all applicable taxes, except for hotel rates, which are usually published without the 15% IVA and the 2% lodging tax.

An **exit tax** of approximately $18 is imposed on every foreigner leaving Mexico. This tax is usually — but not always — included in the price of airline tickets. Be sure to reserve at least this amount in cash for your departure day if you're not certain that it's included in your ticket price.

Chapter 7

Taking Care of the Remaining Details

In This Chapter

▶ Getting your entry and departure documents in order

▶ Considering travel and medical insurance

▶ Ensuring a safe vacation

▶ Deciding whether to rent a car

▶ Packing wisely

A re you ready? Really ready? Before you can string that hammock between the palms, you need to take care of a few final details to get to your personal paradise. In this chapter, I cover the essentials and the requirements of getting into Mexico — and then back home again. I also review the ins and outs of dealing with travel insurance, ensuring a safe trip, deciding whether you should rent a car, and making sure that you pack everything you need for your Yucatán beach vacation.

Arriving In and Departing from Mexico

All travelers to Mexico are required to present **proof of citizenship,** such as an original birth certificate with a raised seal, a valid passport, or naturalization papers. Travelers using a birth certificate should also have a current form of photo identification, such as a driver's license or an official ID card. If your last name on the birth certificate is different from your current name (women using a married name, for example), you should also bring a photo identification card *and* legal proof of the name change, like the *original* marriage license or certificate.

When reentering the United States, you must prove both your citizenship *and* your identification, so always carry a picture ID, such as a driver's license or valid passport.

Although birth certificates enable you to enter Mexico, they don't enable you to reenter the United States. And although you can enter Mexico using a driver's license as identification, this documentation alone is not acceptable identification for reentering the United States. While in Mexico, you must also obtain a **Mexican tourist permit (FMT),** which is issued free of charge by Mexican border officials after proof of citizenship is accepted. These forms are generally provided by the airline aboard your flight into Mexico.

The tourist permit is more important than a passport in Mexico, so guard it carefully. If you lose it, you may not be permitted to leave the country until you can replace it — a bureaucratic hassle that can take anywhere from a few hours to a week. (If you do lose your tourist permit, get a police report from local authorities indicating that your documents were stolen; having one *might* lessen the hassle of exiting the country without all your identification.) You should also contact the nearest consular office to report the stolen papers so that it can issue a reentry document.

Note that children under the age of 18 traveling without parents or with only one parent must have a notarized letter from the absent parent or parents authorizing the travel. The letter must include the duration of the visit, destination, names of accompanying adults, parents' home addresses, telephone numbers, and so on. You must also attach a picture of the child to this letter.

Obtaining a Passport

Although you can enter Mexico without a passport, the only legal form of identification recognized around the world is a valid passport, and for that reason alone, having yours whenever you travel abroad is a good idea. In the United States, you're used to your driver's license being the all-purpose ID card. Abroad, it only proves that some American state lets you drive. Getting a passport is easy, but it takes some time to complete the process.

The U.S. State Department's Bureau of Consular Affairs maintains an excellent Web site (http://travel.state.gov) that provides everything you need to know about passports (including downloadable applications and locations of passport offices). In addition, the Web site provides extensive information about foreign countries, including travel warnings about health and terrorism. You can also call the National Passport Information Center at ☎ **900-225-5674** (35 cents per minute) or ☎ **888-362-8668** ($4.95 per call).

Applying for a U.S. passport

Apply for a passport at least a month, preferably two, before you leave. Although processing generally takes three weeks, during busy periods it can run longer (especially in spring). For people over the age of 15, a passport is valid for ten years.

If you're a U.S. citizen applying for a first-time passport and you're 13 years of age or older, you need to apply in person at one of the following locations:

- ✔ **A passport office:** An appointment is required for a visit to one of the following facilities, and your departure date must be within two weeks: Boston, Chicago, Houston, Los Angeles, Miami, New York City, Philadelphia, San Francisco, Seattle, Stamford (Connecticut), and Washington, D.C. No appointments are required at the offices in Honolulu and New Orleans.

- ✔ **A federal, state, or probate court:** The clerk of court is the office of the court that accepts passport applications.

- ✔ **A major post office, some libraries, and a number of county and municipal offices:** Not all accept applications; call your local post office or log on to the Web site at www.usps.gov for more information.

When you go to apply, bring the following items with you:

- ✔ **Completed passport application:** To apply for your first passport, fill out form DSP-11 (available online at http://travel.state.gov and www.usps.gov). You can complete this form in advance to save time. However, *do not sign* the application until you present it to the person at the passport agency, court, or post office.

- ✔ **Application fee:** For people age 16 or older, a passport costs $70 ($55 plus a $15 handling fee).

- ✔ **Proof of U.S. citizenship:** Bring your old passport if you're renewing (see the following section); otherwise, bring a certified copy of your birth certificate with registrar's seal, a report of your birth abroad, or your naturalized citizenship documents.

- ✔ **Proof of identity:** Among the accepted documents are a valid driver's license, a state or military ID, an old passport, or a naturalization certificate.

- ✔ **Two identical 2-inch by 2-inch photographs with a white or off-white background:** You can get these pictures taken in just about any corner photo shop; these places have a special camera to make the photos identical. Expect to pay up to $15 for them. You *cannot* use the strip photos from one of those photo vending machines.

Renewing a U.S. passport by mail

You can renew an existing, nondamaged passport by mail if it was issued within the past 15 years, *and* you were over age 16 when it was issued, *and* you still have the same name as the passport (or you can legally document your name change).

Include your expired passport, renewal form DSP-82, two identical photos (see the preceding section), and a check or money order for $55 (no extra handling fee). Mail everything (certified, return receipt requested, just to be safe) in a padded envelope to National Passport Center, P.O. Box 371971, Pittsburgh, PA 15250-7971. If you need to change the name on your passport, you must submit a separate form, along with a certified copy of your marriage certificate or name change court decree; consult the Web site http://travel.state.gov for details.

Allow at least one month to six weeks for your application to be processed and your new passport to be sent.

Getting your passport in a hurry

Although processing usually takes about three weeks, it can actually take far longer, especially during busy times of year, such as spring. If you're crunched for time, consider paying an extra $60 (plus the express mail service fee) to have your passport sent to you within seven to ten working days.

In even more of a hurry? Try **Passport Express** (☎ **800-362-8196** or 401-272-4612; Internet: www.passportexpress.com), a nationwide service that can get you a new or renewed passport within 24 hours. Getting a new passport with this service costs $150 plus the $95 government fees if you need it in one to six days, or $100 plus the $95 government fees if you need it in seven to ten days. If you're renewing your passport, the government fees drop to $75. For a rushed passport, you must have proof of travel (your tickets).

For more details about getting a passport, call the **National Passport Agency** (☎ **202-647-0518**). To locate a passport office in your area, call the **National Passport Information Center** (☎ **900-225-5674,** 35¢ per minute). The Web page of the **U.S. State Department** (http://travel.state.gov) also offers information on passport services, and you can download an application. In addition, many post offices and travel agencies keep passport applications on hand.

Applying for passports from other countries

The following list offers more information for citizens of Canada, the United Kingdom, Ireland, Australia, and New Zealand.

Canadian citizens

Passport information and applications are available from the central **Passport Office** in Ottawa (☎ **800-567-6868;** Internet: www.dfait-maeci.gc.ca/passport/). Regional passport offices and travel agencies also offer applications. Valid for five years, a passport costs $85 Canadian. Applications must include two identical passport-sized photographs and proof of Canadian citizenship. Allow five to ten days for processing if you apply in person or about three weeks if you submit your application by mail.

Residents of the United Kingdom

To pick up an application for a ten-year passport, visit your nearest passport office, major post office, or travel agency. You can also contact the **London Passport Office** at ☎ **0171-271-3000** or search its Web site at www.ukpa.gov.uk/. Passports are £30 for adults.

Residents of Ireland

You can apply for a ten-year passport, costing €57, at the **Passport Office** (Setanta Centre, Molesworth St., Dublin 2; ☎ **01-671-1633;** Internet: www.irlgov.ie/iveagh). You can also apply at 1A South Mall, Cork (☎ **021-272-525**) or over the counter at most main post offices. Those under age 18 and over age 65 must apply for a €12 three-year passport.

Residents of Australia

Apply at your local post office, search the government Web site at www.passports.gov.au/, or call toll-free ☎ **131-232.** Passports for adults are A$144 and, for those under age 18, A$72.

Residents of New Zealand

You can pick up a passport application at any travel agency or Link Centre. For more info, contact the **Passport Office** (P.O. Box 805, Wellington; ☎ **0800-225-050;** Internet: www.passports.govt.nz). Passports for adults are NZ$80 and, for those under age 16, NZ$40.

Dealing with lost passports

Keep your passport with you at all times, preferably secured in a money belt. The only times to give it up are at the bank or money exchange (so that tellers can verify information when you change traveler's checks or foreign currency) or to airline reservations agents and immigration officials when entering or leaving a country.

If you lose your passport in a foreign country, go directly to the nearest U.S. embassy or consulate. Bring all forms of identification you have, and they can start arranging for a new passport. This ordeal is a huge hassle that should be avoided at all costs.

Always carry a photocopy of the first page of your passport with you when you travel and keep the copy in a place separate from the original. Doing so greatly speeds up the paperwork in case your passport goes missing.

Clearing U.S. Customs

You *can* take it with you — up to a point. Technically, no limits exist on how much loot U.S. citizens can bring back into the United States from a trip abroad, but the Customs authority *does* put limits on how much you can bring in for free. (This rule is mainly for taxation purposes, to separate tourists with souvenirs from importers.)

U.S. citizens may bring home $400 worth of goods duty-free, providing you've been out of the country at least 48 hours and haven't used the exemption in the past 30 days. This amount includes one liter of an alcoholic beverage (you must, of course, be older than 21), 200 cigarettes, and 100 cigars. Anything you mail home from abroad is exempt from the $400 limit. You may mail up to $200 worth of goods to yourself (marked "for personal use") and up to $100 to others (marked "unsolicited gift") once each day, so long as the package does not include alcohol or tobacco products. You'll have to pay an import duty on anything over these limits.

Note that buying items at a **duty-free shop** before flying home does *not* exempt them from counting toward U.S. Customs limits (monetary or otherwise). The "duty" that you're avoiding in those shops is the local tax on the item (like state sales tax in the United States), not any import duty that may be assessed by the U.S. Customs office.

If you have further questions or for a list of specific items you cannot bring into the United States, look in your phone book (under U.S. Government, Department of the Treasury, U.S. Customs Service) to find the nearest Customs office. Or check out the Customs Service Web site at www.customs.ustreas.gov/travel/travel.htm.

Considering Insurance

You can purchase three primary kinds of travel insurance: trip-cancellation insurance, medical insurance, and lost-luggage insurance.

Trip-cancellation insurance is a good idea if you've paid a large portion of your vacation expenses up front, such as for an air/hotel package deal, an all-inclusive resort, or a cruise. You should strongly consider this coverage particularly if you have young children because you never know when accidents or illnesses may crop up.

But the other two types of insurance — **medical** and **lost luggage** — don't make sense for most travelers. Your existing health insurance should cover you if you get sick while on vacation. (Although, if you belong to an HMO, check to see whether you're fully covered when away from home.) Homeowner's insurance should cover stolen luggage if you have off-premises theft. Check your existing policies before you buy any additional coverage. The airlines are responsible for $2,500 on domestic flights (and $9.07 per pound, up to $640, on international flights) if they lose your luggage; if you plan to carry anything more valuable than that, keep it in your carry-on bag.

Some credit cards (American Express and certain gold and platinum Visa and MasterCard, for example) offer automatic flight insurance against death or dismemberment in case of an airplane crash. If you still feel you need more insurance, try one of the companies in the following list. But don't pay for more insurance than you need. For example, if you only need trip-cancellation insurance, don't purchase coverage for lost or stolen property. Trip-cancellation insurance costs approximately 6% to 8% of the total value of your vacation.

Among the reputable issuers of travel insurance are

- ✔ **Access America** (6600 W. Broad St., Richmond, VA 23230; ☎ **800-284-8300;** Fax: 800-346-9265; Internet: www.accessamerica.com)

- ✔ **Travelex Insurance Services** (11717 Burt St., Ste. 202, Omaha, NE 68154; ☎ **800-228-9792;** Internet: www.travelex-insurance.com)

- ✔ **Travel Guard International** (1145 Clark St., Stevens Point, WI 54481; ☎ **800-826-1300;** Internet: www.travel-guard.com)

- ✔ **Travel Insured International, Inc.** (P.O. Box 280568, 52-S Oakland Ave., East Hartford, CT 06128-0568; ☎ **800-243-3174;** Internet: www.travelinsured.com)

Getting Sick Away from Home

Apart from how getting sick can ruin your vacation, it also can present the problem of finding a doctor you trust when you're away from home. Bring all your medications with you, as well as a prescription for more — you may run out. Bring an extra pair of contact lenses in case you lose one. And don't forget the Pepto-Bismol for common travelers' ailments like upset stomach or diarrhea.

If you have health insurance, check with your provider to find out the extent of your coverage outside of your home area. Be sure to carry your identification card in your wallet. And if you worry that your existing policy isn't sufficient, purchase medical insurance for more comprehensive coverage. (See the "Considering Insurance," section earlier in this chapter.)

If you suffer from a chronic illness, talk to your doctor before taking the trip. If you have epilepsy, diabetes, or a heart condition, wearing a **Medic Alert identification tag** can immediately alert any doctor to your condition and give him or her access to your medical records through Medic Alert's 24-hour hotline. Membership is $35, with a $15 renewal fee. Contact the Medic Alert Foundation (2323 Colorado Ave., Turlock, CA 95382; ☎ **800-432-5378;** Internet: www.medicalert.org).

If you do get sick, ask the concierge at your hotel to recommend a local doctor — even his or her own doctor, if necessary. Another good option is to call the closest consular office and ask for a referral to a doctor. Most consulates have a listing of reputable English-speaking doctors. Most beach destinations in Mexico have at least one modern facility staffed by doctors used to treating the most common ailments of tourists. In the case of a real emergency, a service from the United States can fly people to American hospitals: **Air-Evac (☎ 888-554-9729,** or call collect 510-293-5968) is a 24-hour air ambulance. You can also contact the service in Guadalajara (☎ **01-800-305-9400,** 3-616-9616, or 3-615-2471). Several companies offer air-evac service; for a list, refer to the U.S. State Department Web site at http://travel.state.gov/medical.html.

From my ten years' experience of living in and traveling throughout Mexico, I can honestly say that most health problems that foreign tourists to Mexico encounter are self-induced. If you take in too much sun, too many margaritas, and too many street tacos within hours of your arrival, don't blame the water if you get sick. You'd be surprised how many people try to make up for all the fun they've missed in the past year on their first day on vacation in Mexico.

Avoiding turista!

It's called "travelers' diarrhea" or *turista,* the Spanish word for "tourist." I'm talking about the persistent diarrhea, often accompanied by fever, nausea, and vomiting, that used to attack many travelers to Mexico. Some folks in the United States call this affliction "Montezuma's revenge," but you won't hear it referred to this way in Mexico. Widespread improvements in infrastructure, sanitation, and education have practically eliminated this ailment, especially in well-developed resort areas. Most travelers make a habit of drinking only bottled water, which also helps to protect against unfamiliar bacteria. In resort areas, and generally throughout Mexico, only purified ice is used. Doctors say this ailment isn't caused by just one "bug," but by a combination of consuming different foods and water, upsetting your schedule, being overtired, and experiencing the stresses of travel. A good high-potency (or "therapeutic") vitamin supplement and extra vitamin C can help. And yogurt is good for healthy digestion. If you do happen to come down with this ailment, nothing beats Pepto-Bismol, readily available in Mexico.

Preventing *turista:* The U.S. Public Health Service recommends the following measures for preventing travelers' diarrhea:

✔ Get enough sleep.

✔ Don't overdo the sun.

✔ Drink only purified water, which means tea, coffee, and other beverages made with boiled water; canned or bottled carbonated beverages and water; or beer and wine. Most restaurants with a large tourist clientele use only purified water and ice.

✔ Choose food carefully. In general, avoid salads, uncooked vegetables, and unpasteurized milk or milk products (including cheese). However, salads in a first-class restaurant, or in a restaurant that serves a lot of tourists, are generally safe to eat. Choose food that's freshly cooked and still hot. Peelable fruit is ideal. Don't eat undercooked meat, fish, or shellfish.

✔ In addition, something as simple as washing hands frequently can prevent the spread of germs and go a long way toward keeping *turista* at bay.

Because **dehydration** can quickly become life-threatening, be especially careful to replace fluids and electrolytes (potassium, sodium, and the like) during a bout of diarrhea. Rehydrate by drinking Pedialyte, a rehydration solution available at most Mexican pharmacies, sports drinks, or glasses of natural fruit juice (high in potassium) with a pinch of salt added. Or try a glass of boiled, pure water with a quarter teaspoon of sodium bicarbonate (baking soda) and a bit of lime juice added.

Staying Safe and Healthy

If you find yourself getting friendly with the locals — and I mean friendly to the point of a fling — don't be embarrassed to carry or insist on stopping for condoms and then use them! Too many vacationing men and women are filled with morning-after regrets because they didn't protect themselves. Don't allow your fear of being judged make you do something that's frankly stupid. Also know that Mexico's teen-to-20-something population has a rapidly escalating **AIDS** rate — especially in resort areas — due to the transient nature of the population and poor overall education about this disease.

And when it comes to **drugs,** many outsiders have the impression that the easygoing nature of these tropical towns means an equally laid-back attitude exists toward drug use. Not so. Marijuana, cocaine, ecstasy, and other mood-altering drugs are illegal in Mexico. In some places, police randomly search people — including obvious tourists — who are walking the streets at night.

If you do choose to indulge, don't expect any special treatment if you're caught. In fact, everything bad you've ever heard about a Mexican jail is considered to be close to the truth — if not a rose-colored version of it. Mexico employs the Napoleonic Code of law, meaning that you're guilty until proven innocent. Simply stated, time in jail isn't worth the potential high. That's what tequila's for!

If you're traveling with **infants and/or children** in Mexico, be extra careful to avoid anything that's not bottled. You can purchase infant formulas, baby foods, canned milk, and other baby supplies from grocery stores. Your best bet is to carry extra baby eats when you go out. Most Mexican restaurants will cheerfully warm bottles and packaged goods for your child.

Be especially careful of sun exposure because **sunburn** can be extremely dangerous. Protect the little ones with special SPF bathing suits and cover-ups and regularly apply a strong sunscreen.

Dehydration can also make your child seriously ill. Make sure that your child drinks plenty of water and juices throughout the day. Especially when they're in the pool or at the beach having fun, they may not remember that they're thirsty, so it's up to you to remind them. Sunburn also contributes to and complicates dehydration.

Renting a Car

The first thing you should know is that car-rental costs are high in Mexico because cars are more expensive. However, the condition of rental cars has improved greatly over the years, and clean, comfortable, new cars are the norm. The basic cost for a one-day rental of a Volkswagen (VW) Beetle, with unlimited mileage (but before the 15% tax and $15 to $25 daily for insurance), is $45 in Cancún. Renting by the week gives you a lower daily rate. At press time, Avis was offering a basic seven-day weekly rate for a VW Beetle (before tax or insurance) of $220 in Cancún. Prices may be considerably higher if you rent around a major holiday.

Car-rental companies usually write a credit-card charge in U.S. dollars.

Be careful of deductibles, which vary greatly in Mexico. Some deductibles are as high as $2,500, which immediately comes out of your pocket in case of car damage. Hertz has a $1,000 deductible on a VW Beetle; the deductible at Avis is $500 for the same car.

Always get the insurance. Insurance is offered in two parts. Collision and damage insurance covers your car and others if the accident is your fault, and personal accident insurance covers you and anyone in your car. Read the fine print on the back of your rental agreement and note that insurance may be invalid if you have an accident while driving on an unpaved road.

Finding the best car-rental deal

Car-rental rates vary even more than airline fares. The price depends on the size of the car, the length of time you keep it, where and when you pick it up and drop it off, where you take it, and a host of other factors.

Asking a few key questions can save you hundreds of dollars. For example, weekend rates may be lower than weekday rates. Ask whether the rate is the same for Friday morning pickup as it is for Thursday night. If you're keeping the car five or more days, a weekly rate may be cheaper than the daily rate. Some companies may assess a drop-off charge if you don't return the car to the same renting location; others, notably National, do not. Ask whether the rate is cheaper if you pick up the car at the airport or a location in town. Don't forget to mention membership in AAA, AARP, frequent-flier programs, and trade unions. These memberships usually entitle you to discounts ranging from 5% to 30%. Ask your travel agent to check any and all of these rates. And most car rentals are worth at least 500 miles on your frequent-flier account!

As with other aspects of planning your trip, using the Internet can make comparison shopping for a car rental much easier. All the major booking Web sites — **Travelocity** (www.travelocity.com), **Expedia** (www.expedia.com), **Orbitz** (www.orbitz.com), **Yahoo! Travel** (www.travel.yahoo.com), and **Cheap Tickets** (www.cheaptickets.com), for example — have search engines that can dig up discounted car-rental rates. Just enter the size of the car you want, the pickup and return dates, and the city where you want to rent, and the server returns a price. You can even make the reservation through these sites.

In addition to the standard coverage, car-rental companies also offer additional liability insurance (if you harm others in an accident), personal accident insurance (if you harm yourself or your passengers), and personal effects insurance (if your luggage is stolen from your car). If you have insurance on your car at home, you're probably covered for most of these unlikelihoods. If your own insurance doesn't cover you for rentals or if you don't have auto insurance, you should consider the additional coverage. But weigh the likelihood of getting into an accident or losing your luggage against the cost of these insurance options (as much as $20 per day combined), which can significantly add to the price of your rental.

Some companies also offer refueling packages, in which you pay for an entire tank of gas up front. The price is usually fairly competitive with local gas prices, but you don't get credit for any gas remaining in the tank. If you reject this option, you pay only for the gas you use, but you have to return the car with a full tank or face charges of $3 to $4 a gallon for any shortfall. If a stop at a gas station on the way to the airport will make you miss your plane, by all means take advantage of the fuel purchase option. Otherwise, skip it.

Remembering safety comes first

If you decide to rent a car and drive in Mexico, you need to keep a few things in mind:

- ✔ Most Mexican roads are not up to U.S. standards of smoothness, hardness, width of curve, grade of hill, or safety markings. The roads in and around Cancún are a notable exception, but elsewhere in the Yucatán, this observation generally holds true.

- ✔ Driving at night is dangerous — the roads aren't good, and they're rarely lit; trucks, carts, pedestrians, and bicycles usually have no lights; and you can hit potholes, animals, rocks, dead ends, or uncrossable bridges without warning.

- ✔ Never turn left by stopping in the middle of a highway with your left signal on. Instead, pull off the highway onto the right shoulder, wait for traffic to clear, and then proceed across the road.

- ✔ No credit cards are accepted for gas purchases.

- ✔ Places called *vulcanizadora* or *llantera* repair flat tires. Such places are commonly open 24 hours a day on the most traveled highways. Even if the place looks empty, chances are you'll find someone who can help you fix a flat.

- ✔ When possible, many Mexicans drive away from minor accidents, or try to make an immediate settlement, to avoid involving the police.

- ✔ If the police arrive while the involved persons are still at the scene, everyone may be locked up until responsibility is determined and damages are settled. If you were in a rental car, notify the rental company immediately and ask how to contact the nearest adjuster. (You did buy insurance with the rental, right?)

Packing for the Yucatán

Start packing by taking out everything you think you need and laying it out on the bed. Then get rid of half of it.

It's not that the airlines won't let you take it all — they will, with some limits — but why would you want to get a hernia from lugging half your house around with you? Suitcase straps can be particularly painful when hanging from sunburned shoulders.

So what are the bare essentials? Comfortable walking shoes, a camera, a versatile sweater and/or jacket, a belt, a swimsuit, toiletries and medications (pack these in your carry-on bag so you have them if the airline loses your luggage), and something to sleep in. Unless you're attending a board meeting, a funeral, or one of the city's finest restaurants, you probably don't need a suit or a fancy dress. Even the nicest restaurants tend to be casual when it comes to dress, especially for men. Women, on the other hand, tend to enjoy those sexy resort dresses, and they're definitely appropriate in any of the resorts covered in this book. But when it comes to essentials, you get more use out of a pair of jeans or khakis and a comfortable sweater.

Electricity runs on the same current in Mexico as in the United States and Canada, so feel free to bring a hairdryer, personal stereo, or whatever else you'd like to plug in. Don't bother to bring a travel iron — most hotels offer irons and ironing boards, or they offer the service at a very reasonable rate.

When choosing your suitcase, think about the kind of traveling you're doing. If you'll be walking with your luggage on hard floors, a bag with wheels makes sense. If you'll be carrying your luggage over uneven roads or up and down stairs, wheels don't help much. A fold-over garment bag helps keep dressy clothes wrinkle-free, but it can be a nuisance if you'll be packing and unpacking a lot. Hard-sided luggage protects breakable items better, but it weighs more than soft-sided bags.

When packing, start with the biggest, hardest items (usually shoes) and then fit smaller items in and around them. Pack breakable items in between several layers of clothes or keep them in your carry-on bag. Put things that could leak, like shampoos or suntan lotions, in resealable plastic bags. Lock your suitcase with a small padlock (available at most luggage stores if your bag doesn't already have one) and put a distinctive identification tag on the outside so that your bag is easy to spot on the carousel.

Stricter security measures now dictate that each passenger is only allowed to bring one carry-on bag and one personal item (a purse, backpack, or briefcase) on the plane, and the items you do bring onboard are subject to strict size limitations. Both must fit in the overhead compartment or under the seat in front of you. For specific information about what you can and can't bring on the plane, see Chapter 5.

Among the items you might consider carrying on are a book; any breakable items you don't want to put in your suitcase; a personal stereo with headphones; a snack (in the likely event you don't like the airline food); a bottle of water; any vital documents you don't want to lose in your luggage (your return ticket, passport, wallet, and so on); and some empty space for the sweater or jacket that you won't be wearing while you're waiting for your luggage in an overheated terminal. You should also carry aboard any prescription medications, your glasses or spare contact lenses, and your camera. I always carry a change of clothes (shorts, T-shirt, and swimsuit) — just in case my checked baggage is lost. If the airline loses your luggage, you're likely to have it again within 24 hours, but having these essentials allows you to jump right into vacation fun anyway.

Here's a quick checklist of items you don't want to forget:

- ✔ At least two swimsuits
- ✔ Sunglasses
- ✔ Comfortable walking shoes
- ✔ Sandals
- ✔ Hat or cap
- ✔ Sunscreen
- ✔ Driver's license (if you plan to rent a car)
- ✔ Scuba certification (if you plan to dive)
- ✔ Casual slacks other than jeans (for men, especially if you plan on hitting the trendiest discos, some of which don't allow shorts or jeans)
- ✔ A pareo (sarong) that can double as a long or short skirt, or a wrap (for women)

Tips on what to wear to church

Whenever you visit a church in Mexico, no matter how casual the town is or how close the church is to the ocean, you should never enter wearing just a swimsuit or a pareo. Women should wear something other than short shorts and halter tops. Men should always wear some sort of shirt, even if it's just a tank top.

Part III
Cancún

©RICHTENNANT

"All I know is what the swim-up bartender told me. Wearing these should improve our game by 25 percent."

In this part . . .

The most popular of Mexico's beach resorts, Cancún
perfectly showcases the country's breathtaking natural beauty and the depth of its thousand-year-old history.
Cancún is both the peak of Caribbean splendor and a
modern mega-resort. It boasts translucent turquoise
waters, powdery white-sand beaches, and a wide array of
nearby shopping, dining, and nightlife choices, in addition
to a ton of other activities. Most resorts are offered at
exceptional value, and Cancún is easily accessible by air.

Many travelers who are apprehensive about visiting foreign
soil feel completely at home and at ease in Cancún: English
is spoken, dollars are accepted, roads are well paved, and
lawns are manicured. A lot of the shopping and dining takes
place in malls, and I swear that some hotels seem larger
than a small town. In the following chapters, I introduce you
to this Caribbean-coast jewel and offer lots of tips for
making the most of your stay on this nonstop island.

Chapter 8

The Lowdown on Cancún's Hotel Scene

In 1974, a team of Mexican-government computer analysts selected Cancún as an area for tourism development because of its ideal combination of features to attract travelers — a reliable climate; beautiful, untouched white-sand beaches; clear, shallow water; and proximity to historic ruins. Cancún is actually an island, a 14-mile-long sliver of land shaped roughly like the number "7." Two bridges, spanning the expansive Nichupté Lagoon, connect Cancún to the mainland. (Cancún means "Golden Snake" in the Mayan language.)

With more than 24,000 hotel rooms in the area to choose from, Cancún can no longer claim to be "untouched." But this resort town has an accommodation for every taste and every budget. Here, I review the two main areas — **Cancún Island (Isla Cancún)** and **Cancún City (Ciudad Cancún),** located inland, to the west of the island.

Cancún is definitely the destination to try out an air-hotel package. Although the rack rates at Cancún's hotels are among the highest in Mexico, the package deals are among the best because of the large number of charter companies operating here. I should also point out that if you do arrive without a hotel reservation — not recommended during peak weeks surrounding the Christmas and Easter holidays — you're likely to be able to bargain your way into a great rate. For more information on air-hotel packages, see Chapter 5.

Choosing a Location

Island hotels are stacked along the beach like dominoes; almost all of them offer clean, modern facilities. Extravagance reigns in the more recently built hotels, many of which are awash in a sea of marble and glass. However, some hotels, although they are exclusive, adopt a more relaxed attitude.

The water is placid on the upper end of the island facing Bahía de Mujeres (Bay of the Women), while beaches lining the long side of the island facing the Caribbean are subject to choppier water and crashing waves on windy days. Be aware that the farther south you go on the island, the longer it takes (20 to 30 minutes in traffic) to get back to the "action spots," which are primarily located between the Plaza Flamingo and Punta Cancún on the island — close to the point that connects the two parts of the 7 — and along Avenida Tulum on the mainland. (To get an idea of Cancún's different neighborhoods, see the "Cancún Orientation Map" in Chapter 9.)

Almost all major hotel chains are represented along **Isla Cancún,** also known as the **Hotel Zone,** so you can view my selections as a representative summary, with a select number of notable places to stay. The reality is that Cancún is such a popular package destination from the United States that prices and special deals are often the deciding factor for vacationers traveling here.

Ciudad Cancún is the more authentic Mexican town of the two locations, where the workers in the hotels live and day-to-day business is conducted for those not on vacation. The area offers independently owned, smaller, and much less expensive stays — the difference in prices between these accommodations and their island counterparts is truly remarkable. And many hotels in Ciudad Cancún offer a shuttle service to sister-properties in Isla Cancún, meaning you can still access the beach, and for a fraction of the price in return for a little extra travel time. In my opinion, many of the best restaurants are located here, especially if you're looking for a meal in a type of restaurant other than those you can find back home. It also goes without saying that you get the best value for your meal dollar or peso in Ciudad Cancún.

Living la vida local

For condo, home, and villa rentals as an alternative to hotel stays, check with **Cancún Hideaways,** a company specializing in luxury properties, downtown apartments, and condos — many offered at prices much lower than comparable hotel accommodations. Owner Maggie Rodriguez, a former resident of Cancún, has made this niche market her specialty. You can preview her offerings at **www.cancun-hideaways.com.**

Cancún's Best Accommodations

Each hotel listing includes specific rack rates for two people spending one night in a standard room, double occupancy during high season (Christmas to Easter), unless otherwise indicated. Rack rates simply mean published rates and tend to be the highest rate paid — you can do better, especially if you're purchasing a package that includes airfare. (See Chapter 5 for tips on avoiding paying rack rates.) The rack rate prices quoted here include the 12% room tax — note that this tax is 5% lower than in most other resorts in Mexico, where the standard tax is 17%. Please refer to the Introduction of this book for an explanation of the price categories.

Hotels often double the normal rates during Christmas and Easter weeks, but low-season rates can be anywhere from 20% to 60% below high-season rates. Some rates may seem much higher than others, but many of these higher rates are *all-inclusive* — meaning that your meals and beverages are included in the price of your stay. All tips and taxes and most activities and entertainment are also included in all-inclusive rates.

All hotels listed here have air-conditioning, unless otherwise indicated. Parking is available at all island hotels.

Antillano
$ Ciudad Cancún

A quiet and very clean choice, the Antillano is close to the Ciudad Cancún bus terminal. Rooms overlook either the main downtown street, Avenida Tulum, the side streets, or the interior lawn and pool. The last choice is the most desirable because these rooms are the quietest. Each room has coordinated furnishings, one or two double beds, a sink area separate from the bathroom, and red-tile floors. A bonus: This inexpensive hotel provides guests the use of its beach club on the island. To find Antillano from Avenida Tulum, walk west on Claveles a half block; it's opposite the restaurant Rosa Mexicana. Parking is on the street.

Av. Claveles 1 (corner of Av. Tulum). ☎ *998-884-1532. Fax: 998-884-1878. Internet:* www.hotelantillano.com. *48 units. Street parking. Rack rates: High season $70 double; low season $60 double. AE, MC, V.*

Blue Bay Getaway Cancún
$$$ Isla Cancún

Blue Bay is a spirited yet relaxing all-inclusive resort for adults only — no kids under 16 are allowed — that's favored by young adults in particular. One of its best features is its prime location — right at the northern end of the Hotel Zone, close to the major shopping plazas, restaurants, and nightlife, with a terrific beach with calm waters for swimming. Surrounded by acres of tropical gardens, the comfortable, clean, and modern guest rooms are located in two sections: the central building, where rooms are decorated in rustic wood, and the remaining nine buildings, which feature rooms in a colorful Mexican decor. The main lobby, administrative offices, restaurants, and Tequila Sunrise bar are all located in the central building, meaning you're close to all the action — and more noise — if your room is in this section. Included are all your meals, served at any of the four restaurants, and libations, which you can find in the four bars. During the evenings, guests may enjoy a variety of theme-night dinners, nightly shows, and live entertainment in an outdoor theater with capacity for 150 guests. Activities and facilities include three swimming pools, a tennis court, an exercise room, windsurfing, kayaks, catamarans, boogie boards, complimentary snorkeling and scuba lessons, and a marina. Safes are available for an extra charge, as is dry-cleaning and laundry service. Blue Bay allows guests to use the amenities and facilities at its sister resort, the Blue Bay Club and Marina (a resort for families), located just outside Ciudad Cancún, near the ferry to Isla Mujeres. A free bus and boat shuttle service is provided between both Blue Bay resorts.

Blvd. Kukulcán, km 3.5. ☎ *800-BLUE-BAY in the U.S., or 998-848-7900. Fax: 998-848-7994. Internet:* www.bluebayresorts.com. *385 units. Free parking. Rack rates: High season $280 double; low season $180 double. Rates are all-inclusive (room, food, beverages, and activities). AE, MC, V.*

Calinda Viva Cancún
$$$ Isla Cancún

From the street, the Calinda Viva may not be much to look at, but the location is ideal because it's set on Cancún's best beach for safe swimming. The ocean side has a small but pretty patio garden and pool. Calinda is close to all the shops and restaurants clustered near Punta Cancún and the convention center. You can choose between rooms with either a lagoon or oceanview. The rooms are large and undistinguished in decor, but they're comfortable. They feature marble floors and either two double beds or a king-size bed. Several studios with kitchenettes are also available upon request. In addition to a restaurant and three bars, you also have two lighted tennis courts, watersports equipment rental, and a small marina with its own fishing fleet.

Blvd. Kukulcán, km 8.5, next to the Playa Linda dock. ☎ *800-221-2222 in the U.S., or 998-883-0800. Fax: 998-883-2087. 216 units. Free parking. Rack rates: High season $145–$250 double; low season $138–$158 double. Price includes buffet breakfast. Children under 12 are free. AE, MC, V.*

Camino Real Cancún
$$$$ Isla Cancún

The Camino Real is among the island's most appealing places to stay, located on four acres right at the tip of Punta Cancún. The setting is

Where to Stay in Isla Cancún (Hotel Zone)

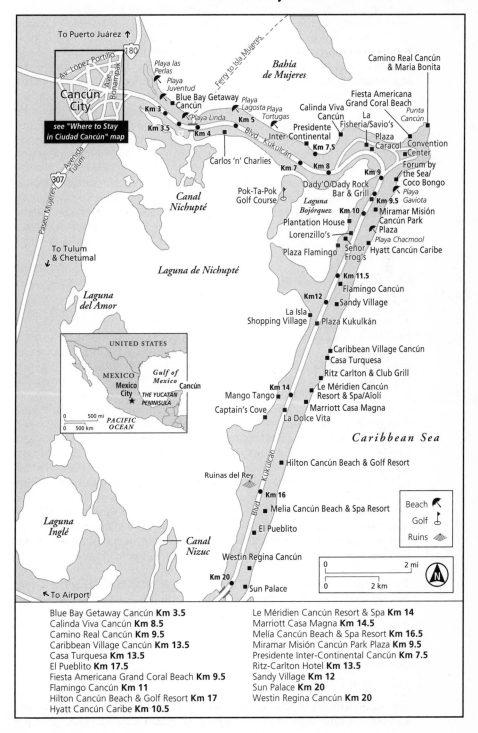

Blue Bay Getaway Cancún **Km 3.5**
Calinda Viva Cancún **Km 8.5**
Camino Real Cancún **Km 9.5**
Caribbean Village Cancún **Km 13.5**
Casa Turquesa **Km 13.5**
El Pueblito **Km 17.5**
Fiesta Americana Grand Coral Beach **Km 9.5**
Flamingo Cancún **Km 11**
Hilton Cancún Beach & Golf Resort **Km 17**
Hyatt Cancún Caribe **Km 10.5**

Le Méridien Cancún Resort & Spa **Km 14**
Marriott Casa Magna **Km 14.5**
Melía Cancún Beach & Spa Resort **Km 16.5**
Miramar Misión Cancún Park Plaza **Km 9.5**
Presidente Inter-Continental Cancún **Km 7.5**
Ritz-Carlton Hotel **Km 13.5**
Sandy Village **Km 12**
Sun Palace **Km 20**
Westin Regina Cancún **Km 20**

sophisticated, but the hotel is very welcoming to children. Camino Real is a favored name among Mexico hotel chains, where vacations are synonymous with family. The architecture of the hotel is trademark Camino Real — contemporary and sleek, with bright colors and strategic angles. Rooms in the newer 18-story Camino Real Club have extra services and amenities, including a complimentary full breakfast each day in the Beach Club lobby. The lower-priced rooms have lagoon views. In addition to the oceanfront pool, the Camino Real has a private saltwater lagoon with sea turtles and tropical fish. Three lighted tennis courts, a fitness center, beach volleyball, a sailing pier, and a watersports center keep things active. The hotel's three restaurants — including the popular María Bonita (see Chapter 10) — and the lively Azucar Cuban dance club are all onsite.

Blvd. Kukulcán, Punta Cancún. ☎ *800-722-6466 in the U.S., or 998-848-7000. Fax: 998-848-7001. Internet:* www.caminoreal.com/cancun. *389 units. Daily fee for guarded parking adjacent to hotel. Rack rates: High season $275 standard double, $320 Camino Real Club double; low season $195 standard double; $230 Camino Real Club double. AE, DC, MC, V.*

Cancún INN Suites El Patio
$ **Ciudad Cancún**

A European-style guesthouse, Cancún INN Suites El Patio caters to travelers looking for more of the area's culture. Many guests at this small hotel stay for up to a month and enjoy its combination of excellent value and warm hospitality. You won't find any bars, pools, or loud parties in this place; what you do find is excellent service and impeccable accommodations. Rooms face the plant-filled interior courtyard, dotted with groupings of wrought-iron chairs and tables. Each room has a slightly different decor and set of amenities, but all have white-tile floors and rustic wood furnishings in their various configurations. Some rooms have light kitchenette facilities, and the guesthouse also offers a common kitchen area with purified water and a cooler for stocking your own supplies. A small restaurant — actually closer to a dining room — serves breakfast and dinner. While a public phone is located in the entranceway, the staff can also arrange for a cellular phone in your room. The game and TV room has a large-screen cable TV, a library stocked with books on Mexican culture, backgammon, cards, and board games. The hotel offers special packages for lodging and Spanish lessons and discounts for longer stays.

Av. Bonampak 51 and Cereza, SM2A, Centro. ☎ *998-884-3500. Fax: 998-884-3540. Internet:* www.cancuninn.com. *18 units. Rack rates: $40–$55 double, includes morning coffee. Ask for discounts for longer stays. AE, MC, V.*

Caribbean Village Cancún
$$$ **Isla Cancún**

Considered one of the best all-inclusive values on Cancún Island, this resort's most notable feature is its location, on one of the island's widest stretches of beach. It's also a convenient 20 minutes form the airport and

Where to Stay in Ciudad Cancún (Cancún City)

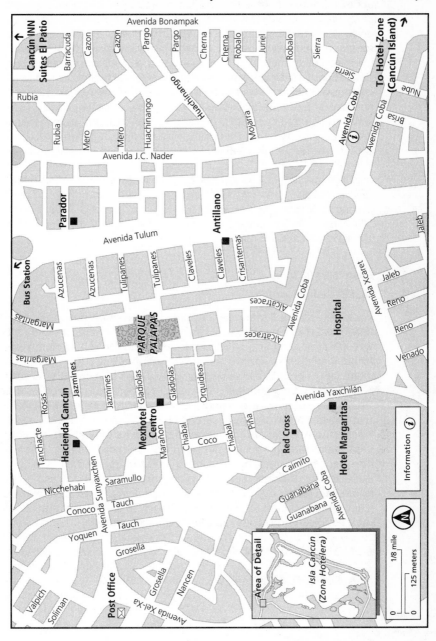

within walking distance of the island's more popular dining and shopping venues. Included in the price of your room are all meals, drinks, and a range of activities and sporting options that include tennis, sailing, windsurfing, boogie boarding, kayaking, and canoeing. This resort attracts a younger, fun-loving, active crowd — the pool area seems to be the scene of one constant party! In addition to the two interconnected beachfront swimming pools, a popular spot is the oversized Jacuzzi — with room enough for a party of 12. Rooms here are standard resort — not remarkable, and small-ish in size, with carpeting and rattan furnishings. All rooms are located in a six-story building that surrounds the pool area and have a view of either the ocean or of Nichupte Lagoon. If you can, reserve one of the 17 higher-priced Junior or Master suites — they're well worth the extra charge, giving you more room as well as your own private terrace overlooking the ocean. Four restaurants are available for dining, plus four bars and a disco that jams until 2 a.m. The resort receives consistently high praise (especially for its friendly service) and welcomes many return guests. For those *very* young travelers, a Little Village kids' club offers supervised activities.

Blvd. Kukulcán, km 13.5. ☎ *800-858-2258 in the U.S., or 998-848-8000. Fax: 998-848-0002. Internet:* www.allegroresorts.com/cv_s/cancun/. *300 units. Free parking. Rack rates: High season $266 double; low season $214 double. Rates are all-inclusive. Children under 2 are complimentary, for children ages 2–12, add $40 per night, per child. AE, MC, V.*

Casa Turquesa
$$$$$ Isla Cancún

Romantic, tranquil, and elegant, Casa Turquesa is an oasis of relaxation in the midst of this playful island. If the Mediterranean-style ambience weren't appealing enough, their exceptional stretch of beach (fronting brilliant turquoise waters) is sure to inspire a positive attitude adjust-ment. Isla Cancún is a true boutique hotel, one that caters to couples and is noted for its exceptional service. All suites feature queen- or king-size beds, plus balconies with Jacuzzis. In-room extras include CD players and bathrobes; bathrooms themselves are extra-large, with double sinks and a separate tub and shower. Blue-and-white canopy shade tents dot the area surrounding the attractive pool area and beach; the adjacent Turquesa Pool Bar is open from 10 a.m. to 5 p.m. daily. For dining, the Belle-Vue restaurant, serving international gourmet fare, is open 24 hours, and the formal Celebrity restaurant serves seafood and angus beef from 6 p.m. to midnight. For those who prefer not to leave the comfort of their room, 24-hour room service is also available.

Blvd. Kukulcán, km 13.5. ☎ *888-528-8300 in the U.S., or 998-885-2925. Fax: 998-885-2922. Internet:* www.slh.com/casaturquesa/. *33 suites. Free parking. Rack rates: $286–$357. AE, DC, MC, V.*

El Pueblito
$$$ Isla Cancún

The El Pueblito looks like a traditional Mexican hacienda and has the gracious, hospitable service to match. Several three-story buildings (no elevators) are terraced in a V-shape down a gentle hillside toward the sea, with a meandering swimming pool with waterfalls running between them, to a beachside, thatched-roof restaurant. Consistent renovations and upgrades and a changeover to an all-inclusive concept have made this hotel more appealing than ever and another exceptional all-inclusive value. Rooms are very large and have rattan furnishings, travertine marble floors, large bathrooms, and either a balcony or terrace facing the pool or sea. In addition to a constant flow of buffet-style meals and snacks, a nightly theme party, complete with entertainment, also awaits guests. Miniature golf and a water slide, plus a full program of kid's activities, make this place an ideal choice for families with children. Baby-sitting services are available for $10 per hour. The hotel is located toward the southern end of the island past the Hilton Resort.

Blvd. Kukulcán, km 17.5, past the Hilton Resort. ☎ ***998-885-0422,*** *998-881-8800. Fax: 998-885-2066. Internet:* www.pueblitohotels.com. *349 units. Free parking. Rack rates: High season $300 double, low season $240 double. Rates are all-inclusive. AE, MC, V.*

Fiesta Americana Grand Coral Beach
$$$$$ Isla Cancún

A spectacularly grand hotel, the Fiesta Americana has one of the best locations in Cancún with its 1,000 feet of prime beachfront property and proximity to the main shopping and entertainment centers — perfect for the traveler looking to be at the heart of all that Cancún has to offer. The great Punta Cancún location (opposite the convention center) has the advantage of facing the beach to the north, meaning that the surf is calm and perfect for swimming. When it comes to the hotel itself, the operative word here is *big* — everything at the Fiesta Americana seems oversized, from the lobby to the rooms. Service is gracious, if cool, as the hotel aims for a more sophisticated ambience. The finishings of elegant dark-green granite and an abundance of marble extend from the lobby to the large guest rooms, all of which have balconies facing the ocean. One meandering pool borders the beach — a 660-foot-long, free-form swimming pool with swim-up bars and a casual poolside snack bar, plus there's a full watersports equipment rental service on the beach. Two additional restaurants, plus five bars, are inside the hotel, along with a mini shopping center. If tennis is your game, this hotel has the best facilities in Cancún. Three indoor tennis courts with stadium seating are part of an extensive fitness center and spa.

Blvd. Kukulcán, km 9.5. ☎ ***800-343-7821*** *in the U.S., or 998-881-3200. Fax: 998-881-3263. Internet:* www.fiestaamericana.com.mx. *602 units. Rack rates: High season $328–$555 double, $529–$650 Club Floors double; low season $222–$424 double, $381–$504 Club Floors double. Up to 2 children included in parents' room at no extra charge. AE, MC, V.*

Flamingo Cancún
$$$ Isla Cancún

The Flamingo seems to have been inspired by the dramatic, slope-sided architecture of the Camino Real, but it's considerably smaller and less expensive. I find it a friendly, accommodating choice for families. The clean, comfortable, and modern guest rooms — all with balconies — border a courtyard facing the interior swimming pools and palapa pool bar. A second pool with a sundeck overlooks the ocean. The Flamingo is in the heart of the island hotel district, opposite the Flamingo Shopping Center and close to other hotels, shopping centers, and restaurants.

Blvd. Kukulcán, km 11 ☎ *998-883-1544. Fax: 998-883-1029. Internet:* www.flamingo cancun.com. *221 units. Free parking on the hotel grounds. Rack rates: High season $170 double; low season $120 double. AE, MC, V.*

Hacienda Cancún
$ Ciudad Cancún

An extremely pleasing little hotel — and a great value — Hacienda Cancún is perfect for travelers on a budget. The facade has been remodeled to look like a hacienda, and rooms continue the theme, with their rustic-style Mexican furnishings. Guest rooms are clean and very comfortable; all have two double beds and windows (but no views). The hotel offers a nice, small pool and cafe under a shaded palapa in the back. To find it from Avenida Yaxchilán, turn west on Sunyaxchen; it's on your right next to the Hotel Caribe International, opposite 100% Natural. Parking is on the street.

Sunyaxchen 39–40. ☎ *998-884-3672. Fax: 998-884-1208. E-mail:* hhda@Cancun. com.mx. *35 units. Rack rates: High season $45 double; low season $38 double. MC, V.*

(Radisson) Hacienda Cancún
$$–$$$ Ciudad Cancún

The nicest hotel in downtown Cancún, the Hacienda Cancún is also one of the very best values in the area, managed by Radisson. It offers all the expected comforts of a chain like Radisson, yet in an atmosphere of Mexican hospitality. Resembling a Mexican hacienda, rooms are set off from a large rotunda-style lobby, lush gardens, and a pleasant pool area, which has a separate wading section for children. All rooms have Talavera tile inlays and brightly colored fabric accents; views of the garden, the pool, or the street; and a small sitting area and balcony. Bathrooms have a combination tub and shower. For the price, I found the extra in-room amenities of a coffeemaker, hairdryer, and iron to be nice extras. In addition to two restaurants, the hotel offers a generally lively lobby bar, as well as tennis courts and a small gym. Guests of the Hacienda may enjoy the facilities of Avalon Bay Hotel with complimentary shuttle service. The hotel is located right behind the state government building and within walking distance of downtown Cancún dining and shopping.

Av. Nader 1, SM2, Centro. ☎ *998-887-4455 Fax: 998-884-7954. Internet:* www. holiday-inn.com. *248 units. Rack rates: High season $100 standard, $125 Jr. suite; low season $90 standard, $115 Jr. suite. AE, MC, V.*

Hilton Cancún Beach & Golf Resort

$$$$ Isla Cancún

The Hilton in Cancún is especially perfect for anyone whose motto is "the bigger the better." Grand, expansive, and fully equipped, this is a true resort in every sense of the word. The Hilton Cancún, formerly the 1994-vintage Caesar Park Resort, is situated on 250 acres of prime Cancún beachfront property with its own 18-hole, par-72 golf course across the street and a location that gives every room a sea view. (Some have both sea and lagoon views.) Like the sprawling resort, rooms are grandly spacious and immaculately decorated in a minimalist style. Area rugs and pale furnishings soften marble floors and bathrooms. The more elegant Beach Club rooms are set off from the main hotel in two- and three-story buildings (no elevators) and have their own check-in and concierge service, plus nightly complimentary cocktails. The hotel is especially appealing to golfers because it's one of only two hotels in Cancún with an onsite course. (The other is the Mélia, which has an 18-hole executive course.) The seven interconnected pools with a swim-up bar, two lighted tennis courts, a large, fully equipped gym, and a beachfront watersports center make the Hilton Cancún a good choice for those looking for an action-packed stay. The Kids Club program is one of the best on the island, making it great for families.

Blvd. Kukulcán, km 17, Retorno Lacandones. ☎ *800-228-3000 in the U.S., or 998-881-8000. Fax: 998-881-8080. Internet:* www.hiltoncancun.com.mx. *426 units. Rack rates: $170 standard double, $230 Beach Club double. AE, DC, MC, V.*

Hotel Margaritas

$–$$ Ciudad Cancún

This four-story hotel (with elevator) in downtown Cancún is comfortable and unpretentious, offering one of the best values in Cancún. Rooms have white tile floors and a small balcony and are exceptionally clean and bright and pleasantly decorated. The attractive pool is surrounded by lounge chairs and has a wading section for children. The hotel offers complimentary safes at the front desk and more services than most budget hotels.

Av. Yaxchilán 41, SM22, Centro. ☎ *998-884-9333. Fax: 998-884-1324. 100 units. Rack rates: $85 double, includes breakfast. AE, MC, V.*

Hyatt Cancún Caribe

$$$$$ Isla Cancún

Although this is one of Cancún's older hotels, it remains a favored choice for travelers wanting a more sophisticated place to stay at a reasonable price. Although the beach is a bit rocky, there's a precious lagoon-style pool above the beach adjoining pool-bar. Rooms are either in a seven-story curved building that backs the pool or in a collection of villas adjacent to the main building. The rooms themselves, though small, are comfortable, decorated in muted colors with light wood furnishings. The combination marble tub has Mexican tile accents, and small furnished balconies overlook the pool and beach (bottom floors have terraces). Rooms are quieter and more private in the villa section; you'll also enjoy larger bathrooms and a large ground-floor terrace. These rooms are all Regency Club rooms, and so offer extra services and amenities. In addition to the pool, the hotel has three lighted tennis courts, a jogging train, and massage services, as well as three restaurants, including the recommended Blue Bayou.

Blvd. Kukulcán, km 10.5. ☎ *800-228-9000 in the U.S., or 998-848-7800. Fax: 998-848-1514. Internet:* www.hyatt.com. *226 rooms and villa suites. Free parking. Rack rates: High season $279–$479 double. AE, MC, V.*

Le Méridien Cancún Resort & Spa

$$$$$ **Isla Cancún**

Of all the luxury properties in Cancún, I find Le Méridien the most inviting, with a polished yet welcoming sense of personal service. Although other hotels tend to overdo a sense of formality in an attempt to justify their prices, Le Méridien has an elegantly casual style that makes you comfortable enough to thoroughly relax. From the intimate lobby and reception area to the most outstanding concierge service in Cancún, guests feel immediately pampered upon arrival. The hotel itself is smaller than others and feels more like an upscale boutique hotel than an immense resort — a welcome relief to those overstressed by activity at home. The decor throughout the rooms and common areas is one of understated good taste — both classy and comforting, not overdone. Rooms are generous in size, and most have small balconies overlooking the pool with a view to the ocean. A very large marble bathroom has a separate tub and a glassed-in shower. The hotel attracts many Europeans and younger, sophisticated travelers, and is ideal for a second honeymoon or romantic break. Certainly, a highlight of — or even a reason for — staying here is time spent at the **Spa del Mar,** one of Mexico's finest and most complete European spa facilities, featuring two levels and more than 15,000 square feet of services dedicated to your body and soul. A complete fitness center with extensive cardio and weight machines is found on the upper level. The spa is located below and comprised of a healthy snack bar, a full-service salon, and 14 treatment rooms, as well as separate men's and women's steam rooms, saunas, whirlpools, cold plunge pools, inhalation rooms, tranquility rooms, lockers, and changing areas.

The health club may become a necessity if you fully enjoy the gourmet restaurant, **Aioli,** with its specialties based on Mediterranean and Provençal cuisines. (Check out Chapter 10 for a detailed listing of this restaurant.) The menu is simply delicious — not pretentious. Adjoining the spa is a large swimming pool that cascades down three levels. Above the spa is a tennis center with two championship tennis courts with lights. Watersports equipment is available for rent on the beach. A supervised children's program has its own Penguin Clubhouse, play equipment, and a wading pool. Baby-sitting services are also available for $12 per hour; after 10 p.m,. add a $10 taxi charge.

Retorno del Rey, km 14, Zona Hotelera. ☎ *800-543-4300 in the U.S., or 998-881-2200. Fax: 998-881-2201. Internet:* www.meridiencancun.com.mx. *213 units. Free parking. Rack rates: High season $290 standard, $450 suite; low season $220 standard, $350 suite. Ask for special spa packages. AE, DC, MC, V. Small pets accepted, with advanced reservation.*

Marriott Casa Magna
$$$$ **Isla Cancún**

This property is quintessential Marriott. Travelers who are familiar with the chain's standards feel at home here and appreciate the hotel's attention to detailed service. In fact, if you're on your first trip to Mexico, and you're looking for a little familiarity of home, this hotel is a great choice because it feels like a slice of the United States transported to a stunning stretch of Caribbean beach. Guest rooms have contemporary furnishings, tiled floors, and ceiling fans; most have balconies. All suites occupy corners and have enormous terraces, oceanviews, and TVs in both the living room and the bedroom. The Marriott Casa Magna offers five on-site restaurants to choose from, plus a lobby bar with live music. Alongside the meandering oceanfront pool are two lighted tennis courts. The hotel caters to family travelers with specially priced packages (up to two children can stay free with parents) and the Club Amigos supervised children's program. A more deluxe offering from Marriott, the 450-room luxury **JW Cancún Resort & Spa** (☎ **998-848-9600**), recently opened on the beach next to the Casa Magna. Its hallmark is a 20,000-square-foot European spa and fitness center.

Blvd. Kukulcán, km 14.5. ☎ *800-228-9290 in the U.S., or 998-881-2000. Fax: 998-881-2071. Internet:* www.marriott.com. *452 units. Rack rates: High season $225–$254 double, $350 suite; low season $139–$160 double, $300 suite. Ask about available packages. AE, DC, MC, V.*

Melía Cancún Beach & Spa Resort
$$$$ **Isla Cancún**

The large, ultra-modern Melía is popular for weddings, conventions, and other group events, but is also a great option for individual travelers looking for a lively place to stay. The resort is a landmark of sorts, known for its spectacular nine-story, pyramid-shaped lobby atrium, with cascading waterfalls and a bevy of palms. Guest rooms are small but adequate, with marble floors, bright decor, and balconies — about half offer ocean or lagoon view. Opt for the Royal Beach floor, and you'll enjoy larger rooms and upgraded amenities and services. Two unique pools, an executive 18-hole golf course, three tennis courts, two paddle tennis courts lit for night, and a 6,000-square-foot spa and fitness center mean it has among the broadest range of amenities on the island. Dining choices are also ample, with five restaurants to choose from, as well as three bars and 24-hour room service.

Blvd. Kukulcán, km 16.5. ☎ *800-336-3542 in the U.S., or 998-885-1114. Fax: 998-885-1963. Internet:* www.solmelia.com. *400 rooms. Free parking. Rack rates: $190–$330. AE, DC, MC, V.*

Mexhotel Centro

$$ **Ciudad Cancún**

One of the perennially popular hotels in downtown Cancún, Mexhotel Centro has the warmth and style of a small hacienda. Three floors (with elevator) of rooms front a lovely palm-shaded pool area with comfortable tables and chairs and a restaurant. Standard rooms are extra-clean with muted decor, two double beds framed with wrought-iron headboards, large tile bathrooms with separate sinks, desks, and over-bed reading lights. Although prices may seem high for the location, beach and pool privileges at its sister resort in the Hotel Zone, Mexhotel Resort Cancún, make it a great bargain. (Guest do have an extra charge for transportation, but the hotel is close to the bus route.) The hotel is between Jazmines and Gladiolas, kitty-corner from Perico's.

Yaxchilan 31, SM 22. ☎ */Fax: 988-884-3078. 81 units. Free parking. Rack rates: $50–$100. MC, V.*

Miramar Misión Cancún Park Plaza

$$$ **Isla Cancún**

Another good choice for travelers looking for well-priced rooms right on the beach, the ingeniously designed Miramar offers partial views of both the lagoon and ocean from all its rooms. A notable feature is the large, rectangular swimming pool that extends through the hotel and down to the beach and contains built-in, submerged sun chairs. The hotel also offers an oversized whirlpool (the largest in Cancún), a sundeck, and a snack bar on the seventh-floor roof. Rooms are on the small side but are bright and comfortable with a small balcony and bamboo furniture; bathrooms have polished limestone vanities. In addition to three restaurants, **Batacha,** a popular nightclub features live music for dancing from 9 p.m. to 4 a.m. Tuesday to Sunday.

Blvd. Kukulcán, km 9.5. ☎ *998-883-1755. Fax: 998-883-1136. Internet:* www.hotelesmision.com. *300 units. Rack rates: High season $220; low season $160 double. AE, MC, V.*

Parador

$ **Ciudad Cancún**

The convenient location and rock-bottom prices make this otherwise nondescript hotel among the most popular downtown hotels. Guest rooms, located on one of three floors, are arranged around two long, narrow garden courtyards leading back to a small pool (with an even smaller, separate children's pool) and grassy sunning area. The rooms are contemporary and basic, each with two double beds and a shower. The hotel is next to Pop's restaurant, almost at the corner of Uxmal. Street parking is limited.

*Av. Tulum 26. ☎ **998-884-1043**, 998-884-1310. Fax: 998-884-9712. 66 units. Rack rates: High season $56 double; low season $45 double. Ask about promotional rates. MC, V.*

Presidente Inter-Continental Cancún

$$$$–$$$$$ **Isla Cancún**

On the island's best beach, facing the placid Bahía de Mujeres, the Presidente's location is reason enough to stay here, and it's just a two-minute walk to Cancún's public Pok-Ta-Pok Golf Club. Cool and spacious, the Presidente sports a postmodern design with lavish marble and wicker accents and a strong use of color. Guests have a choice of two double beds or one king-size bed. All rooms have tastefully simple unfinished pine furniture. The expansive pool has a pyramid-shaped waterfall and is surrounded by cushioned lounge chairs. In addition to lighted tennis courts and a small fitness center, the marina has watersports equipment rentals. Coming from Cancún City, the Presidente is on the left side of the street before you get to Punta Cancún. For its ambience, I feel that the Presidente is an ideal choice for a romantic getaway or for couples who enjoy indulging in the sports of golf, tennis, or even shopping.

*Blvd. Kukulcán, km 7.5. ☎ **800-327-0200** in the U.S., or 998-848-8700. Fax: 998-883-2602. Internet:* www.interconti.com. *299 units. Rack rates: High season $240–$300 double; low season $150–$230 double. Ask about special promotional packages. Rates include buffet breakfast for two adults, and children under 17 are free in their parents' room. AE, MC, V.*

Ritz-Carlton Hotel

$$$$$ **Isla Cancún**

The grand-scale Ritz-Carlton is a fountain of formality in this casual beach resort, perfect for someone who wants a Palm Beach–style experience in Mexico. The decor — in both public areas as well as guest rooms — is sumptuous and formal with thick carpets, elaborate chandeliers, and fresh flowers throughout. The hotel fronts a 1,200-foot white-sand beach, and all rooms overlook the ocean, pool (heated during winter months), and tropical gardens. In all rooms, marble bathrooms have telephones, separate tubs and showers, and lighted makeup mirrors. Ritz-Carlton Club floors offer guests five mini-meals a day, private butler service, and Hermés bath products. **The Club Grill,** a fashionable English pub, is one of the best restaurants in the city, and the **Lobby Lounge** is the original home of proper tequila tastings, featuring one of the world's most extensive menus of fine tequilas, as well as Cuban cigars. I love its white-draped cabañas for two on the beach! There's a very good fitness center with spa services, plus three lighted tennis courts. The Ritz Kids program has supervised activities for children, and baby-sitting services are also available. The hotel has won countless recognitions and accolades for service. Special packages for golfing, spa, and weekend getaways are worth exploring.

Retorno del Rey 36, off Blvd. Kukulcán, km 13.5. ☎ *800-241-3333 in the U.S. and Canada, or 998-881-0808. Fax: 998-881-0815. Internet:* www.ritzcarlton.com. *365 units. Free guarded parking. Rack rates: High season $369–$475 double; $389–$850 Club floors; low season $189–$279 double; Club floors $295–$429. AE, MC, V.*

Sandy Village

$$ **Isla Cancún**

Sandy Village (The Hotel Formerly Known As Aristos) is my pick for a quality inexpensive hotel on Isla Cancún. One of the island's first hotels, it continues to welcome repeat guests, especially younger (read: spring breakers), European, and senior travelers. The location is prime — near the central shopping, dining, and nightlife centers. The rooms, though small, are kept updated and are clean and cool, with red-tile floors and small balconies. All rooms face either the Caribbean or the *paseo* (boulevard) and lagoon; the best views are the Caribbean side (and with no noise from the *paseo*). A central pool overlooks the ocean and a wide stretch of beach one level below the lobby. The hotel has a restaurant and three bars, plus two lighted tennis courts and a small marina with watersports equipment. At press time, the ownership (and also the name) of this hotel had just been changed, and an upgrade was planned, so rates may increase in the future.

Blvd. Kukulcán, km 12. ☎ *800-527-4786 in the U.S., or 998-883-0011. Fax: 998-883-0078. 245 units. Free, unguarded parking. Rack rates: High season $120 double; low season $100 double. AE, MC, V.*

Sun Palace

$$$$$ **Isla Cancún**

If you're looking for an all-inclusive resort on a great stretch of Caribbean beach, this member of the popular Palace Resorts is a prime pick — and the most elegant of their options in Cancún. Here what you get is a fantastic beach, one of the widest on the island. Located toward the southern end of the island, next to the Westin Regina, it's further away from hotel zone action, which may be what you want, in order to revel in all of the included goodies that go with staying here. Suites feature modern Mexican decor, and all have marble floors and a combination bath with whirlpool tub. All also have either oceanview balconies or terraces, and come with premium extras like bathrobes and hairdryers. In addition to the beachside pool, the resort offers an indoor pool, plus a large Jacuzzi with a waterfall. A nicely equipped health club and tennis court complement the ample activities program. For dining, you can choose from one of three restaurants or order in from 24-hour room service. Sun Palace also has weekly theme parties. One of the best perks to staying here is that excursions to Tulum, Chichén-Itzá, or Isla Mujeres are also included in their activities program. When you stay at any of the Palace resorts, you have the option of visiting any other members of their chain — and you have two others in Cancún to choose from.

Blvd. Kukulcán, km 20. ☎ *800-346-8225, 998-85-0533. Fax: 998-885-1593. Internet:* www.palaceresorts.com. *237 suites. Free parking. Rack rates: $310–$398, double. Rates are all-inclusive. AE, DC, MC, V.*

Westin Regina Cancún
$$$$$ Isla Cancún

A stunning hotel, the Westin Regina is great for anyone wanting the beauty of Cancún's beaches and a little distance between them and the more boisterous, flashy parts of Cancún's hotel strip. The strikingly austere but grand architecture of the Westin Regina is the stamp of leading Latin-American architect Ricardo Legorreta. A series of five swimming pools front the beach, and the Westin offers two lighted tennis counts and a small fitness center with limited spa services. The hotel is divided into two sections, the main building and the more exclusive six-story, hot-pink, tower section. Standard rooms are unusually large and beautifully furnished with cool, contemporary furniture. The rooms on the sixth floor have balconies, and first-floor rooms have terraces. Rooms in the tower all have ocean or lagoon views and extensive use of marble, furniture with Olinalá lacquer accents, Berber-carpet area rugs, oak tables and chairs, and terraces with lounge chairs. Note that this hotel is a 15- to 20-minute ride from the lively strip that lies between the Plaza Flamingo and Punta Cancún, so it's a better choice for those who want to relish a little more seclusion than Cancún typically offers. However, you can easily join the action when you're so inclined — buses stop in front, and taxis are readily available.

Blvd. Kukulcán, km 20. ☎ *800-228-3000 in the U.S., 800-215-7000 in Mexico, or 998-848-7400. Fax: 998-885-0296. Internet:* www.westin.com. *293 units. Rack rates: High season $285–$450 double; low season $160–$299 double. AE, DC, MC, V.*

Chapter 9

Settling into Cancún

. . . .

In This Chapter

▶ Knowing what to expect when you arrive

▶ Finding your way around

▶ Discovering helpful information and resources

. . . .

*Y*es, you need a passport or other appropriate credentials (see Chapter 7) to enter Cancún, but after that, you couldn't be in a more American-friendly foreign destination if you tried. If this trip is your first to Mexico — or to a foreign country — you'll probably find that any sense of culture shock is practically nonexistent. But you'll be more comfortable knowing a few details before you arrive. In this chapter, I take you from the plane, through the airport, and to your hotel, helping you quickly get your bearings in this easy-to-navigate resort. I continue with tips on everything from taxis to taxes.

Arriving in Cancún

Cancún has one of Mexico's busiest and most modern airports, which seems to be in a constant state of construction to improve and expand its services. Still, it's easy to navigate — both international and national flights are under the same roof. After checking in with immigration, collecting your bags, and passing through the Customs checkpoint, you're ready to enjoy your holiday!

Navigating passport control and Customs

Immigration check-in can be a lengthy wait, depending on the number of planes arriving at the same time, but it's a generally easy and unremarkable process in which officials ask you to show your passport and complete a tourist card, known as the **FMT.** (See Chapter 7 for more information.)

Your FMT is an important document, so take good care of it. You're supposed to keep the FMT with you at all times, as you may be required to
show it if you run into any sort of trouble. You also need to turn the
FMT back in upon departure, or you may be unable to leave without
replacing it.

Next is the baggage claim area. Here, porters stand by to help with your
bags, and they're well worth the price of the tip — about a dollar a bag.
After you collect your luggage, you pass through another checkpoint.
Something that looks like a traffic light awaits you here — otherwise
known as Mexico's random search procedure for Customs. You press a
button, and if the light turns green, you're free to go. If it turns red, you
need to open each of your bags for a quick search. If you have an unusu-
ally large bag or an excessive amount of luggage, you may be searched
regardless of the traffic-light outcome.

Getting to your hotel

Just past the traffic light, you exit to the street, where you can find transportation to your hotel. Choose between a *colectivo* (shared minivan) and
a private taxi. If three or more of you are traveling together, you're probably better off opting for the private cab service. With so many hotels for
the collective van to stop at, it can easily take an hour to get to your room,
and believe me, the drivers wait until the vans are fully packed before
departing! Check out the Cancún Orientation Map in this chapter to see
where your hotel is positioned relative to the airport.

The airport is on the mainland, close to the southern end of the
Cancún area. It's about 9 miles to downtown **Ciudad Cancún** (Cancún
City), which is also on the mainland. The start of the **Zona Hotelera
(Hotel Zone),** located on **Isla Cancún** (Cancún Island), is 6½ miles from
the airport — about a 20-minute drive east from the airport along wide,
well-paved roads.

Riding with a colectivo

If you do choose the colectivo service, which consists of air-conditioned
vans, buy your ticket at the booth that's located to the far right as you
exit the baggage claim area. You can purchase tickets for private cab
service at a booth inside the airport terminal. Tickets for both the colectivo vans and the private taxis are based on a fixed rate depending on
the distance to your destination. A taxi ticket is good for up to four
passengers.

Hiring a taxi

Rates for a **private taxi** from the airport are around $20 to downtown
Cancún or $28 to $40 to the Hotel Zone, depending on your destination.
The colectivos run from Cancún's international airport into town
and the Hotel Zone and cost about $8 per person. There's minibus

Cancún Orientation Map

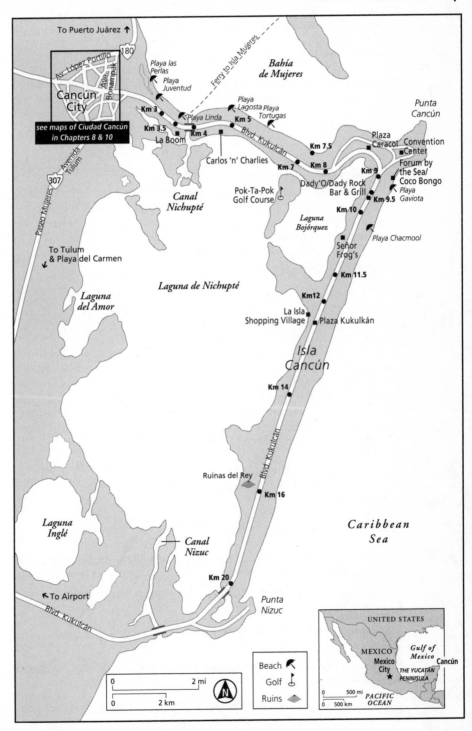

To Puerto Juárez ↑

180

Av. López Portillo

Ave. Bonampak

Cancún City

see maps of Ciudad Cancún in Chapters 8 & 10

Playa las Perlas
Playa Juventud

Ferry to Isla Mujeres

Bahía de Mujeres

Punta Cancún

Km 3
Playa Linda
Km 3.5
Km 4
La Boom

Playa Lagosta
Playa Tortugas
Km 5

Blvd. Kukulcán

Carlos 'n' Charlies

Km 7
Km 8
Km 7.5

Plaza Caracol
Convention Center

Forum by the Sea/ Coco Bongo

Km 9
Dady'O/Dady Rock Bar & Grill
Playa Gaviota
Km 9.5

Avenida Tulum

307

Canal Nichupté

Pok-Ta-Pok Golf Course

Km 10

Laguna Bojórquez

Playa Chacmool

To Tulum & Playa del Carmen

Paseo Mujeres

Señor Frog's

Km 11.5

Laguna de Nichupté

Km12

Laguna del Amor

La Isla Shopping Village
Plaza Kukulkán

Isla Cancún

Km 14

Ruinas del Rey

Blvd. Kukulcán

Km 16

Laguna Inglé

Caribbean Sea

Canal Nizuc

Km 20

Punta Nizuc

←To Airport

Blvd. Kukulcán

Beach
Golf
Ruins

0   2 mi

0   2 km

N

UNITED STATES

MEXICO

Mexico City

Gulf of Mexico
Cancún

THE YUCATÁN PENINSULA

0   500 mi
0   500 km

PACIFIC OCEAN

transportation (for $9.50) from the airport to the Puerto Juárez passenger ferry that takes you to Isla Mujeres. You can also hire a private taxi for this trip for about $40.

No colectivo service returns to the airport from Ciudad Cancún or the Hotel Zone, so you must hire a taxi, but the rate should be much less than the trip from the airport. The reason? Only federally chartered taxis may take fares *from* the airport, but any local taxi may bring passengers *to* the airport. Ask for a fare estimate at your hotel, but expect to pay about half what you were charged to get from the airport to your hotel.

Renting a car

Most major car-rental firms have outlets at the airport, so if you're renting a car, consider picking it up and dropping it off at the airport to save on airport-transportation costs. Another way to save money is to arrange for the rental before you leave home. If you wait until you arrive, the daily cost of a rental car may be around $65 to $75 for a Volkswagen Beetle.

Although you certainly don't have to rent a car here — taxis and buses are plentiful — this destination is one where having a car may make sense for a day or two. First, it can be a convenience, although it's not likely to save you bundles on transportation costs, based on the high relative prices of car rentals in Cancún. The roads in and around Cancún are excellent, and parking is readily available in most of the shopping/entertainment malls. The main reason for renting a car, however, is the flexibility that it provides in exploring the surrounding areas — a day-trip down the coast or to nearby sights is definitely recommended. But if you're not comfortable driving, you can easily cover this ground in one of the many sightseeing tours available.

If you do rent a car, keep any valuables out of plain site. Although Cancún's crime rate is very low, the only real problem tends to be rental-car break-ins.

Major car rental services include

- ✓ **Avis** (☎ **800-331-1212** in the U.S., or 998-883-0803; Internet: www.avis.com)
- ✓ **Budget** (☎ **800-527-0700** in the U.S., or 998-884-4812; Fax: 998-884-5011; Internet: https://rent.drivebudget.com/)
- ✓ **Dollar** (☎ **800-800-4000** in the U.S., or 998-886-0775; Internet: www.dollar.com)
- ✓ **Hertz** (☎ **800-654-3131** in the U.S. and Canada, or 998-884-4692; Internet: www.hertz.com)
- ✓ **National** (☎ **800-328-4567** in the U.S., or 998-886-0655; Internet: www.nationalcar.com)

Looking for more information?

Here's a list of the best Web sites for additional information about Cancún:

✓ **All About Cancún** (www.cancunmx.com)

Before taking off on a vacation, every traveler has a few questions. If Cancún is your destination, this site is a good place to start. It contains a database of answers to the most commonly asked questions. Just look for "The Online Experts" section. The site can be slow, but it has input from lots of recent travelers to the region.

✓ **Cancún Convention and Visitors Bureau** (www.gocancun.com)

The official site of the Cancún Convention and Visitors Bureau provides excellent information on events and area attractions. The site's hotel guide is one of the most complete listings I've seen, and it also offers online booking.

✓ **Cancún Online** (www.cancun.com)

Cancún Online is a comprehensive guide that has lots of information about things to do and see in Cancún. Just remember that advertisers pay to be included and provide most of the details. Highlights include forums, live chats, property-swaps, and bulletin boards, plus information on local Internet access, news, and events. You can even reserve a golf tee time or plan your wedding online.

✓ **Cancún Travel Guide** (www.go2cancun.com)

This group specializing in online information about Mexico has put together an excellent resource for Cancún rentals, hotels, and area attractions. Note that only paying advertisers are listed, but you can find most of the major players here.

✓ **Mexico Web Cancún Chat** (www.mexicoweb.com/travel/chat.html)

This site features one of the more active online chats specifically about Cancún with several different topics to select from. The users share inside information on everything from the cheapest beers to the quality of food at various all-inclusive resorts.

Getting Around Cancún

As I discuss a bit in the "Getting to your hotel" section earlier in this chapter, there are really two Cancúns: **Isla Cancún** (Cancún Island) and **Ciudad Cancún** (Cancún City). The latter, on the mainland, has restaurants, shops, and less expensive hotels, as well as all the other establishments that make life function — pharmacies, dentists, automotive shops, banks, travel and airline agencies, car-rental firms, and so on — which are all located within an approximately nine-square-block area. The city's main thoroughfare is **Avenida Tulum.** Heading south, Avenida Tulum becomes the highway to the airport, Playa del Carmen, and Tulum. (It actually runs all the way down to Belize.) Heading north, Avenida Tulum intersects the highway to Mérida and the road to Puerto Juárez and the Isla Mujeres ferries.

The famed **Zona Hotelera** (Hotel Zone, also called the **Zona Turística,** or Tourist Zone) stretches out along Isla Cancún, which is a sandy strip of land 14 miles long and shaped like a "7." The Playa Linda Bridge, at the north end of the island, and the Punta Nizuc Bridge, at the southern end, connect Isla Cancún to the mainland. Between these two bridges lies **Laguna Nichupté.** Avenida Cobá, coming from Cancún City, becomes Blvd. Kukulcán, the island's main traffic artery. Actually, Blvd. Kukulcán is the only main road on the island, so getting lost here would really take some effort! To get the hang of pronouncing it quickly enough, say koo-cool-*can* (as in, *Cancún* is sooo cool!). Cancún's international airport is located just inland from the south end of the island.

Ciudad Cancún's street-numbering system is a holdover from its early days. Addresses in the city are still expressed by the number of the building lot and the *manzana* (block) or *supermanzana* (group of city blocks). The city is still relatively compact, and you can easily cover the downtown commercial section on foot. Streets here are named after famous Mayan cities. Chichén-Itzá, Tulum, and Uxmal are the names of the boulevards in downtown Cancún, as well as nearby archeological sites.

On the island, addresses are given by their kilometer (km) number on Blvd. Kukulcán or by reference to some well-known location. The point on the island closest to Ciudad Cancún is km 1; km 20 is found at the very bottom of the "7" at Punta Nizuc, where the Club Med is located.

Taking a taxi

Taxi prices in Cancún are clearly set by zone, although keeping track of what's in which zone can take some work. Taxi rates within the Hotel Zone are a minimum fare of $5 per ride, making it one of the most expensive taxi areas in Mexico.

In addition, taxis operating in the Hotel Zone feel perfectly justified in having a discriminatory pricing structure: Local residents pay about half of what tourists pay, and guests at higher-priced hotels pay about twice the fare that guests in budget hotels are charged. You can thank the taxi union for this discrepancy — it establishes the rate schedule. Rates should be posted outside your hotel; however, if you have a question, all taxi drivers are required to have an official rate card in their taxi, although it's generally in Spanish.

Within the downtown area, the cost is about $1.50 per cab ride (not per person); within any other zone, it's $5. Traveling between two zones also costs $5. If you cross two zones, the cost is $7.50. Settle on a price in advance or check at your hotel where destinations and prices are generally posted. Trips to the airport from most zones cost $14. Taxis also have a rate of $18 per hour for travel around the city and Hotel Zone, but you can generally negotiate this rate down to $10 to $12.

If you want to hire a taxi to take you to Chichén-Itzá or along the Riviera Maya, expect to pay about $30 per hour — many taxi drivers feel that they're also providing guide services.

Catching a bus

Bus travel within Cancún continues to improve and is increasingly the most popular way of getting around for both residents and tourists. Air-conditioned and rarely crowded, the Hotel Zone buses run 24 hours a day. You can easily spot the bus stops using the signs posted along the road that have a bus on them. Bus stops are in front of most of the main hotels and shopping centers. Most buses cost 50 cents. In town, almost everything is within walking distance. Ruta 1 and Ruta 2 *("Hoteles")* city buses travel frequently from the mainland to the beaches along Avenida Tulum (the main street) and all the way to Punta Nizuc at the far end of the Hotel Zone on Isla Cancún.

Ruta 8 buses go to Puerto Juárez/Punta Sam, where you can catch ferries to Isla Mujeres. The buses stop on the east side of Avenida Tulum. These buses operate between 6 a.m. and 10 p.m. daily. Beware of private buses along the same route; they charge far more than the public ones. The public buses have the fare amount painted on the front; at the time of publication, the fare was 5 pesos (50 cents).

Zipping around on a moped

Mopeds are a convenient and popular way to cruise around through the very congested traffic, but they can be dangerous. Rentals start at $25 for a day, and the shops require a credit-card voucher as security for the moped.

When you rent a moped, you should receive a crash helmet (it's the law) and instructions on how to lock the wheels when you park. Be sure to read the fine print on the back of the rental agreement regarding liability for repairs or replacement in case of accident, theft, or vandalism.

Fast Facts: Cancún

American Express

The local office is located in Ciudad Cancún at Avenida Tulum 208 and Agua (☎ 998-881-4000, 998-881-4055; Internet: www.american express.com/mexico/), one block past the Plaza México. The office is open Monday to Friday 9 a.m. to 6 p.m. and Saturday 9 a.m. to 1 p.m.

Area Code

The telephone area code is **988.** *Note:* The area code changed from 9 in November 2001

Baby Sitters

Most of the larger hotels can easily arrange for baby sitters, but many sitters speak limited English. Rates range from $3 to $10 per hour.

Banks, ATMs, and Currency Exchange

Most banks are downtown along Avenida Tulum and are usually open Monday to Friday 9:30 a.m. to 5 p.m., and many now have automatic teller machines for after-hours cash withdrawals. In the Hotel Zone, you can find banks in the Plaza Kukulcán and next to the convention center. Many *casas de cambio* (exchange houses) are in the Hotel Zone, in the plazas, and near the convention center. Avoid changing money at the airport as you arrive, especially at the first exchange booth you see — its rates are less favorable than any in town or others farther inside the airport concourse. In general, the best exchange rates are found at ATMs, casas de cambio, and hotels.

Business Hours

Most downtown offices maintain traditional Mexican hours of operation (9 a.m. to 2 p.m. and 4 to 8 p.m., daily), but shops remain open throughout the day from 10 a.m. to 9 p.m. Offices tend to close on Saturday and Sunday, but shops are open on Saturday, at least, and increasingly offer limited hours of operation on Sunday. Malls are generally open from 10 a.m. to 10 p.m. or later.

Climate

It's hot but not overwhelmingly humid. The rainy season is May through October. August through October is the hurricane season, which brings erratic weather. November through February is generally sunny but can also be cloudy, windy, somewhat rainy, and even cool, so a sweater and rain protection are handy.

Consular Agents

The **U.S. consular agent** is located in the Playa Caracol 2, 3rd level, rooms 320–323, Boulevard Kukulcán, km 8.5 (☎ 998-883-0272). The office is open Monday to Friday 9 a.m. to 1 p.m. The **Canadian** consulate is located in the Plaza Caracol 2, 3rd level, room 330, Boulevard Kukulcán km 8.5 (☎ 998-883-3360). The office is open from Monday to Friday 9 a.m. to 5 p.m.

Emergencies/Hospitals

To report an emergency, dial ☎ **060,** which is supposed to be similar to 911 emergency service in the United States. For first aid, the **Cruz Roja** (Red Cross; ☎ 998-884-1616; Fax: 998-883-9218) is open 24 hours a day on Avenida Yaxchilán between avenidas Xcaret and Labná, next to the Telmex building. **Total Assist,** a small, nine-room emergency hospital with English-speaking doctors (Claveles 5, SM 22, at Avenida Tulum; ☎ 998-884-1058, 998-884-8017; E-mail: totalassist@prodigy. net.mx, is also open 24 hours. American Express, MasterCard, and Visa are accepted. Desk staff may have limited command of English. An **air ambulance service** is also available by calling ☎ 800-305-9400 (toll-free within Mexico). *Urgencias* means "Emergencies."

Information

The **State Tourism Office** (☎ 998-881-9000) is centrally located downtown on the east side of Avenida Pecari 23, next to Banco Bancomer, immediately left of the Ayuntamiento Benito Juárez building, The office is open Monday to Friday 9 a.m. to 5 p.m., and it has maps, brochures, and information on the area's popular sights, including Tulum, Xcaret, Isla Mujeres, and Playa del Carmen. A second tourist information office, the Convention and Visitors Bureau (☎ 998-884-6531, 998-881-0400), is located on Avenida Cobá at Avenida Tulum, next to Pizza Rolandi, and is open Monday to Friday 9 a.m. to 2 p.m. and 4 to 7 p.m. Hotels and their rates are listed at each office, as are ferry schedules. For information prior to your arrival in Cancún, call ☎ 800-CANCUN-8 from the United States or visit the Convention Bureau's Web site at www.gocancun.com.

Pick up copies of the free monthly *Cancún Tips* or the Cancun Tips booklet, which is published four times a year. Both contain lots of useful information and great maps. The publications are owned by the same people who own the Captain's Cove restaurants, a couple of sightseeing boats, and timeshare hotels, so the information, though good, is not completely unbiased.

Internet Access

C@ncunet (☎ 998-885-0055), located in a kiosk on the second floor of Plaza Kukulcán (Blvd. Kukulcán km 13), offers Internet access for 10 pesos per 10 minutes or 70 pesos per hour from 10 a.m. to 10 p.m. In downtown Cancún, **Sybcom** (☎ 998-884-6807) offers Internet access for 20 pesos per hour, although daily package specials are also available. Its minimum charge is 12 pesos for 15 minutes. It is located in the Plaza Alconde, Local 2, at Avenida Náder, just in front of Clinica AMAT and is open from 9 a.m. to 9 p.m., Monday to Saturday.

Maps

One of the best around is the free American Express map, usually found at the tourist information offices and the local American Express office. *Cancún Tips* (see "Information") also have excellent maps and are generally available through your hotel concierge.

Newspapers/Magazines

Most hotel gift shops and newsstands carry English-language magazines and English-language Mexican newspapers.

Pharmacy

Next to the Hotel Caribe Internacional, **Farmacia Canto** (Avenida Yaxchilán 36, at Sunyaxchen; ☎ 998-884-9330) is open daily 8 to 12 a.m. American Express, MasterCard, and Visa are accepted. Plenty of drugstores are in the major shopping malls, open until 10 p.m., in the Hotel Zone. You can stock up on Retin-A, Viagra, and many other prescription drugs without a prescription.

Police

To reach the **police** *(seguridad pública),* dial ☎ 998-884-1913 or 998-884-2342.

Post Office

The **main post office** (☎ 998-884-1418) is downtown at the intersection of avenidas Sunyaxchen and Xel-Ha. It's open Monday to Friday 9 a.m. to 4 p.m. and Saturday 9 a.m. to 1 p.m.

Safety

Cancún has very little crime. People are generally safe late at night in tourist areas; just use ordinary, common sense. As at any other beach resort, don't take money or valuables to the beach.

Car break-ins are about the only crimes here, although they do happen frequently, especially around the shopping centers in the Hotel Zone. VW Beetles and Golfs are frequent targets.

Swimming on the Caribbean side presents a danger from undertow. Pay attention to the posted flag warnings on the beaches.

Special Events

The annual **Cancún Jazz Festival,** featuring internationally known musicians, is held each year over the U.S. Memorial Day weekend in late May. The **Cancún Marathon** takes place each December and attracts world-class athletes as well as numerous amateur competitors. Additional information is available through the Convention and Visitors Bureau.

Taxes

There's a 10% value-added tax (IVA) on goods and services, and it's generally included in the posted price. Cancún's IVA is 5% lower than most of Mexico due to a special exemption that dates back to its origins as a duty-free port.

Taxis

Taxi prices in Cancún are set by zone, although keeping track of what's in which zone can take some work. Taxi rates within the Hotel Zone are a minimum fare of $5 per ride, making it one of the most expensive taxi areas in Mexico. Rates within the downtown area are between $1.50 and $2. You can also hire taxis by the hour or day for longer trips, when you'd prefer to leave the driving to someone else. Rates run between $12 and $18 per hour with discounts available for full-day rates, but an extra charge applies when the driver doubles as a tour guide. Always settle on a price in advance or check at your hotel, where destinations and prices are generally posted.

Telephone

Avoid the phone booths that have signs in English advising you to call home using a special 800 number — these booths are absolute rip-offs and can cost as much as $20 per minute. The least expensive way to call is by using a Mexican prepaid phone card called Telmex (LADATEL), available at most pharmacies and mini-supermarkets, using the official public phones, Telmex (Lada). Remember, in Mexico, you need to dial 001 prior to a number to reach the United States, and you need to preface long-distance calls within Mexico by dialing 01.

Time Zone

Cancún operates on Central Standard Time, but Mexico's observance of daylight savings time varies somewhat from that in the United States.

Chapter 10

Dining in Cancún

● ●

In This Chapter

▶ Discovering Cancún's best restaurants

▶ Finding a restaurant with true Mexican ambience

● ●

*T*he restaurant scene in Cancún is populated in large part by U.S.-based franchise chains, which need no introduction — Hard Rock Cafe, Planet Hollywood, Rainforest Cafe, Tony Roma's, TGI Fridays, Ruth's Chris Steak House, and the usual fast-food burger places. And surprisingly, contrary to the conventional travel wisdom, many of the best restaurants in Cancún are located either in hotels or shopping malls.

Most restaurants are located in the Hotel Zone in Isla Cancún, which is logical because that's where most of the tourists who dine out are staying. However, don't dismiss the charms of dining in Ciudad Cancún. You're likely to find a great meal — at a fraction of the price of an Isla Cancún eatery — accompanied by a dose of local color.

As in many of Mexico's beach resorts, even the finest restaurants in town can be comfortably casual when it comes to dress. Men rarely wear jackets, although ladies are frequently seen in dressy resort wear — basically, everything goes, attire-wise.

For those traveling with kids, Cancún has no shortage of options. From Johnny Rockets to McDonald's, this destination has plenty of kid-friendly — and kid-familiar — places.

Prices in Cancún restaurants can cover an extended range, boosted by shrimp and lobster dishes, which can top $20 for an entree. If you're watching your budget, even the higher-priced places generally have less-expensive options — you just need to avoid the premium seafood dishes. Tips generally run about 15% of the bill, and most wait staff really depend on tips for their income, so be generous if the service warrants.

Cancún's Best Restaurants

The restaurants listed here are either locally owned, one-of-a-kind restaurants, or exceptional selections at area hotels. Many feature live music as an accompaniment to the dining experience. I arrange the restaurants alphabetically and note their location and general price category. Please refer to the Introduction of *Cancún & the Yucatán For Dummies* for an explanation of the price categories.

Please see Chapter 18 and Appendix B for more information on Mexican cuisine.

100% Natural

$ Isla Cancún VEGETARIAN/MEXICAN

If you want a healthy reprieve from an overindulgent night — or if you just like your meals as fresh and natural as possible — this restaurant is your oasis. No matter what your dining preference, you owe it to yourself to try a true Mexican tradition, the fresh fruit *liquado* (lee-*qwa*-doe) — a blended drink that combines fresh fruit, ice, and either water or milk. (Think combos of mango and milk, or mango and watermelon, juiced in an icy tall glass.) Of course, other creative combinations mix in yogurt, granola, or other goodies. But 100% Natural is more than just drinks — the restaurant offers a bountiful selection of basic Mexican fare and terrific sandwiches served on whole-grain breads. (Look for numerous vegetarian options, too.) Breakfast here is a delight, as well as a good value. The atmosphere is abundant with plants and bright colors. The restaurant has two locations; the Plaza Terramar store is open 24 hours.

Plaza Kukulcán, Blvd. Kukulcán 13, ☎ 998-885-2904. Also at Plaza Terramar, ☎ 998-883-3636. Reservations not accepted. Main courses: $2.80–$12.50. MC, V. Open: Daily 8 a.m.–11 p.m.

Aïoli

$$$$ Isla Cancún FRENCH

Aïoli, in Le Méridien Hotel, is a Provençal — but definitely not provincial — restaurant that offers exquisite French and Mediterranean gourmet specialties in a warm and cozy country French setting. Though it offers perhaps the best breakfast buffet in Cancún (for $15), most visitors outside the hotel come only for dinner, where low lighting and superb service make for a romantic evening. Starters include traditional pâtés and delightful escargots served in the shell with a white wine and herb butter sauce. A specialty is duck breast served in a honey and lavender sauce. Equally scrumptious is the rack of lamb, prepared in a Moroccan style and served with couscous. Pan-seared grouper is topped with a paste of black olives, crushed potato, and tomato, and the bouillabaisse is laden with an exceptional array of seafood. Desserts are decadent in true French style,

Isla Cancún (Hotel Zone) Dining

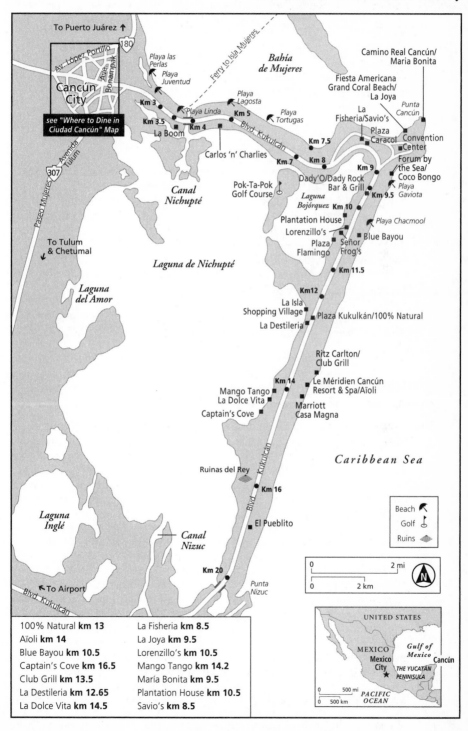

To Puerto Juárez ↑

Av. López Portillo

Ave Bonampak

Cancún City

see "Where to Dine in Ciudad Cancún" Map

Playa las Perlas

Playa Juventud

Ferry to Isla Mujeres

Km 3

Playa Linda

Km 3.5

Km 4

La Boom

Carlos 'n' Charlies

Avenida Tulum

307

Paseo Mujeres

To Tulum & Chetumal

Canal Nichupté

Pok-Ta-Pok Golf Course

Playa Lagosta

Km 5

Playa Tortugas

Blvd. Kukulcán

Km 7

Km 7.5

Km 8

Bahía de Mujeres

Fiesta Americana Grand Coral Beach/ La Joya

La Fisheria/Savio's

Camino Real Cancún/ Maria Bonita

Punta Cancún

Plaza Caracol

Convention Center

Forum by the Sea/ Coco Bongo

Dady'O/Dady Rock Bar & Grill

Km 9

Km 9.5

Playa Gaviota

Laguna Bojórquez

Km 10

Plantation House

Lorenzillo's

Plaza Flamingo

Señor Frog's

Blue Bayou

Playa Chacmool

Km 11.5

Laguna de Nichupté

Laguna del Amor

Km12

La Isla Shopping Village

La Destileria

Plaza Kukulkán/100% Natural

Ritz Carlton/ Club Grill

Km 14

Le Méridien Cancún Resort & Spa/Aïoli

Mango Tango
La Dolce Vita

Captain's Cove

Marriott Casa Magna

Blvd. Kukulcán

Caribbean Sea

Ruinas del Rey

Km 16

Laguna Inglé

El Pueblito

Canal Nizuc

Km 20

To Airport

Blvd. Kukulcán

Punta Nizuc

Beach ☂
Golf ⛳
Ruins 〰

0   2 mi
0   2 km

N

UNITED STATES

MEXICO

Gulf of Mexico

Mexico City

Cancún

THE YUCATÁN PENINSULA

0   500 mi
0   500 km

PACIFIC OCEAN

100% Natural **km 13**	La Fisheria **km 8.5**
Aïoli **km 14**	La Joya **km 9.5**
Blue Bayou **km 10.5**	Lorenzillo's **km 10.5**
Captain's Cove **km 16.5**	Mango Tango **km 14.2**
Club Grill **km 13.5**	María Bonita **km 9.5**
La Destileria **km 12.65**	Plantation House **km 10.5**
La Dolce Vita **km 14.5**	Savio's **km 8.5**

including the signature Fifth Element, a sinfully delicious dish rich with chocolate. For the quality and the originality of the cuisine, coupled with the excellence in service, Aïoli gets my top pick for the best fine-dining value in Cancún.

Le Méridien Hotel, Retorno del Rey, km 14. ☎ 998-881-2200. Internet: www. meridiencancun.com.mx. *Free parking. Reservations required. Main courses: $14–$30. AE, DC, MC, V. Open: Mon–Sun 6:30 a.m.–11 p.m.*

Blue Bayou
$$$$ Isla Cancún   CAJUN

You may not associate Cancún with Cajun dining, but this restaurant receives plenty of raves — not to mention repeat diners. Crawfish are flown in daily from Louisiana, and the signature Maya Blackened Seafood Platter is a favorite, combining the Caribbean with the Cajun's best. The restaurant serves certified Angus beef, and the Ribeye with Green Goddess sauce is excellent. The bi-level setting is remarkable — the lower level has a lush hanging garden with waterfall. Adding to the ambience is live jazz, played nightly, as well as a special "dine and dance" every Thursday through Saturday.

Blvd. Kukulcán, km. 10.5, in the Hyatt Cancún Caribe Hotel. ☎ 998-848-7800. Reservations not necessary. Main courses: $15–$33. AE, MC, V. Open: Daily 6 p.m.–11 p.m.

Captain's Cove
$$ Isla Cancún   INTERNATIONAL/SEAFOOD

Captain's Cove's multilevel dining room is a draw for diners who come for the good value, heaping servings, friendly service, and the consummate tropical ambience. Diners face big, open windows overlooking the lagoon and Royal Yacht Club Marina. (Sunsets from the upper-level deck are particularly stunning.) For breakfast, an extremely popular all-you-can-eat buffet beats the price and quality of most hotel offerings. Main courses of USDA Angus steak and seafood — such as Islander coconut shrimp — are top bets at lunch and dinner, and a menu catering especially to children is available. Dessert standouts include flaming coffees, crêpes, and Key lime pie. Captain's Cove sits almost at the end of Blvd. Kukulcán, on the lagoon side opposite the Omni Hotel.

Blvd. Kukulcán, km 16.5 ☎ 998-885-0016. Reservations recommended. Main courses: $12–$40; breakfast buffet $10 and up. AE, MC, V. Open: Daily 7 a.m.–11 p.m.

Club Grill
$$$$ Isla Cancún   INTERNATIONAL

Cancún's most elegant and stylish restaurant, located in the Ritz-Carlton Hotel, is also among its most delicious. The gracious service and the old-world charm begin the moment you enter the anteroom, with its

Ciudad Cancún (Cancún City) Dining

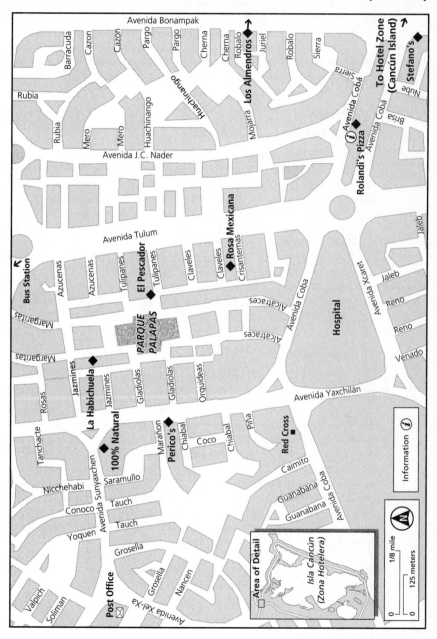

comfortable couches and chairs and selection of fine tequilas and Cuban cigars. The scene continues into a candlelit dining room with padded side chairs and tables that shimmer with silver and crystal. Elegant plates of peppered scallops, truffles, and potatoes in tequila sauce; grilled lamb; or mixed grill arrive at a leisurely pace after the appetizer. The restaurant has both smoking and nonsmoking sections. After dinner, take a turn on the dance floor, as a band plays romantic music starting at 8 p.m. Club Grill is the place for that truly special night out. A dress code is enforced: No sandals or tennis shoes, and gentlemen must wear long pants.

Ritz-Carlton Hotel, Blvd. Kukulcán, km 13.5. ☎ *998-881-0808. Reservations required. Main courses: $11–$40. AE, DC, MC, V. Open: Tues–Sun 7–11 p.m.*

El Pescador
$$ Ciudad Cancún   SEAFOOD

El Pescador is the best spot for fresh seafood in Cancún. A line often forms here for the well-prepared fresh seafood served in a street-side patio and upstairs venue. Feast on shrimp cocktail, conch, octopus, *camarones à la criolla* (Creole-style shrimp), charcoal-broiled lobster, and stone crabs. Can't decide? Try a little of everything with the *Zarzuela* combination seafood plate, cooked in white wine and garlic. El Pescador also features a Mexican specialty menu as well. Another branch, **La Mesa del Pescador,** is located in the Plaza Kukulcán on Cancún Island and is open the same hours, but it's more expensive.

Tulipanes 28, off Av. Tulum. ☎ *998-884-2673. Fax: 998-884-3639. Reservations not accepted. Main courses: $5–$30. AE, MC, V. Open: Daily 11 a.m.–11 p.m.*

La Destileria
$$$ Isla Cancún   MEXICAN

If you want to experience tequila in its native habitat, then don't miss this place — although technically, this restaurant is across the country from the region where the beverage is produced. But La Destileria is more than a tequila-inspired restaurant, it's a mini-museum that honors the "spirit" of Mexico. Over 150 brands of tequila are served here, including some true treasures that never see their way across the country's northern border — so be adventurous! The margaritas are among the best on the island as well. When you decide it's time to pair some food with your tequila, choose from dishes on the refined Mexican menu, anything from quesadillas with squash blossom flowers to shrimp in a delicate tequila-lime sauce.

Blvd. Kukulcán, km. 12.65, across from Kukulcán Plaza. ☎ *998-885-1086 or 998-885-1087. Reservations not necessary. Main courses: $8–$30. AE, MC, V. Open: Daily 1 p.m. to midnight.*

La Dolce Vita
$$$ Isla Cancún   ITALIAN/SEAFOOD

The casually elegant La Dolce Vita is known as Cancún's favorite Italian restaurant. Appetizers include pâté of quail liver and carpaccio in vinaigrette or gnocchi in a four-cheese sauce. The chef specializes in homemade pastas combined with fresh seafood. You can order green tagliolini with lobster medallions, linguine with clams or seafood, or rigatoni Mexican-style (with *chorizo,* mushrooms, and jalapeños) as a main course, or as an appetizer for half price. Choose between dining in air-conditioned comfort or on an open-air terrace with a view of the lagoon. Dinner is accompanied by live jazz from 7:00 p.m. to 11:30 p.m., Monday through Saturday.

Blvd. Kukulcán, km 14.5 (on the lagoon, across from the Marriott Casamagna). ☎ *998-885-0150 or 998-885-0161. Fax: 998-885-0590. Internet:* www.cancun. com/dining/dolce. *Reservations required for dinner. Main courses: $9–$29. AE, MC, V. Open: Daily noon to 11:30 p.m.*

La Fisheria
$$ Isla Cancún   SEAFOOD

La Fisheria is one of the exceptions to the rule about never finding good food in a shopping mall eatery. The expansive menu at La Fisheria includes grouper fingers with a jalapeño dip, stir-fried seafood with fresh vegetables and roasted peanuts, Cancún-style ceviche, shrimp bisque, steamed mussels in marinara sauce, Caribbean-style red snapper — you get the idea. The menu changes daily, but there's always *tikin xik,* that great Yucatecan grilled fish marinated in *achiote* sauce (made from the paste of the achiote chile). If seafood isn't your bag, a wood-burning, oven-made pizza may do, or perhaps one of the grilled chicken or beef dishes. If you're at the mall shopping, La Fisheria is your best bet — but even if you're not, it's also a reason to stop by.

Plaza Caracol, Shopping Center 2nd floor. ☎ *998-883-1395. Reservations not necessary. Main courses: $6.50–$21. AE, MC, V. Open: Daily 11 a.m.–11 p.m.*

La Habichuela
$$–$$$ Ciudad Cancún   GOURMET SEAFOOD/CARIBBEAN/ MEXICAN

Enjoy some of downtown Cancún's finest food as you dine alfresco in this romantic garden setting. Tables in pink-and-white linens sit on a vine-draped patio, as stars twinkle overhead and soft music plays in the background. For an all-out culinary adventure, try *habichuela* (string bean) soup; shrimp in any number of sauces, including Jamaican tamarind, tequila, and a ginger-and-mushroom combination; and the Maya coffee with *xtabentun* (a strong, sweet, anise-based liquor). The grilled seafood and steaks are excellent as well, but La Habichuela is a good place to try a Mexican specialty such as *enchiladas suizas (Swiss crepes)* or *tampiqueña*-style beef (thinly sliced, marinated, and grilled). A more unusual — and divine — choice is the *Cocobichuela,* lobster and shrimp in curry sauce served in a coconut shell and topped with fruit.

Margaritas 25. ☎ *998-884-3158. E-mail:* habichuela@infosel.net.mx. *Free parking. Reservations recommended in high season. Main courses: $10–$32. AE, MC, V. Open: Daily noon to midnight.*

Dining at sea

One unique way to combine dinner with sightseeing is to board the **Lobster Dinner Cruise** (☎ 998-849-4621). Cruising around aboard a pirate-style ship in the tranquil, turquoise waters of the lagoon, passengers feast on lobster dinners accompanied by wine. The cost is $49 per person, and the cruise departs two times daily from the Royal Mayan Marina. A sunset dinner cruise leaves at 4:30 p.m. during winter months and 5:30 p.m. during the summer. A moonlight cruise leaves at 7:30 p.m. during the winter and 8:30 p.m. during the summer. Another option is the **Captain Hook Lobster Dinner Cruise** (☎ 998-849-4451), which is similar, but with the added attraction of a pirate show. It costs $58 and departs at 7 p.m. from El Embarcadero.

La Joya
$$$$ Isla Cancún   MEXICAN/INTERNATIONAL

La Joya (the Jewel) is truly a gem of a dining experience, with a menu of gourmet Mexican cuisine in a suitably upscale atmosphere. For starters, try the lobster quesadillas, made with mellow panela cheese. Baked pumpkin flower soup or a rich, lobster-infused version of the Mexican classic *pozole* are equally tempting first courses. Main dishes range from red snapper Cozumel (grilled and topped with a rainbow of coconut-infused sauces) to beef medallions on a bed of sautéed cactus petals in a creamy chipotle sauce. Entertaining touches include a cigar show, guided Tequila tastings, and live music nightly, ranging from mariachis to classical piano. This restaurant was Mexico's first to earn the Five Diamond Award by AAA.

Blvd. Kukulcán, km. 9.5, at the Fiesta Americana Grand Coral Beach hotel. ☎ *998-881-3200. Reservations not necessary. Main courses: $25–$40. AE, MC, V. Open: Daily 6:30 p.m. to midnight.*

Los Almendros
$$ Ciudad Cancún   YUCATECAN

To steep yourself in Yucatecan cuisine and music, head directly to this large, colorful, air-conditioned restaurant. Regional specialties served here include lime soup, *poc chuc* (marinated, barbecue-style pork), chicken or pork *pibil* (sweet and spicy barbeque sauce served over shredded meat), and appetizers such as *panuchos* (soft, fried tortillas with refried beans and either shredded turkey or pork *pibil*). The *combinado Yucateco* is a sampler of four typically Yucatecan main courses.

Av. Bonampak and Sayil, across from the bullring. ☎ *998-887-1332. Reservations recommended during Christmas and Easter weeks. Main courses: $5–$9. AE, MC, V. Open: Daily 11 a.m.–9:30 p.m.*

Lorenzillo's

$$–$$$ Isla Cancún   SEAFOOD

A personal favorite; I never miss a stop here when I'm in Cancún. Live lobster is the overwhelming favorite here, and part of the appeal is the chance to select your dinner out of the giant lobster tank. A dock leads down to the main dining area, overlooking the lagoon and topped by a giant palapa. When the place is packed (which is often), a wharf-side bar handles the overflow. In addition to the lobster — it comes grilled, steamed, or stuffed — good bets are the shrimp stuffed with cheese and wrapped in bacon, the admiral's fillet coated in toasted almonds and a light mustard sauce, or the seafood-stuffed squid. Desserts include the tempting "Martinique": Belgian chocolate with hazelnuts, almonds, and pecans, served with vanilla ice cream. A new sunset pier offers a lighter menu of cold seafood, sandwiches, and salads. The atmosphere is festive and friendly, and children are very welcome — after all, most of the patrons are wearing bibs!

Blvd. Kukulcán, km 10.5. ☎ *998-883-1254. Internet:* www.lorenzillos.com.mx. *Free parking in lot across the street, plus valet parking. Reservations recommended. Main courses: $12–$50. AE, MC, V. Open: Daily noon to midnight.*

Mango Tango

$$–$$$ Isla Cancún   INTERNATIONAL

Mango Tango has sizzling floor shows (featuring salsa, tango, and other Latin dancing) and live reggae music, but the kitchen is the real star here. Try the peel-your-own shrimp, Argentine-style grilled meat with *chimichurri* sauce (sauce with roasted vegetables and spices), and other tropical specialties. The restaurant serves a fixed-price menu that includes your choice of a soup or salad, entrée, and dessert, with three hours of domestic open bar, for $40 (half-price for children ages 4 to 12). The beauty of dining here is that you can stay and enjoy one of the current hot nightspots in Cancún.

Blvd. Kukulcán, km 14.2, opposite the Ritz-Carlton Hotel. ☎ *998-885-0303. Reservations recommended. Three-course dinner, $40. AE, MC, V. Open: Daily 6 p.m.–1 a.m.*

María Bonita

$$$ Isla Cancún   REGIONAL/MEXICAN/NOUVELLE MEXICAN

Possibly the most "Mexican" of Isla Cancún's dining options, María Bonita combines the music, food, and atmosphere of Mexico's various regions — it's like taking a condensed food tour of this vast country. María Bonita is a hotel restaurant, so prices are higher and the flavors more institutionalized than at the traditional Mexican restaurants found in Ciudad Cancún, but the restaurant is still a good choice for those who want to taste more of Mexico without leaving the Hotel Zone. The restaurant overlooks the water, and the hacienda-style interior is divided into rooms that reflect different cuisine types. My favorite is *La Cantina Jalisco,* which features an open, colorful Mexican kitchen (with pots and pans on the wall) and tequila bar (with more than 50 different tequilas). For the less adventurous, a few international dishes are thrown in for variety. Trios, marimba, and jarocho music — and the ever-enchanting mariachis — serenade diners. The different peppers used are explained on the front of the menu, and each dish is rated for its heat quotient (from zero to two chilies). The restaurant is to the left of the hotel entrance; you can enter from the street.

Hotel Camino Real, Punta Cancún. ☎ *998-848-7000, ext. 8060 or 8061. Reservations recommended. Main courses: $25–$31. AE, DC, MC, V. Open: Daily 6:30–11 p.m.*

Périco's

$$–$$$ Ciudad Cancún   MEXICAN/SEAFOOD/STEAKS

Perico's is arguably the most tourist-friendly spot in Ciudad Cancún. With colorful murals that almost dance off the walls, a bar area overhung with baskets (and saddles for bar stools), inviting leather tables and chairs, and waiters dressed like Pancho Villa, it's no wonder the place is always booming and festive. The extensive menu offers well-prepared steak, seafood, and traditional Mexican dishes for moderate rates (except for the lobster), but the food here is less the point than the fun. Périco's is a place not only to eat and drink, but also to let loose and join in the fun. Don't be surprised if everybody drops their forks, dons huge Mexican sombreros, and snakes around the dining room in a conga dance. You can still have fun whether or not you join in, but Périco's is definitely not the place for that romantic evening alone. There's marimba music from 7:30 to 9:30 p.m. and mariachis from 9:30 p.m. to midnight. Expect a crowd.

Yaxchilán 61. ☎ *998-884-3152. Reservations recommended only in high season. Main courses: $9–$40. AE, MC, V. Open: Daily 1 p.m.–1 a.m.*

Pizza Rolandi

$ Ciudad Cancún   ITALIAN

Surprised to find great pizza in Cancún? Don't be — Pizza Rolandi is an institution, and the Rolandi name is synonymous with dining in both Cancún and neighboring Isla Mujeres. At this shaded outdoor sidewalk cafe, you can choose from almost two dozen different wood-oven pizzas and a full selection of spaghetti, calzones, Italian-style chicken and beef, and desserts. A full bar list is available as well. Another Rolandi's Pizza is located in Isla Mujeres and has the same food and prices. Both locations have become standards for dependably good casual fare in Cancún. For a more formal, Italian-dining affair, try the elegant **Casa Rolandi** in Plaza Carocal, Isla Cancún (☎ **988-883-1817**). See Chapter 12 for reviews of both Isla Mujeres restaurants.

Cobá 12. ☎ *998-884-4047. Fax: 998-884-3994. Reservations not necessary. Internet:* www.rolandi.com. *Main courses and pizza: $7–$14; pasta $5–$8. AE, MC, V. Open: Daily 12:30 p.m. to 12:30 a.m.*

Plantation House
$$$$ Isla Cancún CARIBBEAN/FRENCH

Elegant Caribbean fare — styled after the time when it was infused with European influences — is served up in this pale yellow-and-blue clapboard restaurant overlooking Nichupté lagoon. The decor combines island-style colonial charm with elegant touches of wood and crystal. The service is excellent, but the food is only mediocre, especially considering the price. For starters, try the signature poached shrimp with lemon juice and olive oil or a creamy crabmeat soup. Move on to the main event, which may consist of classic veal chop grilled and served in a hunter's mushroom sauce, baked fish fillet with crab and shrimp, topped with a hollandaise sauce, or lobster Rockefeller with oysters and spinach. Flambéed desserts are a specialty, and the Plantation House has one of the most extensive wine lists in town. Plantation House is generally quite crowded, which makes it a bit loud for a truly romantic evening.

Blvd. Kukulcán, km 10.5, Zona Hotelera, 77500, Cancún, Q. Roo. ☎ *998-883-1433, 998-885-1455. Reservations recommended. Main courses: $13–$40. AE, MC, V. Open: Daily 5 p.m. to midnight.*

Rosa Mexicana
$$$ Ciudad Cancún MEXICAN HAUTE

Rosa Mexicana is a simply stylish bistro and a top choice for downtown dining. Candlelit tables are set indoors and surrounded by colorful *piñatas* and paper streamers and located on a plant-filled patio in back. The menu features "refined" Mexican specialties. Try the *pollo almendro,* which is chicken covered in a cream sauce sprinkled with ground almonds, or the pork baked in a banana leaf with a sauce of oranges, lime, *chile ancho (smoky flavored chile pepper),* and garlic. The more traditional steak *tampiqueño* is a huge platter that comes with guacamole salad, quesadillas, beans, salad, and rice. Dine to live, romantic Mexican music most nights.

Claveles 4. ☎ *998-884-6313. Fax: 998-884-2371. Reservations recommended for parties of 6 or more. Main courses: $9–$17; lobster $30. AE, MC, V. Open: Daily 5–11 p.m.*

Savio's
$$$ Isla Cancún ITALIAN

Savio's is a great place to stop for a quick meal or coffee, and it's centrally located in the heart of the Hotel Zone. A stylish bi-level with a black-and-white decor and tile floors, Savio's faces Blvd. Kukulcán through two stories of awning-shaded windows. The bar is always crowded with patrons sipping everything from cappuccino to imported beer. A loyal crowd returns time and again for the large, fresh salads and richly flavored, subtly spiced Italian dishes. Among my favorites are the ravioli stuffed with ricotta and spinach, served in a delicious tomato sauce; and savory wild mushroom and saffron risotto. Live music plays nightly from 7:30 to 10:30 p.m.

*Plaza Caracol. ☎ and fax: **998-883-2085**. Reservations not accepted. Main courses: $8.25–$26. AE, MC, V. Open: Daily 10 a.m. to midnight.*

Stefano's
$$ Ciudad Cancún   ITALIAN/PIZZA

Stefano's began primarily as a local restaurant, serving Italian food with a few Mexican accents — call it "Mexitalian," if you will — and it seems to be a winning combination. Among the menu items are ravioli stuffed with *huitlacoche* (a delicious, mushroom-type fungus that grows on a cornstalk); rigatoni in tequila sauce; and seafood with chile peppers. The Stefano special pizza is made with fresh tomato, cheese, and pesto. The ricotta strudel dessert is something out of the ordinary. Stefano's offers lots of different coffees and mixed drinks, plus an expanded wine list.

*Bonampak 177. ☎ **998-887-9964**. Reservations not necessary. Main courses: $8–$10; pizza $6–$16.50. MC, V. Open: Daily 1 p.m.–1 a.m.*

Chapter 11

Having Fun On and Off the Beach in Cancún

*Y*ou're likely to run out of vacation days before you run out of things to do in Cancún. Snorkeling, jet skiing, jungle tours, and visits to ancient Mayan ruins or modern ecological theme parks are among the most popular diversions in this resort that has a little of everything. Beyond Cancún's renowned beaches are over a dozen malls with name-brand retailers and duty-free shops (featuring European goods with better prices than you can find in the United States), plus a seemingly endless supply of nightclubs to revel in.

In addition to Cancún's own attractions, the resort is a convenient distance from the more Mexican-feeling beach towns in **Isla Mujeres** (see Chapter 12), **Cozumel** (see Chapter 13), and **Playa del Carmen** (see Chapter 14). The **Mayan ruins** at Tulum and Chichén-Itzá are also close by (see Chapter 15). All these diversions are within driving distance for a spectacular day-trip.

So what's worth your time? To help you decide, I devote this chapter to giving you an overview of the best beaches in this mecca of white sand and crystalline waters. I also give you the rundown on the area's popular day-trips and diversions.

Finding Water Fun for Everyone

Face it: If you're in Cancún, you probably decided to come here based on the vision of powdery, white-sand beaches and turquoise waters. If you're in search of a beautiful beach, Cancún may be your nirvana.

With the added bonus of the Nichupté Lagoon on the other side of the island, Cancún is packed with ways to make the most of your time in the water.

Basking on a Cancún beach

The big hotels dominate the best stretches of beaches, so you likely have a fine patch of sand at your hotel. All of Mexico's beaches are public property, so technically, you can use the beach of any hotel by accessing it directly from the sand. *Technically* is the key word here. Although this is the law, the reality is that hotel security guards regularly ask nonguests to relocate. You choose if you want to suffer the potential embarrassment of being asked to leave or, if asked, standing your ground — or beach, as it were.

If you're intent on swimming, be careful on beaches fronting the open Caribbean, where the undertow can be quite strong. By contrast, the waters of **Bahía de Mujeres** at the north end of the island are usually calm and ideal for swimming. Get to know Cancún's water-safety pennant system and make sure to check the flag at any beach or hotel before entering the water.

Here's what each flag means:

- ✔ **White:** Excellent
- ✔ **Green:** Normal conditions (safe)
- ✔ **Yellow:** Changeable, uncertain (use caution)
- ✔ **Black or red:** Unsafe (use the swimming pool instead)

In the Caribbean, storms can arrive quickly, and conditions can change from safe to unsafe in a matter of minutes, so be alert: If you see dark clouds heading your way, head to shore and wait until the storm passes.

The public beaches located along the stretch of Cancún Island on the calm, Bahía de Mujeres side include **Playa Linda** (Pretty Beach), **Playa Langosta** (Lobster Beach), **Playa Tortuga** (Turtle Beach), and **Playa Caracol** (Snail Beach). Playa Linda (at km 4) has a shuttle service to Isla Mujeres, as well as a few dive shops and snack bars. Playa Langosta (at km 5) is a protected cove near the Hotel Casa Maya that features a tour-boat pier and a watersports concession, plus some shops and restaurants. Next up is Playa Tortuga (at km 7.5), a popular public beach with changing rooms, public restrooms, and restaurants. This bit of sand is frequently overrun with families on weekends. The last beach before the island curves toward the Caribbean is Playa Caracol, which stretches for about a mile and passes the Fiesta Americana and Camino Real hotels — a lovely stretch with a few restaurants but no public facilities.

The Caribbean side of Cancún faces the open sea, and it's subject to frequent riptides and strong currents. The beaches here include the regally named **Playa Chac-Mool** (named after the Mayan deity of rain) and **Playa del Rey** (Beach of the King). Playa Chac-Mool (at km 13) has showers, restrooms, and other facilities that make it as popular as Playa Tortuga on weekends. Playa del Rey, the last public beach on the island before Punta Nizac, is an unspoiled treasure. This remarkable stretch of sand ends at the entrance to Club Med.

At most beaches, in addition to swimming, you can rent a sailboard and take lessons, ride a parasail, or partake in a variety of other watersports.

To locate these beaches on a map, please see the map of Isla Cancún in Chapter 9.

Skiing and surfing

Many beachside hotels offer watersports concessions that include the rental of rubber rafts, kayaks, and snorkeling equipment. Outlets for renting **sailboats, Jet Skis, windsurfers,** and **water skis** are located on the calm Nichupté Lagoon. Prices vary and are often negotiable, so check around.

For windsurfing, go to the Playa Tortuga public beach where a **windsurfing school** (no phone) has equipment for rent.

A very popular option for getting wet and wild is a **jungle cruise,** offered by several companies. The cruise takes you by Jet Ski or WaveRunner through Cancún's lagoon and mangrove estuaries out into the Caribbean Sea and by a shallow reef. The excursion runs about 2½-hours (you drive your own watercraft) and is priced from $35 to $45, with snorkeling and beverages included. Some of the motorized mini-boats seat you side by side; other crafts seat one person behind the other. The difference? The second person can see the scenery or the back of his or her companion's head, depending on your choice.

The operators and names of boats offering excursions change often. The popular **Aquaworld** (Blvd. Kukulcán, km 15.2; ☎ **998-885-2288;** Internet: www.aquaworld.com.mx) calls its trip the Jungle Tour and charges $45 for the 2½-hour excursion, which includes 45 minutes of snorkeling time. The company even gives you a free snorkel, but its watercrafts have the less-desirable seating configuration of one behind the other. Departures are 8:00 a.m., 8:30 a.m., 9:00 a.m., 10:30 a.m., 11:30 a.m., 12 p.m., 1 p.m., 2 p.m., 2:30 p.m., 3:30 p.m., and 4:30 p.m. daily. To find out what's available when you're there, check with a local travel agent or hotel tour desk; you should find a wide range of options. You can also go to the Playa Linda pier either a day ahead or the day of your intended outing and buy your own tickets for trips on the *Nautibus* or to Isla Mujeres (see information later in this chapter). If you go on the day of your trip, arrive at the pier around 8:45 a.m.; most boats leave by 9 or 9:30 a.m.

Exploring the deep blue

Known for its shallow reefs, dazzling colors, and diversity of life, Cancún is one of the best places in the world for beginning **scuba diving.** Punta Nizuc is the northern tip of the **Gran Arrecife Maya (Great Mesoamerican Reef),** the largest reef in the Western Hemisphere and one of the largest in the world. In addition to the sea life present along this reef system, several sunken boats add a variety of dive options. Inland, a series of caverns and wellsprings, known as *cenotes,* are fascinating venues for the more experienced diver. Drift diving is the norm here, with popular dives going to the reefs at **El Garrafón** and the **Cave of the Sleeping Sharks.** For those unfamiliar with the term, *drift diving* occurs when divers drift with the strong currents in the waters and end up at a point different than where they started. The dive boat follows them. In traditional dives, the divers resurface where they began.

Resort courses that teach the basics of diving — enough to make shallow dives and slowly ease your way into this underwater world of unimaginable beauty — are offered in a variety of hotels. Scuba trips run around $60 for two-tank dives at nearby reefs and $100 and up for locations farther out. **Scuba Cancún** (Blvd. Kukulcán, km 5; ☎ **998-849-7508,** 998-849-4736; Internet: www.scubacancun.com.mx), on the lagoon side, offers a four-hour resort course for $84. In addition to calling or visiting, you can make reservations in the evenings from 7:30 to 10:30 p.m. using the preceding phone numbers. Full certification takes four to five days and costs around $368. Scuba Cancún is open from 8:30 a.m. to 6 p.m. and accepts major credit cards.

The largest operator is **Aquaworld,** across from the Meliá Cancún hotel at Blvd. Kukulcán, km 15.2 (☎ **998-885-2288,** 998-848-8300; Internet: www.aquaworld.com.mx). Aquaworld offers resort courses and diving from a manmade, anchored dive platform, Paradise Island. Aquaworld also has the **Sub See Explorer,** a submarine-style boat with picture windows that hang beneath the surface. The boat doesn't actually submerge — it's more like an updated version of the glass-bottom boat concept — but it does provide nondivers with a look at life beneath the sea. This outfit is open from 6:30 a.m. to 10 p.m. and accepts all major credit cards.

Scuba Cancún (☎ **998-849-7808,** 998-849-4736; e-mail: scuba@cancun. com.mx) also offers diving trips to 20 nearby reefs, at 30 feet, and the open ocean at 30 to 60 feet (offered in good weather only). The average dive is around 35 feet. One-tank dives cost $50, and two-tank dives cost $64. Discounts apply if you bring your own equipment. Dives usually start around 10 a.m. and return by 2:15 p.m. Snorkeling trips cost $27 and leave every afternoon after 1:30 p.m. for shallow reefs located about a 20-minute boat ride away.

The Great Mesoamerican Reef also offers exceptional snorkeling opportunities near Cancún, for those who don't want to go too deep. In Puerto Morelos (23 miles south of Cancún; see Chapter 14) this reef hugs the coastline for 9 miles. The closeness of the reef to the shore (about 500 yards) is a natural barrier for the village and keeps the waters calm on the inside of the reef. The depth of the water here is shallow, between 5 to 30 feet, resulting in ideal conditions for snorkeling. The reef here has remained unspoiled due to the stringent environmental regulations implemented by the local community. Only a select few companies are allowed to offer snorkel trips here and must adhere to guidelines that will ensure the ecological preservation of the reef. Among these companies, **Cancún Mermaid** is considered the best — it's a family-run eco-tour company that has been operating in the area since the '70s, known for its highly personalized service. Its tour typically takes snorkelers to two sections of the reef, spending about an hour in each area, however, when conditions allow, the company will have the boat drop off snorkelers and then follow them along with the current — an activity known as *drift snorkeling* — which enables snorkelers to see as much of the reef as possible. The price of the trip is $45 for adults, $35 for children, and includes boat, snorkeling gear, life jackets, a light lunch, bottled water, sodas and beer, plus round-trip transportation to and from Puerto Morelos from Cancún hotels. Departures are Monday through Saturday at 9 a.m. and noon (minimum of four snorkelers required for a trip), and reservations are required; ☎ **998-843-6517,** 998-886-4117; Internet: www. cancunmermaid.com.

Reeling in the big one

You can arrange a day of **deep-sea fishing** at one of the numerous piers or travel agencies for around $200 to $360 for four hours, $420 for six hours, and $520 for eight hours for up to four people. Marinas sometimes assist in putting together a group. Charters include a captain, a first mate, bait, gear, and beverages. Rates are lower if you depart from Isla Mujeres or from Cozumel Island, and frankly, the fishing is better closer to these departure points.

Swimming with dolphins

In Cancún, the **Parque Nizuc** (☎ **998-881-3030**) marine park offers guests a chance to swim with dolphins and view these wonderful creatures in their dolphin aquarium, Atlántido. It's a fun place for a family to spend the day, with its numerous pools, waterslides, and rides. Another attraction offers the chance to snorkel with manta rays, tropical fish, and tame sharks. Open 10 a.m. to 5:30 p.m., the park is located on the southern end of Cancún at km 25, between the airport and the Hotel Zone. Admission is $27 for adults and $21 for kids.

La Isla Shopping Center, Blvd. Kukulcán, km 12.5, also has an **Interactive Aquarium** (☎ **998-883-0413,** 998-883-0436, or 998-883-0413) with dolphin swims and the chance to feed a shark. Interactive encounters and swims start at $50.

In my opinion, the best option for doing the dolphin thing is found on Isla Mujeres, where you can swim with dolphins at **Dolphin Discovery** (☎ **998-849-4757;** Fax: 998-849-4758; Internet: www.dolphindiscovery. com). Each session lasts one hour, with an educational introduction followed by 30 minutes of swim time. The price is $119, and transportation to Isla Mujeres is an additional $15. Reservations are required because capacity is limited each day. Assigned swimming times are 10 a.m., 12 a.m., 2 p.m., and 3:30 p.m., and you must arrive 1½ hours before your scheduled swim time.

What to See and Do on Dry Land

Even by land, Cancún has its share of winning ways to spend the day. Although golf is a latent developer here, more courses are popping up along the coast south of Cancún. Tennis, however, is tops as a hotel amenity, and you can find courts throughout Cancún. Horseback riding and all-terrain vehicle tours are also great choices for land adventures.

Teeing off

Although the golf options are limited, the most well-known — and well-used — facility is the 18-hole **Club de Golf Cancún** (☎ **998-883-0871;** e-mail: poktapok@sybcom.com), also known as the Pok-Ta-Pok Club. Designed by Robert Trent Jones, Sr., it's located on the northern leg of the island. Greens fees run $105 per 18 holes. Clubs rent for $27, shoes run $16, and caddies charge $20 per bag. The club is open daily; American Express, MasterCard, and Visa are accepted. The club also has tennis courts.

The **Melía Cancún** (☎ **998-881-1100**) offers a nine-hole executive course; the fee is $25, and the club is open daily from 8 a.m. to 4 p.m. American Express, MasterCard, and Visa are accepted.

The most interesting option is at the **Hilton Cancún Golf & Beach Resort** (☎ **998-881-8016;** Fax: 998-881-8084). Its championship 18-hole, par-72 course was designed around the Ruinas del Rey (Ruins of the King) archeological site. Greens fees for the public are $110 for 18 holes and $88 for 9 holes; Hilton Cancún guests receive a 20% discount off these rates. Greens fees include a golf cart. Golf clubs and shoes are available for rent as well, and the club is open daily from 6 a.m., with closing time varying depending upon the season, and available daylight.

Making time for tennis

Many hotels in Cancún offer excellent **tennis** facilities, and many of the courts are lit for night play. Among the best are the facilities at Le Méridien and the Fiesta Americana Coral Beach hotels.

Galloping along on horseback

Rancho Loma Bonita (☎ **998-887-5465,** 998-887-5423) is Cancún's most popular option for **horseback riding.** Five-hour packages are available for $65. The packages include two hours of riding to caves, *cenotes* (spring-fed, underground caves), lagoons, and Mayan ruins and along the Caribbean coast. After the ride, you have some time for relaxing on the beach. The ranch also offers a four-wheeler ride on the same route as the horseback tour for $55. Ranch Loma Bonita is located about 30 minutes south of Cancún. The prices include transportation to the ranch, riding, soft drinks, and lunch, plus a guide and insurance. Only cash is accepted.

Trailing away through the jungle

Cancún Mermaid (☎ **998-843-6517,** 998-886-4117; Internet: www. cancunmermaid.com), in Cancún, offers all-terrain-vehicle (ATV) jungle tours priced at $49 per person. The ATV tours travel through the jungles of Cancún and emerge on the beaches of the Riviera Maya. The 2½-hour tour includes equipment, instruction, the services of a tour guide, and bottled water; it departs daily at 8 a.m. and 1:30 p.m.

Getting a bird's-eye view

Get the best possible view of Cancún atop the new **La Torre Cancún** (☎ **998-849-4848,** 998-889-7777), the rotating scenic tower located at the El Embarcadero park and entertainment complex. One ride will cost you $9, or opt for a day and night pass for $14. The company is located at Blvd. Kukulcán, km 4, and is open daily from 9 a.m. to 11 p.m.

Sightseeing in Cancún

To the right side of the entrance to the Cancún Convention Center is the small **Museo Arqueológico de Cancún** (☎ **998-883-0305**), a small but interesting museum with relics from archaeological sites around the state. Admission is $3, with no charge for children under 13 (free for all on Sundays and holidays). The museum is open Tuesday to Friday from 9 a.m. to 8 p.m., and Saturday and Sundays from 10 a.m. to 7 p.m.

Another cultural enclave is the **Museo de Arte Popular Mexicano**
(☎ **998-849-4848,** 849-5580; Internet: www.elembarcadero.com/
museo.html), located at El Embarcadero, km 4, Blvd. Kukulcán. It displays a representative collection of masks, regional folkloric costumes,
nativity scenes, religious artifacts, musical instruments, Mexican toys,
and gourd art, spread over 4,500 feet of exhibition space. Admission is
$10, with kids under 12 paying half price. The museum is open Monday
to Saturday from 10 a.m. to 11 p.m. and Sunday from 10 a.m. to 7 p.m.

During the winter tourist season, **bullfights** are held every Wednesday
at 3:30 p.m. in Cancún's small bullring **Plaza de Toros** (☎ **998-884-8372,**
884-8248), which is located near the northern end of Blvd. Kukulcán
opposite the Restaurant Los Almendros (Ave. Bonampak and Sayil).
A sport introduced to Mexico by the Spanish viceroys, bullfighting is
now as much a part of Mexican culture as tequila. The bullfights usually
include four bulls, and the spectacle begins with a folkloric dance exhibition, followed by a performance by the *charros* (Mexico's sombrero-
wearing cowboys). You're not likely to see Mexico's best bullfights in
Cancún — the real stars are in Mexico City.

Keep in mind that if you go to a bullfight, *you're going to see a bullfight,*
so stay away if you're an animal lover or you can't bear the sight of
blood. Travel agencies in Cancún sell tickets: $30 for adults, with chil-
dren admitted free of charge. Seating is by general admission.
American Express, MasterCard, and Visa are accepted.

Panoramic **helicopter tours** allow you to see a complete overview of
this island paradise and the surrounding areas. Both day and evening
flights are available. Tours to the ruins and flights south along the
Riviera Maya are also an option. **Heli Data** offers customized tours
with hourly rates depending upon the length of flight and time of day.
Hotel pickup is provided. For details, call ☎ **998-883-3104. HeliTours**
(☎ **998-849-4222,** 849-4230) also offers a 15-minute ride over the
Cancún Hotel Zone for $79.

Cancún has its own Mayan ruins, **Ruinas del Rey,** a small site that's less
impressive than the ruins at Tulum or Chichén-Itzá. Mayan fishermen
built this small ceremonial center and settlement very early in the history of Mayan culture and then abandoned it. The site was resettled
again near the end of the post-classic period, not long before the arrival
of the conquistadors. The platforms of numerous small temples are visible amid the banana plants, papayas, and wildflowers. The ruins are
about 12 miles from town, at the southern reaches of the Hotel Zone,
close to Punta Nizuc. Look for the Hilton hotel on the left (east) and
then the ruins on the right (west). Admission is $2.50 (free on Sundays
and holidays); the hours are 8 a.m. to 4:30 p.m. daily.

A new theme restaurant, **El Rey Mundo Maya,** is adjacent to the ruins,
offering visitors a more comprehensive "taste" of what life was like on
Cancún Island years ago. The restaurant is styled like an ancient Mayan

village, complete with an astronomical observatory and market.
A three-course dinner of traditional cooking is served in its Royal
Dining Room (Monday through Saturday), accompanied by a folkloric
show, and nocturnal tour of the ruins. Dinner starts at 7 p.m., and the
cost is $62 per person, including drinks, the show, and the tour. It's an
unusual alternative to other nighttime attractions here.

Nearby Attractions and Side Trips

One of the best ways to spend a vacation day in Cancún is by exploring
one the nearby archeological ruins or new ecological theme parks or
by sailing away for the day to the quaint, nearby island, Isla Mujeres
(Island of Women). Historical and natural treasures unlike any you may
have encountered before are within easy driving distance. Cancún is a
perfect base for day-trips to these places, which provide a great introduction to Mexico's rich historical past and diverse natural attractions.

The Maya ruins to the south of Cancún at **Tulum** should be your first
goal. Then perhaps, you can check out the *caleta* (cove) of **Xel-Ha** or
take the day-trip to **Xcaret.** See Chapter 15 for more information on the
ruins at Tulum and Chapter 14 for more on Xcaret and Xel-Ha.

For day-trips by land, the organized trips are popular and easy to book
through any travel agent in town, or you can plan a journey on your
own via bus or rental car.

Day-trips to Isla Mujeres

One of the most popular — and in my mind, best — ways to spend the
day is to check out a real Mexican beach town across the narrow channel from Cancún. **Isla Mujeres** (the name means "Island of Women" in
Spanish), just 10 miles offshore, is one of the most pleasant day-trips
from Cancún. At one end of the island is **El Garrafón National
Underwater Park,** which is excellent for snorkeling and diving. At the
other end is a captivating village with small shops, restaurants, and
hotels, along with **Playa Norte (North Beach),** the island's best beach.

To get from Cancún to Isla Mujeres, you have four options:

- ✔ The **public ferries** from Puerto Juárez take between 15 and 45
  minutes and make frequent trips.
- ✔ Traveling by **shuttle boat** from Playa Linda or Playa Tortuga is an
  hour-long ride. The boats offer irregular service.
- ✔ The **watertaxi** is a more expensive but faster option than the public
  ferry or a shuttle boat. It's located next to the Xcaret terminal.
- ✔ Daylong **pleasure-boat trips** to the island leave from the Playa
  Linda pier.

Pleasure-boat cruises to Isla Mujeres include practically every conceivable type of vessel: Modern motor yachts, catamarans, trimarans, and even old-time sloops — more than 25 boats a day — take swimmers, sun lovers, snorkelers, and shoppers out into the translucent waters. Some tours include a snorkeling stop at Garrafón, lunch on the beach, and a short time for shopping in downtown Isla Mujeres. Most cruises leave at 9:30 or 10 a.m., last about five or six hours, and include continental breakfast, lunch, and rental of snorkel gear. Others, particularly the sunset and night cruises, go to beaches away from town for pseudo-pirate shows and include a lobster dinner or Mexican buffet. If you want to actually see Isla Mujeres, take a morning cruise or go on your own using the public ferry at Puerto Juárez. Prices for the day cruises run around $45 per person.

The inexpensive Puerto Juárez **public ferries** are just a few miles from downtown Cancún and give you greater flexibility in planning your day. From Isla Cancún or Cancún City, take either a taxi or the Ruta 8 bus (from Avenida Tulum) to Puerto Juárez. Choose the fast ferry (a 15-minute ride) that costs $3.50 per person over the slower one (a 45-minute ride) that costs $2. Departures are every half-hour from 6 to 8:30 a.m. and then every 15 minutes until 8:30 p.m. Upon arrival, the ferry docks in downtown Isla Mujeres near all the shops, restaurants, hotels, and Norte beach. Take a taxi or rent a golf cart to get to Garrafón Park at the other end of the island. You can stay on the island as long as you like (even overnight) and return by ferry, but be sure to check the time of the last returning ferry — the hours are clearly posted.

For more on Isla Mujeres, see Chapter 12.

Scenic boat trips

The glass-bottomed *Nautibus* (☎ **998-883-3732,** 998-883-2119; $29 adults, $14.50 children ages 6 to 12) has been around for years. The morning and afternoon trips (9:30 a.m., 11 a.m., 12:30 p.m., and 2 p.m.) take about 1 hour and 20 minutes, including about 50 minutes of transit time back and forth. You travel in a glass-bottom boat from the El Embarcadero pier to the Chitale coral reef and see colorful fish.

The **Atlantis Submarine** (☎ **987-872-5671;** $71 adults, $35.50 children ages 6 to 12) provides a front-row seat to the underwater action. Departures vary, depending on weather conditions, and the submarine descends to a depth of 100 feet. Atlantis Submarine departs Monday to Saturday every hour from 9 a.m. until 1 p.m.; the tour lasts about an hour. The submarine departs from Cozumel, so you either need to take a ferry to get there or purchase the package that includes round-trip ground and water transportation from your hotel in Cancún ($103 adults, $63.50 children ages 6 to 12). For more information, see Chapter 13.

You can call any travel agent or see any hotel tour desk to get a wide selection of boat tours to **Isla Contoy.** Prices range from $44 to $65, depending on the length of the trip. Still other boat excursions visit **Isla Contoy, a national bird sanctuary** that's well worth the time. However, if you plan to spend time in Isla Mujeres, the Contoy trip is easier and more pleasurable to take from there.

Seeing the archeological sites

Three great archeological sites are within close proximity to Cancún: Tulum, Ruinas del Rey, and Chichén-Itzá. You can arrange day-trips from Cancún through your hotel or through a travel agent in the United States (before you go) or in Mexico.

✔ **Tulum:** Poised on a rocky hill overlooking the transparent, turquoise Caribbean Sea, ancient **Tulum** is a stunning site. Hours are 8 a.m. to 6 p.m. daily in the summer and 7 a.m. until 5 p.m. daily in the winter. Admission is $4, with free admission on Sunday. For more information, see Chapter 15.

✔ **Chichén-Itzá:** The fabled pyramids and temples of Chichén-Itzá are the region's best-known ancient monuments. Hours are 8 a.m. to 5 p.m. daily. Admission is $11 free for children under 12, and free for all on Sundays and holidays. For more information, see Chapter 15.

✔ **Ruinas del Rey:** Cancún has some ruins of its own, which are convenient though far less impressive. The hours are 8 a.m. until 4:30 p.m. dailyAdmission is $2.50. For more information, see "Sightseeing in Cancún," later in this chapter.

Exploring an ecotheme park

The popularity of the Xcaret and Xel-Ha ecoparks has inspired a growing number of entrepreneurs to ride the wave of interest in ecological and adventure theme parks. Be aware that "theme park" more than "ecological" is the operative part of the phrase. The newer parks of Aktun Chen and Tres Ríos are — so far — less commercial and more focused on nature than their predecessors.

Aktun Chen

This nature park, with its large, well-lit caverns and abundant wildlife, is the first time that above-the-ground cave systems in the Yucatán have been open to the public. The main cave contains three rivers and a deep underground *cenote* (sinkhole).

Traveling to Aktun Chen on your own is easy. From Cancún, go south on Highway 307 (the road to Tulum). Just past the turn-off for Akumal, a sign on the right side of the highway indicates the turn-off for Aktun Chen (at km 107, Cancún-Tulum road). From there, it's a 3-km (1.9-mile) drive west along a smooth but unpaved road. Travel time from Cancún is about an hour. For more on Aktun Chen, see Chapter 14.

Tres Ríos

Tres Ríos — meaning three rivers — is the most "natural" of the area's nature parks. Just 25 minutes south of Cancún on more than 150 acres of land, this park is a true nature reserve that offers guests a beautiful area for kayaking, canoeing, snorkeling, horseback riding, or biking along jungle trails. Essentially, Tres Ríos is just one big natural spot for participating in these activities. Most Cancún travel agencies sell a half-day Kayak Express tour to Tres Ríos. Priced at $45, it includes admission and activities, plus round-trip transportation, lunch, and two nonalcoholic drinks. For more information, see Chapter 14.

Xcaret

Xcaret (pronounced *ish*-car-et), located 50 miles south of Cancún, is a specially built ecological and archaeological theme park and one of the area's most popular tourist attractions. Xcaret has become almost a reason in itself to visit Cancún. With a ton of attractions — most of them participatory — in one location, it's the closest thing to Disneyland in Mexico. In Cancún, signs advertising Xcaret and folks handing out Xcaret leaflets are everywhere. The park has its own bus terminal in Cancún where buses pick up tourists at regular intervals. Plan to spend a full day here; children love it, and the jungle setting and palm-lined beaches are beautiful. Past the entrance booths (built to resemble small Mayan temples) are pathways that meander around bathing coves, the snorkeling lagoon, and the remains of a group of real Mayan temples.

Xcaret may celebrate Mother Nature, but its builders rearranged quite a bit of her handiwork in completing it. If you're looking for a place to escape the commercialism of Cancún, this park may not be it. The park is relatively expensive and may be very crowded, thus diminishing the advertised "natural" experience.

Travel agencies in Cancún offer day-trips to Xcaret that depart at 8 a.m. and return at 6 p.m. The cost starts at $89 for adults ($45 for children), which includes transportation, admission, and a guide. You can also buy a ticket to the park at the **Xcaret bus terminal** (☎ **998-883-0654,** 998-883-3143; Internet: www.xcaretcancun.com), located next to the Fiesta Americana Coral Beach hotel on Cancún Island. The "Xcaret at Night" trip includes round-trip transportation from Cancún, a *charreada* festival (where horse riding and roping skills are showcased), lighted pathways to Mayan ruins, dinner, and a folkloric show. The cost is $79 for adults and $40 for children age 6 to 11 (free for kids age 5 and younger). Buses leave the terminal at 9 and 10 a.m. daily, with the "Night" tour departing at 3 p.m. The park, itself, is open daily 8:30 a.m. to 10 p.m. For more on Xcaret, see Chapter 14.

Xel-Ha

The sea has carved the Caribbean coast of the Yucatán into hundreds of small *caletas,* or coves. Many *caletas* along the coast remain undiscovered and pristine, but Xel-Ha (shell-*hah*), near Tulum, plays host daily to throngs of snorkelers and scuba divers who come to luxuriate in its warm waters and swim among its brilliant fish. Xel-Ha is a swimmers' paradise with no threat of undertow or pollution. It's a beautiful, completely calm cove that's a perfect place to bring kids for their first snorkeling experience. Experienced snorkelers, on the other hand, may be disappointed because the crowds seem to have driven out the living coral and many of the fish here. For more information, see Chapter 14.

Shopping in Cancún

Despite the surrounding natural splendor, shopping has become a favored activity in Cancún, and the place is known throughout Mexico for its diverse array of shops and festive malls catering to large numbers of international tourists. Tourists arriving from the United States may find apparel more expensive in Cancún, but the selection here is much broader than in other Mexican resorts.

Numerous duty-free shops offer excellent value on European goods. The largest shop is **UltraFemme** (☎ **998-884-1402,** 998-885-0804), specializing in imported cosmetics, perfumes, and fine jewelry and watches. Its downtown-Cancún location on Avenida Tulum, Supermanzana (intersection) 25, offers lower prices than the locations in Plaza Caracol, Kukulcán Plaza, Plaza Mayafair, and Flamingo Plaza.

Handcrafts and other *artesanía* works are more limited and more expensive in Cancún than in other regions of Mexico because they're sold but not produced here. Several **open-air crafts markets** are easily visible on Avenida Tulum in Cancún City and near the convention center in the Hotel Zone. One of the biggest markets is **Coral Negro,** located at Blvd. Kukulcán, km 9.5 (☎ **998-883-0758;** Fax: 998-883-0758). It's open daily from 9 a.m. to 10 p.m.

The main venue for shopping in Cancún are the **malls** — not quite as grand as the typical U.S. counterparts, but close. All of Cancún's malls are air-conditioned, sleek, and sophisticated, with most located on Avenida Kukulcán between km 7 and km 12. You can find everything from fine crystal and silver to designer clothing and decorative objects, along with numerous restaurants, clubs, and multiplex movie theaters for an afternoon out of the sun. Stores are generally open daily from 10 a.m. to 10 p.m., with clubs and restaurants remaining open much later. Here's a brief rundown on the malls, running from the northern to the southern end of the island — and some of the shops they contain.

The long-standing **Plaza Caracol** (Blvd. Kukulcán, km 8.5; ☎ 998-883-1038) holds Cartier jewelry, Guess, Waterford Crystal, Señor Frogs clothing, Samsonite luggage, Gucci, and La Fisheria restaurant. It's just before you reach the convention center as you come in from downtown Cancún.

The entertainment-oriented **Forum by the Sea** (Blvd. Kukulcán, km 9; ☎ 998-883-4425; Internet: www.cancunshoppingmalls.com) has shops including Tommy Hilfiger, Levi's, Diesel, Swatch, and Harley Davidson, but most people come here for the food and fun. You can choose from Hard Rock Cafe, Coco Bongo, Rainforest Cafe, Sushi-ito, and Santa Fe Beer Factory, plus an extensive food court. It's open 10 a.m. to midnight (bars remain open later).

Planet Hollywood anchors the **Plaza Flamingo** (Blvd. Kukulcán, km 8.5; ☎ 998-883-2945), but branches of Bancrecer, Subway, and La Casa del Habano (for Cuban cigars) are located inside.

Maya Fair Plaza/Centro Comercial Maya Fair, frequently called "Mayfair" (Blvd. Kukulcán, km 8.5; ☎ 998-883-2801), is Cancún's oldest mall and features a lively, bricked center with open-air restaurants and bars, such as Tequila Sunrise, and several stores selling silver, leather, and crafts.

Inside **Plaza Kukulcán** (Blvd. Kukulcán, km 12; ☎ 998-885-2200; Internet: www.KukulcanPlaza.com) is a large selection of more than 300 shops, restaurants, and entertainment venues. It houses a branch of Banco Serfin; OK Maguey Cantina Grill; a movie theater showing U.S. movies; an Internet-access kiosk; Tikal, a shop with Guatemalan textile clothing; several crafts stores; a liquor store; several bathing-suit specialty stores; record and tape outlets; a leather-goods store (including shoes and sandals); and a store specializing in silver from Taxco. In the food court are a number of U.S. franchise restaurants, including Ruth's Chris Steak House, plus a specialty-coffee shop. For entertainment, the plaza has a bowling alley, the Q-Zar laser game pavilion, and a videogame arcade. There's also a large indoor garage. The mall is open 10 a.m. to 10 p.m.

The newest and most intriguing mall is the **La Isla Shopping Village** (Blvd. Kukulcán, km 12.5; ☎ 998-883-5025, 883-5725, Internet: www.cancunshoppingmalls.com), an open-air festival mall that looks like a small village, where walkways lined with shops and restaurants crisscross over little canals. The mall also has a "riverwalk" alongside the Nichupté Lagoon with an interactive aquarium and dolphin-swim facility, as well as the Mayaventura Labyrinth — great for kid-friendly fun. Shops include Zara clothing, Benetton, Guess, Swatch, H. Stern, Ultra Femme, and the first Warner Brothers Studios store in Mexico. Dining choices include Johnny Rockets, The Food Court (not actually a "food court," but an Anderson's restaurant), and the beautiful Mexican restaurant, La Casa de las Margaritas. You also can find a movie theater, a video arcade, and several nightclubs, including Max-O's and Alebrejes. The mall is across from the Sheraton, on the lagoon side.

Enjoying Cancún's Nightlife

Ready to party? The nightlife in Cancún is as hot as the sun at noon on a cloudless July day, and clubbing is one of the main attractions of this let-loose town. The current hotspots are centralized in **Forum by the Sea** and **La Isla Village,** but it's not hard to find a party anywhere in town. Hotels also compete for your pesos with happy-hour entertainment and special drink prices as they try to entice visitors and guests from other resorts to pay a visit. (Lobby-bar hopping at sunset is one great way to plan next year's vacation.)

Partying at a club

Clubbing in Cancún can go on each night until the sun rises over that incredibly blue sea. Several of the big hotels have nightclubs — sometimes still called discos here — and others entertain in their lobby bars with live music. On weekends, expect to stand in long lines for the top clubs, pay a cover charge of $10 to $20 per person, and spend $5 to $8 on a drink. Some of the higher-priced clubs include an open bar or live entertainment.

What's hot now? As any good clubber knows, popularity can shift like the sands on the beach, but Cancún clubs do seem to have staying power. So take this list as a starting point — extensive research showed me that these were the current hot spots at press time, listed alphabetically:

- ✔ **Bulldog Café** (formerly the opulent disco, Christine), in the Hotel Krystal on the island (☎ **998-848-9800**), is this former hot-spot's attempt at luring back the nightlife crowds. The owners have taken the impressive space, signature laser-light shows, infused oxygen, and large video screens and have updated the music. They've also made the overall ambience much more casual and funky — and therefore more popular for the typical Cancún partier. The music ranges from Hip-Hop to Latino rock, with a heavy emphasis on infectious dance tunes. Bulldog opens at 10 p.m. nightly and stays open until the party winds down. The cover charge is $12 per person or pay $25 for open bar all night long (domestic drinks only).

- ✔ **Coco Bongo** in Forum by the Sea (Blvd. Kukulcán, km 9.5; ☎ **998-883-5061;** Internet: www.cocobongo.com.mx) continues its reputation as the hottest spot in town. This spot's main appeal is that it has no formal dance floor, so you can dance anywhere you can find the space — that includes on the tables, on the bar, or even on stage with the live band! Coco Bongo can pack in up to 3,000 people — and regularly does. Despite its capacity, lines are long on weekends and in the high season. The music alternates between Caribbean, salsa, techno, and classics from the 1970s and '80s.

✔ **Dady'O** (Blvd. Kukulcán, km 9.5; ☎ **998-883-3333;** Internet: www. dady-o.com) is a highly favored rave with frequent, long lines. It opens nightly at 10 p.m. and generally charges a cover of $15. **Dady Rock Bar and Grill** (Blvd. Kukulcán, km 9.5; ☎ **998-883-1626**), the offspring of Dady'O, opens early (6 p.m.) and goes as long as any other nightspot, offering a new twist on entertainment with a combination of live bands and DJ-orchestrated music. It also features an open bar, full meals, a buffet, and dancing.

✔ **La Boom** (Blvd. Kukulcán, km 3.5; ☎ **998-883-1152;** Fax: 998-883-1458; Internet: www.laboom.com.mx) has two sections: One side is a video bar, and the other is a bilevel disco with cranking music. Both sides are air-conditioned. Each night finds a special deal going on: no cover, free bar, ladies' night, bikini night, and other promos. Popular with 20-somethings, it's open nightly from 10 p.m. to 6 a.m. A sound-and-light show begins at 11:30 p.m. in the disco. The cover varies for the disco and the bar depending on the night — ladies get in free most nights, and men pay covers that vary between $20 and $35 with an open bar.

Numerous restaurants, such as **Carlos 'n Charlie's, Planet Hollywood, Hard Rock Cafe, Señor Frog's, TGI Friday's,** and **Iguana Wana,** double as nighttime party spots offering wild-ish fun at much lower prices than the clubs. Check these out:

✔ **Carlos 'n Charlie's** (Blvd. Kukulcán, km 5.5; ☎ **998-849-4052**) is a reliable place to find both good food and frat-house-type entertainment in the evenings. A dance floor goes along with the live music that starts nightly around 8:30 p.m. A cover charge kicks in if you're not planning to eat. It's open daily 11 to 2 a.m.

✔ **Hard Rock Cafe,** in Plaza Lagunas Mall and Forum by the Sea (☎ **998-881-8120,** 998-883-2024; Internet: www.hardrock.com), entertains with a live band at 10:30 p.m. every night except Wednesday. At other times, you get lively recorded music to munch by. It's open daily 11 to 1 a.m.

✔ **Planet Hollywood** (Flamingo Shopping Center, Blvd. Kukulcán, km 11; ☎ **998-883-0527;** Internet: www.planethollywood.com) is the still-popular brainchild (and one of the last-remaining) of Sylvester Stallone, Bruce Willis, and Arnold Schwarzenegger. It's both a restaurant and a nighttime music/dance spot with mega-decibel live music. It's open daily 11 to 2 a.m.

Not into the party scene? The most refined and upscale of all Cancún's nightly gathering spots is the **Lobby Lounge** at the **Ritz-Carlton Hotel** (☎ **998-881-0808**). Live dance music and a list of more than 120 premium tequilas for tasting or sipping are the highlights here.

Enjoying a cultural event

Nightly performances of the **Ballet Folklórico de Cancún** (☎ **998-849-7777**) are held at the Teatro de Cancún, at the El Embarcadero Pier. The show, **Voces y Danzas de Mexico (Voices and Dances of Mexico),** takes place each night, Monday through Friday, at 7 p.m. The cost is $29 per person and includes an open bar of national drinks.

Another show, **Tradicion del Caribe (Caribbean Traditions),** also takes place at the Teatro de Cancún (☎ **998-849-7777**), Mondays through Fridays at 9 p.m. The cost of $29 per person includes the show of more than 80 performers showcasing the dance and music of the Mexican Caribbean, Trinidad and Tobago, Costa Rica, Cuba, and Puerto Rico, plus an open bar of national drinks. At the conclusion of the show, guests are welcome to dance to these tempting tropical rhythms.

Several hotels host **Mexican fiesta nights,** which include a buffet dinner and a folkloric dance show; the price, including dinner, ranges from $35 to $50, but the quality of the performance is likely to be less professional than the show performed at the convention center.

In the Costa Blanca shopping center, **El Mexicano** restaurant (☎ **998-884-4207**) hosts a tropical dinner show every night and also features live music for dancing. The entertainment alternates each night — *mariachis* entertain off and on from 7:30 to 8:30 p.m., and a folkloric show takes place from 8:30 to 10:30 p.m.

You can also get in the party mood at **Mango Tango** (Blvd. Kukulcán, km 14.2; ☎ **998-885-0303**), a lagoon-side restaurant/dinner-show establishment opposite the Ritz-Carlton Hotel. Diners can choose from two seating levels, one nearer the music and the other overlooking the whole production. The music is loud and varied but mainly features Caribbean or salsa. A 45-minute floor show starts nightly at 8:30 p.m. A variety of packages is available — starting at $40 per person — depending on whether you want dinner and the show, open bar and the show, or the show alone. For music and dancing, which starts at 9:30 p.m., you pay a $10 cover charge.

Part IV
Isla Mujeres and Cozumel

The 5th Wave   By Rich Tennant

In this part...

If you're looking for a low-key place that doesn't have the hustle and bustle of Cancún or the boomtown feel of the big towns along the Riviera Maya (covered in Part V), Isla Mujeres and Cozumel may be right for you.

Isla Mujeres, only a few miles off the Cancún mainland, is nevertheless a world apart. Quiet beaches and casual, open-air restaurants lend the island a relaxed, get-away-from-it-all feel.

Cozumel, while a bit busier than Isla Mujeres, is so laid-back, the name may as well be the Mayan translation for cozy and mellow — you definitely get a tropical-island vibe here. This town is where you come to take the plunge into scuba diving; the offshore reefs are top-notch, and the island has more dive shops than any town on the mainland. If scuba is too challenging, the snorkeling is great as well. Throw in some duty-free shopping and a little low-key nightlife, and you've got yourself a great "Cozymello" vacation.

Chapter 12

Isla Mujeres

- -

In This Chapter

▶ Hopping the ferry to Isla Mujeres

▶ Choosing a hotel

▶ Finding the best meals

▶ Having fun and chilling out while you're there

- -

*I*sla Mujeres (Island of Women) is a casual, laid-back refuge from the hyper-commercial action of Cancún, visible across a narrow channel. This island of white-sand beaches is surrounded by turquoise waters and complemented by a town filled with Caribbean-pastel-colored clapboard houses and rustic, open-air seafood restaurants. Just 5 miles long and 2½ miles wide, this fish-shaped island is known as the best value in the Caribbean, assuming that you favor an easy-going vacation pace and prefer simplicity to pretense.

Located just 8 miles northeast of Cancún, "Isla" — as the locals call it — is a quick boat ride away, making it a popular daytime excursion. However, to fully explore the small village of shops and cafes, relax at the broad, tranquil Playa Norte, or snorkel or dive El Garrafón Reef (a national underwater park), more time is needed. Overnight accommodations range from rustic to offbeat chic on this small island where relaxation rules.

Francisco Hernández de Córdoba landed here in 1517 and gave the island its name upon seeing small statues of partially clad females along the shore. These objects are now believed to have been offerings to the Mayan goddess of fertility and the moon, Ixchel. Their presence is an indication that the island was probably sacred to the Maya.

At midday, suntanned visitors hang out in open-air cafes and stroll streets lined with frantic souvenir vendors. Calling out for attention to their bargain-priced wares, the vendors provide a carnival atmosphere to the hours when tour-boat traffic is at its peak. Befitting the size of the island, most of the traffic consists of golf carts, *motos* (also called mopeds), and bicycles. Once the tour boats leave, however, Isla

Mujeres reverts back to its more typical, tranquil way of life, where taking a *siesta* in a hammock is a favored pastime.

In the last few years, Isla has seen the emergence of several smaller but decidedly upscale places to stay. Anyone wanting the proximity and ease of arrival that Cancún offers — but not the excesses for which Cancún is famous — should seriously consider these new options in Isla Mujeres, where a trip to the mainland is less than an hour if you do choose to enjoy its shopping or dining. Isla's budget-priced hotels as well as their more luxury-oriented offerings both offer excellent values — Isla tends to be one of the better bargains among Mexico's resorts. Its location, so close to the excellent air access of Cancún, make this spot a great choice for travelers wanting an authentic Mexican beach experience at a great price.

Settling into Isla Mujeres

Isla Mujeres is so small, it's easy to get your bearings and find your way around. It's so comfortably casual that a friendly soul is always around to help you out if you do happen to need a little guidance.

The island is about 5 miles long and 2½ miles wide, with the town located at its northern tip. "Downtown" is a compact 4 blocks by 6 blocks, so it's very easy to get around. The **ferry docks** (☎ 998-877-0065) are right at the center of town, within walking distance of most hotels, restaurants, and shops. The street running along the waterfront is Avenida **Rueda Medina,** commonly called the **malecón.** The **market** (Mercado Municipal) is by the post office on **Calle Guerrero,** an inland street at the north edge of town, which, like most streets in the town, is unmarked.

Arriving to Isla Mujeres by ferry

To get to Isla Mujeres, you need to first fly into Cancún's International Airport (CUN). Once inside the terminal, you enter the immigration clearance area where you're asked to show your passport and completed tourist card, called an FMT (see Chapter 5). Once you claim your baggage, you exit the terminal, where taxis or other transportation services are waiting. (See Chapter 9 for details.)

Puerto Juárez (☎ 998-877-0618 for the Isla Mujeres office), just north of Cancún, is the dock where you catch a passenger ferry to Isla Mujeres. This choice is the least expensive way to travel to Isla. The air-conditioned *Caribbean Express* makes the trip in 20 minutes, has storage space for luggage, and costs about $4, running every hour on the half hour between 6:30 a.m. and 8:30 p.m. Pay at the ticket office — or, if the ferry is about to leave, you can pay onboard.

Isla Mujeres

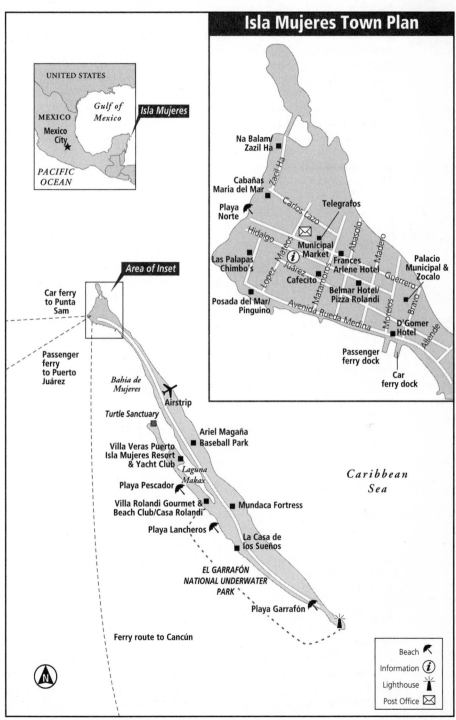

Isla Mujeres Town Plan

UNITED STATES

Gulf of Mexico

MEXICO

Mexico City

Isla Mujeres

PACIFIC OCEAN

Na Balam/ Zazil Ha

Zacil Ha

Cabañas Maria del Mar

Carlos Lazo

Telegrafos

Playa Norte

Hidalgo

Municipal Market

Abasolo

Madero

Las Palapas Chimbo's

Lopez Mateos

Juarez

Frances Arlene Hotel

Cafecito

Matamoros

Palacio Municipal & Zocalo

Guerrero

Belmar Hotel/ Pizza Rolandi

Posada del Mar/ Pinguino

Avenida Rueda Medina

Morelos

Bravo

Allende

D'Gomer Hotel

Passenger ferry dock

Car ferry dock

Area of Inset

Car ferry to Punta Sam

Passenger ferry to Puerto Juárez

Bahia de Mujeres

Airstrip

Turtle Sanctuary

Villa Veras Puerto Isla Mujeres Resort & Yacht Club

Ariel Magaña Baseball Park

Laguna Makax

Playa Pescador

Caribbean Sea

Villa Rolandi Gourmet & Beach Club/Casa Rolandi

Mundaca Fortress

Playa Lancheros

La Casa de los Sueños

EL GARRAFÓN NATIONAL UNDERWATER PARK

Playa Garrafón

Ferry route to Cancún

N

Beach

Information (i)

Lighthouse

Post Office

When you arrive by taxi or bus to Puerto Juárez, be wary of "guides" who offer advice and tell you either that the ferry is cancelled or that it's several hours until the next ferry. They offer the services of a private *lancha* (small boat) for about $40 — but it's nothing but a scam. Small boats are available and, on a co-op basis, are priced much cheaper — $15 to $25 for a one-way fare, based on the number of passengers. They take about 50 minutes for the trip over and are not recommended on days with rough seas. Check with the ticket office for information — this (clearly visible) office is the only accurate source.

Taxi fares for the trip from Puerto Juarez back to Cancún are now posted by the street where the taxis park, so be sure to check the rate before agreeing to a ride. Rates generally run $12 to $15, depending upon your final destination. Moped and bicycle rentals are also readily available as you depart the ferryboat. This small complex also has public bathrooms, luggage storage, a snack bar, and souvenir shops.

Isla Mujeres is so small that a vehicle isn't necessary, but if you're taking one, you have to use the **Punta Sam** port, just beyond Puerto Juárez. The ferry runs the 40-minute trip five or six times daily between 8 a.m. and 8 p.m., year-round except in bad weather. Times are generally as follows: Cancún to Isla at 8 a.m., 11 a.m., 2:45 p.m., 5:30 p.m., and 8:15 p.m., with returns from Isla to Cancún at 6:30 a.m., 9:30 a.m., 12:45 p.m., 4:15 p.m., and 7:15 p.m.; however, you should check with the tourist office in Cancún to verify this schedule. Cars should arrive an hour before the ferry departure to register for a place in line and pay the posted fee, which varies depending on weight and type of vehicle. You can find the only gas pump in Isla at the intersection of Avenida Rueda Medina and Abasolo Street, just northwest of the ferry docks.

Ferries also travel to Isla Mujeres from the **Playa Linda,** known as the Embarcadero pier in Cancún, but they're less frequent and more expensive than those from Puerto Juárez. A **Water Taxi** (☎ **998-886-4270** or 998-886-4847; e-mail: asterix1@prodigy.net.mx) to Isla Mujeres operates from Playa Caracol, between the Fiesta Americana Coral Beach Hotel and the Xcaret terminal on Isla Cancún, with prices about the same as those from Playa Linda and about four times the cost of the public ferries from Puerto Juárez. Scheduled departures are 9 a.m., 11 a.m., and 1 p.m., with returns from Isla Mujeres at noon and 5 p.m. Adult fares are $15; kids ages 3 to 12 are half price, and those under age 3 ride free.

Getting from the ferry dock to your hotel

Ferries arrive at the ferry dock (☎ **998-877-0065**) in the center of town. The main road that passes in front of the ferry dock is Avenida Rueda Medina. Most hotels are close by. Tricycle taxis are the least expensive and most fun way to get to your hotel; you and your luggage pile in the open carriage compartment while the driver peddles through the streets. Regular taxis are always lined up in a parking lot to the right of the pier, with their rates posted.

If someone on the ferry offers to arrange a taxi for you, politely decline, unless you'd like some help with your luggage down the short pier — it just means an extra, unnecessary tip for your helper.

Getting around

A popular form of transportation on Isla Mujeres is the electric **golf cart,** available for rent at many hotels for $12 per hour or $35 per day. El Sol Golf Cart Rental will deliver one to you (☎ **998-877-0791**), or you can stop by the office at Avenida Francisco Madero 5 if you're just visiting for the day. The golf carts don't go more than 20 miles per hour, but they're fun. And you don't come to Isla Mujeres to hurry around. They accept MasterCard and Visa, with an added 6% if you pay by credit card.

Many people enjoy touring the island by **"moto,"** the local name for motorized bikes and scooters. Fully automatic versions are available for around $25 per day or $7 per hour. They come with seats for one person, but some are large enough for two. There's only one main road with a couple of offshoots, so you won't get lost. Be aware that the rental price doesn't include insurance, and any injury to yourself or the vehicle comes out of your pocket. **Bicycles** are also available for rent at some hotels for $3 per hour or $7 per day, including a basket and a lock.

If you prefer to use a taxi, rates are about $2.50 for trips within the downtown area, or $4.50 for a trip to the southern end of Isla. You can also rent taxis for about $12 per hour.

Staying in Isla

You can find plenty of hotels in all price ranges on Isla Mujeres. Rates are at their peak during high season, which is the most expensive and most crowded time to go. Those interested in private home rentals or longer-term stays can contact **Mundaca Travel and Real Estate** in Isla Mujeres (☎ **998-877-0025;** Fax: 998-877-0076; Internet: www.mundaca travel.com).

With the exception of a few upscale places to stay along the western shore of the island, Isla's hotel offerings are clustered throughout the downtown area, or along Playa Norte. Although you'll have to walk to the beach from the downtown hotels, remember it's relatively close by, and getting around is both easy and inexpensive.

As far as prices go, I note rack rates (the maximum that a hotel or resort charges for a room) for two people spending one night in a double room. You can usually do better, especially if you're purchasing a package that includes airfare. (See Chapter 5 for tips on avoiding paying rack rates.) Prices quoted here include the 12% room tax.

A kid-friendly icon highlights hotels that are especially good for families.

I note all hotels that have air-conditioning, but this feature is not standard in Isla hotels.

Belmar Hotel
$$ Downtown

Situated in the center of Isla's small-town activity, above Pizza Rolandi (consider the restaurant noise), this hotel is run by the same people who serve up those wood-oven pizzas. (See "Dining in Isla Mujeres," later in this chapter, for a review.) Each of the simple but stylish rooms comes with two twin or double beds and tile accents. Prices are high for no views, but the rooms are very pleasant. On the other hand, this hotel is one of the few on the island with televisions (that receives U.S. channels) in the room. One large colonial-decorated suite with a whirlpool and a patio is available.

Av. Hidalgo 110 (between Madero and Abasolo, 3½ blocks from the passenger-ferry pier) ☎ *998-877-0430. Fax: 998-877-0429. E-mail:* hotel.belmar@mail. caribe.net.mx. *High season $56–$95 double. Low season $28–$45 double. AE, MC, V.*

Cabañas María del Mar
$$ Playa Norte

A good choice for simple accommodations on the beach, the Cabañas María del Mar is located on the popular Playa Norte. The older two-story section behind the reception area and beyond the garden offers nicely outfitted rooms facing the beach, all with two single or double beds, refrigerators, and balconies strung with hammocks and oceanviews. Eleven single-story *cabañas* closer to the reception and pool were all completely remodeled in late 1999, in a rustic Mexican style, with new bathroom fixtures and the addition of a minifridge. The newest addition, **El Castillo,** is across the street, built over and beside Buho's restaurant. It contains all "deluxe" rooms, but some are larger than others; the five rooms on the ground floor all have large patios. Upstairs rooms have small balconies. All have oceanviews, blue-and-white tile floors, and tile baths and are outfitted in colonial-style furniture. A small pool is in the garden.

Av. Arq. Carlos Lazo 1 (on Playa Norte, a half block from the Na Balam hotel). ☎ *800-223-5695 in the U.S., or* ☎ *998-877-0179. Fax: 998-877-0213. High season $109–$123 double. Low season $87–$111 double. MC, V. To get here from the pier,* *walk left 1 block and then turn right on Matamoros. After 4 blocks, turn left on Lazo, the last street. The hotel is at the end of the block.*

D'Gomar Hotel

$ **Downtown**

This hotel is known for comfort at reasonable prices. You can hardly beat the value for basic accommodations, which were completely remodeled inside and out just a few years ago. Rooms — each with two double beds — have new mattresses, drapes, and a paint job, and bathrooms have been retiled, with new fixtures added. A wall of windows offers great breezes and picture views. The higher prices are for air-conditioning, which is hardly needed with fantastic breezes and ceiling fans. The only drawback is that the hotel has five stories and no elevator. But it's conveniently located kitty-corner (look right) from the ferry pier, with exceptional rooftop views. The name of the hotel is the most visible sign on the "skyline."

Rueda Medina 150. ☎ *998-877-0541. High season $40 double. Low season $35 double. No credit cards.*

Francis Arlene Hotel

$ **Downtown**

The Magaña family operates this neat little two-story inn built around a small, shady courtyard. This hotel is very popular with families and seniors, and it welcomes many repeat guests. You'll notice the tidy cream-and-white façade of the building from the street. Some of the rooms have oceanviews, and each year they're all remodeled or updated. They're clean and comfortable, with tile floors, all-tile bathrooms, and a very homey feel to them. Each downstairs room has a coffeemaker, refrigerator, and stove; each upstairs room comes with a refrigerator and toaster. Some rooms have either a balcony or a patio. Telephone service is available through the front desk only. Rates are substantially better if quoted in pesos and are reflected as follows. In dollars, they're 15% to 20% higher.

Guerrero 7 (5½ blocks inland from the ferry pier, between Abasolo and Matamoros). ☎ */Fax: 998-877-0310; 998-877-0861. High season $45–$55 double. Low season $35–$40 double (higher prices are for rooms with A/C). No credit cards.*

La Casa de los Sueños

$$$$$ **Western Coast**

This "house of dreams" is easily Isla Mujeres's most intimate, sophisticated, and romantic property, and one of a few luxury B&Bs in Mexico. Though it was originally built as a private residence, luckily it became an upscale, adults-only B&B in early 1998. Its location on the southern end of the island, adjacent to El Garrafón National Park, makes it ideal for snorkeling and diving enthusiasts. The captivating design features vivid sherbet-colored walls — think watermelon, lime, and blueberry — and a sculpted architecture. You find a large, open interior courtyard; tropical gardens; a sunken living area; and an infinity pool that melts into the cool Caribbean waters. All rooms have balconies or terraces and face west, offering stunning views of the sunset over the sea, as well as the night lights of Cancún. In addition, the rooms — which have names such as "Serenity," "Passion," and "Love" — also have large, marble bathrooms, and luxury amenities. One master suite ideal for honeymooners has an exceptionally spacious bathroom area, complete with whirlpool and steam room shower, plus other deluxe amenities. Geared to a healthful, stress-free vacation, the B&B forbids smoking and encourages casual dress and no shoes. A telephone is available at the office for messages. You can request private boat transportation from Cancún to the B&B's dock.

Carretera Garrafón s/n. ☎ ***998-877-0651.*** *Fax: 998/877-0708. Internet:* www.lossuenos.com. *E-mail:* info@lossuenos.com. *High season $250–$375 double. Low season $215–$335 double. Rates include full American breakfast. MC, V. No children.*

Na Balam
$$$ **Playa Norte**

Increasingly, Na Balam is becoming known as a haven for yoga students or those interested in an introspective vacation. This popular, two-story hotel near the end of Playa Norte has comfortable rooms on a quiet, ideally located portion of the beach. Rooms are in three sections, with some facing the beach and others across the street in a garden setting with a swimming pool. All rooms have either a terrace or a balcony, with hammocks. Each spacious suite contains a king-size bed or two double beds, a seating area, and folk-art decorations. Though other rooms are newer, the older section is well kept, with a bottom-floor patio facing the peaceful, palm-filled, sandy inner yard and Playa Norte. Guests can enjoy complimentary yoga classes. (For more, see "Exploring your inner self in Isla," later in this chapter.) The restaurant, **Zazil Ha,** is one of the island's most popular (see "Dining in Isla Mujeres," later in this chapter), serving Mexican and Caribbean cuisine, with abundant vegetarian specialties. A beachside bar serves a selection of natural juices and is known as one of the most popular spots for sunset watching during the evenings.

Zazil Ha 118. ☎ ***998-877-0279.*** *Fax: 998-877-0446. Internet:* www.nabalam.com. *High season $175–$225. Low season $135–$200 suite. Ask about special weekly and monthly rates. AE, MC, V. Free unguarded parking.*

Posada del Mar
$$ **Playa Norte**

Simply furnished, quiet, and comfortable, this long-established hotel faces the water and a wide beach 3 blocks north of the ferry pier, and it has one of the few swimming pools on the island. This hotel is probably the best choice in Isla for families, and children younger than age 12 stay free of charge with paying adults. The ample-size rooms are in either a three-story building or one-story bungalow units. For the spacious quality of the rooms and the location, this hotel is among the best values on the island and is very popular, though I consistently find the staff to be the least gracious on the island. A wide, seldom-used but appealing stretch of Playa Norte is across the street, where watersports equipment is available for rent. A great, casual palapa-style bar and a lovely pool are set on the back lawn, and the restaurant **Pinguino** (see "Dining in Isla Mujeres," later in this chapter) is by the sidewalk at the front of the property. From the pier, go left for 4 blocks; the hotel is on the right.

Av. Rueda Medina 15 A. ☎ 800-544-3005 in the U.S., or 998-877-0044. Fax: 998-877-0266. Internet: www.mexhotels.com/psm.html. *High season $57–$73 double. Low season $30–$40 double. Rates include 2 children free in the same room. AE, MC, V.*

Villa Rolandi Gourmet & Beach Club
$$$$$ Western Coast

This hotel is ideal for guests who enjoy Isla's tranquility — but also like being pampered. Villa Rolandi is an exceptional value, with rooms styled in a Mediterranean decor that offer every conceivable amenity, as well as its own small, private beach in a sheltered cove. Each of the 20 oversized suites has an oceanview — across the infinity pool, with its waterfall that flows over to the cove below. Each suite also has a large terrace or balcony with a full-size private whirlpool. (Staff change the water with each guest's arrival.) Floors are made of stone, and ceilings are vaulted. TVs offer satellite music and movies, and rooms all have a sophisticated in-room sound system. A recessed seating area extends out to the balcony or terrace. Bathrooms are large and tastefully decorated in deep-hued Tikal marble. The stained-glassed shower has dual showerheads, stereo speakers, and jet options, and it even converts into a steam room.

Dining is an integral part of a stay at Villa Rolandi. Its owner is a Swiss-born restaurateur who made a name for himself with his family of Rolandi restaurants on Isla Mujeres and in Cancún (see "Dining in Isla Mujeres," later in this chapter). It also offers 24-hour room service to guests. This intimate hideaway with highly personalized service is ideal for honeymooners, who receive a complimentary bottle of domestic champagne upon arrival, when notified in advance. Only children older than age 13 are welcome.

Fracc. Lagunamar SM 7 Mza. 75 L 15 & 16. ☎ 998-877-0700. Fax: 998-877-0100. Internet: www.villarolandi.com. *High season $320 double. Low season $260 double. Rates include round-trip transportation from the dock at Playa Linda in Cancún aboard a private catamaran yacht, Cocoon; daily continental breakfast; and à la carte lunch or dinner in the onsite restaurant. AE, MC, V.*

Villa Vera Puerto Isla Mujeres Resort & Yacht Club
$$$$$ **Western Coast**

The concept here — an exclusive glide-up yachting/sailing resort — is unique not only to Isla Mujeres, but also to most of Mexico. Facing an undeveloped portion of the glass-smooth, mangrove-edged Macax Lagoon, Puerto Isla Mujeres is a collection of modern suites and villas with sloping white-stucco walls and red-tile roofs spread across spacious palm-filled grounds. Beautifully designed with Scandinavian and Mediterranean elements, guest quarters feature tile, wood-beam ceilings, natural teakwood, and marble accents. Suites have a large, comfortable living area with minibar on a lower level, with the bedroom set above, loft-style. Villas have two bedrooms upstairs with a full bathroom and a small bathroom downstairs with a shower. Each villa also features a small stylish kitchen area with a dishwasher, microwave, refrigerator, and coffee-maker. A whirlpool is on the upper patio off the master bedroom. Nightly turndown service leaves the next day's weather forecast on the pillow beside the requisite chocolate. The beach club, with refreshments, is a water-taxi ride across the lagoon on a beautiful stretch of beach, and the resort has two restaurants. A staff biologist can answer questions about birds and water life on Isla Mujeres.

Puerto de Abrigo Laguna Macax. ☎ ***998-877-0093*** *or 998-877-0330. Internet:* www. differentworld.com/mexico/hotels/puerto_isla_mujeres/pages/ entrance.htm. *High season $290–$550. Low season $203–$385. Rates include transportation from office in Playa Linda and daily continental breakfast, plus include up to 2 children younger than 12 in same room. AE, MC, V.*

Dining in Isla Mujeres

Dining in Isla — as most everything else — is a casual affair. The most common options you find are known as **cocinas económicas,** literally meaning an "economic kitchen." Usually aimed at the local population, these spots are great places to find good food at rock-bottom prices, most of which feature regional specialties. But be aware the hygiene is not what you'll find at more established restaurants, so you're dining at your own risk. The places I include here cater to a more established tourist clientele, so although they're higher priced, they also offer a much better overall dining experience.

Here, even the best restaurants are very casual when it comes to dress. Any man wearing a jacket would be looked at suspiciously, however, ladies are frequently seen in dressy resort wear — basically, everything goes, but shorts and T-shirts are typical.

The restaurants I include are arranged alphabetically, with their location and general price category noted. Remember that tips generally run about 15%, and most wait-staff really depend on these for their income, so be generous if the service warrants.

Cafecito
$$ CRÈPES/ICE CREAM/COFFEE/FRUIT DRINKS

Sabina and Luis Rivera own this cute, Caribbean-blue corner restaurant where you can begin the day with flavorful coffee and a croissant and cream cheese or end it with a hot-fudge sundae. Terrific crêpes are served with yogurt, ice cream, fresh fruit, or chocolate sauces, as well as ham and cheese. The two-page ice-cream menu satisfies most any craving, even one for waffles with ice cream and fruit. The three-course fixed-price dinner starts with soup, includes a main course such as fish or curried shrimp with rice and salad, and is followed by dessert.

Calle Matamoros 42, corner of Juárez (4 blocks from the pier). ☎ 998-877-0438. Crêpes $2.10–$4.50; breakfast $2.50–$4.50; sandwich $2.80–$3.50. No credit cards. Daily 8 a.m.–2 p.m. During high season also open Fri–Wed 5:30–10:30 or 11:30 p.m., depending on the crowd.

Casa Rolandi
$$ ITALIAN/SEAFOOD

The gourmet Casa Rolandi restaurant and bar has become the favored fine-dining experience in Isla, with a view overlooking the Caribbean and the most sophisticated menu in the area. It has a colorful main dining area, as well as a more casual, open-air terrace seating for drinks or light snacks. Food is the most notable on the island, although the overall experience falls short, especially with lights that are a bit too bright and music that is a bit too close to what you'd hear on an elevator ride. Along with seafood and northern Italian specialties, the famed wood-burning oven pizzas are a good bet. Careful — the wood-oven baked bread, which arrives looking like a puffer fish, is so divine that you're likely to fill up on it. This restaurant is a great place to enjoy the sunset, and you have a selection of more than 80 premium tequilas.

On the pier of Villa Rolandi, Lagunamar SM 7. ☎ 998-877-0700. Dinner $8–$35. AE, MC, V.

Las Palapas Chimbo's
$$ SEAFOOD

If you're looking for a beachside palapa-covered restaurant where you can wiggle your toes in the sand while relishing fresh seafood, this one is the best of them. Locals recommend it as their favorite on Playa Norte. Try the delicious fried fish (a whole one), which comes with rice, beans, and tortillas. You'll notice a bandstand and dance floor in the middle of the restaurant, and especially the sex-hunk posters all over the ceiling — that is, when you aren't gazing at the beach and the Caribbean. Chimbo's becomes a lively bar and dance club at night, drawing a crowd of drinkers and dancers. (See the section "Isla Mujeres after dark," later in this chapter.)

Norte Beach (from the pier, walk left to the end of the malecón, and then right onto the Playa Norte; it's about half a block on the right). No phone. Sandwiches and fruit $2.50–$4.50; seafood $6–$9. No credit cards. Daily 8 a.m.–midnight.

Pinguino
$$ MEXICAN/SEAFOOD

The best seats on the waterfront are on the deck of this restaurant/bar, especially in late evening, when islanders and tourists arrive to dance and party. This is the place to feast on lobster — you get a beautifully presented, large, sublimely fresh lobster tail with a choice of butter, garlic, and secret sauces. The grilled seafood platter is spectacular, and fajitas and barbecue ribs are also popular. Breakfasts include fresh fruit, yogurt, and granola, or sizable platters of eggs, served with homemade wheat bread. Both free parking and nonsmoking areas are available.

In front of the Hotel Posada del Mar (3 blocks west of the ferry pier), Av. Rueda Medina 15. ☎ 998-877-0044, 998-877-0878. Main courses $4–$7; daily special $7; all-you-can-eat buffets $5. AE, MC, V. Daily 7 a.m.–10 p.m.; bar open to midnight.

Pizza Rolandi
$$ ITALIAN/SEAFOOD

Practically an institution in Isla, you're bound to dine at least one night at Rolandi's. The plate-sized pizzas or calzones are likely to lure you with exotic ingredients — including lobster, black mushrooms, pineapple, or roquefort cheese, as well as more traditional tomatoes, olives, basil, and salami. A wood-burning oven provides the signature flavor of the pizzas, as well as baked chicken, roast beef, or mixed seafood casserole with lobster. The extensive menu also offers a selection of salads and light appetizers, along with an ample array of pasta dishes, steaks, fish, and scrumptious desserts. The setting is the open courtyard of the Belmar Hotel, with a porch overlooking the action on Hidalgo Street.

Av. Hidalgo #10 (3½ blocks inland from the pier, between Madero and Abasolo). ☎ 998-877-0430. Main courses $3.70–$12.70. AE, MC, V. Daily 11 a.m.–11:30 p.m.

Zazil Ha
$$ CARIBBEAN/INTERNATIONAL

You can enjoy some of the island's best food at this restaurant while sitting at tables on the sand among palms and gardens. The serene environment is enhanced by the food — terrific pasta with garlic, shrimp in tequila sauce, fajitas, seafood pasta, and delicious molé enchiladas. Caribbean specialties include cracked conch, coconut sailfish, jerk chicken, and stuffed squid. The vegetarian menu is complemented by a selection of fresh juices, and even a special menu is available for those participating in yoga retreats. Between the set hours for meals, you can have all sorts of enticing food, such as vegetable and fruit drinks, tacos and sandwiches, *ceviche,* and terrific nachos. It's likely you'll stake this place out for several meals before you leave.

At the Na Balam hotel (at the end of Playa Norte and almost at the end of calle Zazil Ha). ☎ ***998-877-0279.*** *Fax: 998-877-0446. Main courses $8.50–$15.75. AE, MC, V. Daily 7:30 am–10:30 a.m., 12:30–3:30 p.m., and 6:30–10 p.m.*

Fun On and Off the Beach in Isla Mujeres

Days in Isla can alternate between adventurous activity and absolute repose. Trips to the Isla Contoy bird sanctuary are popular, as is the excellent diving, fishing, and snorkeling — in 1998, the island's coral coast was made part of Mexico's new Marine National Park. In the evenings, most people find the slow, casual pace one of the island's biggest draws. The cool night breeze is a perfect accompaniment to casual open-air dining and drinking in small street-side restaurants. Most people turn in as early as 9 or 10 p.m., when most businesses close. Those in search of a party, however, can find kindred souls at the bars on Playa Norte that stay open late.

Isla's best beaches

The most popular beach in town used to be called Playa Cocoteros ("Cocos," for short). Then, in 1988, Hurricane Gilbert destroyed the coconut palms on the beach. Gradually, the name has changed to **Playa Norte,** referring to the long stretch of beach that extends around the northern tip of the island, to your left as you get off the boat. This beach is splendid — a wide stretch of fine white sand and calm, translucent, turquoise-blue water and is definitely where you want to go to rack up serious beach time. Topless sunbathing is permitted, and the row of bordering beach bars adds to the festive atmosphere. You can easily reach the beach on foot from the ferry and from all downtown hotels. You can also rent watersports equipment, beach umbrellas, and lounge chairs. The umbrellas and chairs in front of restaurants usually cost nothing if you use the restaurant as your headquarters for drinks and food. New palms are growing back all over Playa Norte, and it won't be long before it deserves to get its old name back.

Garrafón National Park is known best as a snorkeling area, but a nice stretch of beach is on either side of this park, which now offers food service, diving platforms, and a full range of affiliated services, for one admission fee (see "Deep blue explorations in Isla," the following section). **Playa Lancheros** is on the Caribbean side of Laguna Makax. Local buses go to Lancheros and then turn inland and return to downtown. The beach at Playa Lancheros is nice, but the few restaurants there are high-priced.

Wide Playa Norte is the best swimming beach, with Playa Lancheros second. No lifeguards are on duty on Isla Mujeres, and the system of water-safety flags used in Cancún and Cozumel isn't used here.

Deep blue explorations in Isla

By far the most popular place to snorkel is **Garrafón National Park,** at the southern end of the island, where you can see numerous schools of colorful fish. The well-equipped park has beach chairs, a swimming pool, kayaks, changing rooms, rental lockers, showers, a gift shop, and snack bars. Once a public national underwater park, Garrafón, since late 1999, has been operated by the same people who manage Xcaret, south of Cancún. Public facilities have been vastly improved, and two restaurant/bars have been added. Admission is $25 for adults and $13 for children. (AE, MC, and V are accepted.) You can also choose an all-inclusive option for $40, which includes food, beverages, locker rental, and snorkeling gear rental. Day-trip packages from Cancún are now also available, priced at $25 and up, including round-trip transportation (☎ **998-884-9422** in Cancún and 984-875-4070 at the park). The park is open daily 8:30 a.m. to 6 p.m.

Also good for snorkeling is the **Manchones Reef,** where a bronze cross was installed in 1994. The reef is just offshore and can be reached by boat.

Another excellent location is around the lighthouse (*el faro*) in the **Bahía de Mujeres** at the southern tip of the island, where the water is about 6 feet deep. Boatmen will take you for around $25 per person if you have your own snorkeling equipment, or $30 if you use theirs.

Several dive shops have opened on the island, most offering the same trips. **Bahía Dive Shop,** on Rueda Medina 166, across from the car-ferry dock (☎ **998-877-0340**), is a full-service shop with dive equipment for sale or rent, and resort and certification classes. The shop is open daily 9 a.m. to 7 p.m. and accepts Visa and MasterCard only. Another respected dive shop is **Coral Scuba Center** (☎ **998-877-0061** or 998-877-0763), located at Matamoros 13A and Rueda Medina. It offers discounted prices for those who bring their own gear, and it also has rental bungalows available for short-term and long-term stays.

Cuevas de los Tiburones (Caves of the Sleeping Sharks) is Isla's most renowned dive site — but the name is slightly misleading, as shark sightings are rare these days. Two sites where you could traditionally see the sleeping shark are the Cuevas de Tiburones and **La Punta,** but the sharks have obviously moved on to a more secluded site — after all, would *you* want to have dozens of gawkers watching you snooze? Sharks have no gills and so must constantly move to receive the oxygen they need. (Remember the line in *Annie Hall* equating relationships to sharks: "They must constantly move forward or die"?) The phenomenon here is that the high salinity and lack of carbon monoxide in the caves, combined with strong and steady currents, allow the sharks to receive the oxygen they need without moving. Your chance of actually seeing sleeping sharks is about 1 in 4. The best time to see them, though, is from January to March.

Other dive sites include a wreck 9km (14.4 miles) offshore; Banderas reef, between Isla Mujeres and Cancún, where there's always a strong current; Tabos reef on the eastern shore; and Manchones reef, 1km (1.6 miles) off the southeastern tip of the island, where the water is 15 to 35 feet deep. Another underwater site, "The Cross of the Bay," is close to Manchones reef. A bronze cross, weighing 1 ton and standing 39 feet high, was placed in the water between Manchones and Isla in 1994, as a memorial to those who have lost their lives at sea. The best season for diving is from June to August, when the water is calm.

To arrange a day of **fishing,** ask at the **Sociedad Cooperativa Turística** (the boatmen's cooperative) located on Avenida Rueda Medina (☎ **998-877-0118**), next to Mexico Divers and Las Brisas restaurant. You can share the cost with four to six others, and it includes lunch and drinks. Captain Tony Martínez (☎ **998-877-0274**) also arranges fishing trips aboard his *lancha, **Marinonis,*** with advanced reservations recommended. Year-round, you can find bonito, mackerel, kingfish, and amberjack. Sailfish and sharks (hammerhead, bull, nurse, lemon, and tiger) are in good supply in April and May. In winter, larger grouper and jewfish are prevalent. Four hours of fishing close to shore costs around $110; 8 hours farther out goes for $250. The cooperative is open from Monday to Saturday 8 a.m. to 1 p.m. and 5 to 8 p.m., and Sunday 7:30 to 10 a.m. and 6 to 8 p.m.

You can **swim with dolphins** at Dolphin Discovery, located at Treasure Island, on the side of Isla Mujeres that faces Cancún. Swims take place in groups of six people with two dolphins and one trainer. First, swimmers listen to an educational video and spend time in the water with the trainer and the dolphins before enjoying 15 minutes of free swimming time with them. Reservations are recommended, and you must arrive an hour before your assigned swimming time, at 9 a.m., 11 a.m., 1 p.m., or 3 p.m. Make your reservations at ☎ **998-877-0207** or in Cancún at ☎ **998-849-4748** (Fax: 998-849-4751). Additional information is available at the Web site www.dolphindiscovery.com. Cost is $119 per person, plus $15 if round-trip transportation from Cancún is required.

A worthwhile outing on the island is to a **Turtle Sanctuary,** dedicated to preserving Caribbean sea turtles and to educating the public about them. As recently as 20 years ago, fishermen converged on the island nightly from May to September waiting for these monster-size turtles to lumber ashore to deposit their Ping-Pong ball-shaped eggs. Totally vulnerable once they begin laying their eggs and exhausted when they have finished, the turtles were easily captured and slaughtered for their highly prized meat, shell, and eggs. Then a concerned fisherman, Gonzalez Cahle Maldonado, began convincing others to spare at least the eggs, which he protected. It was a start. Following his lead, the fishing secretariat founded this **Centro de Investigaciones** ten years ago; both the government and private donations help to support it. Since then, at least 28,000 turtles have been released, and every year local schoolchildren participate in the event, thus planting the notion of protecting the turtles for a new generation of islanders.

Six different species of sea turtles nest on Isla Mujeres. An adult green turtle, the most abundant species, measures 4 to 5 feet in length and can weigh as much as 450 pounds when grown. At the center, visitors walk through the indoor and outdoor turtle pool areas, where the creatures paddle around. The turtles are separated by age, from newly hatched up to 1 year. Besides protecting the turtles that nest on Isla Mujeres of their own accord, the program also captures turtles at sea, brings them to enclosed compounds to mate, and later frees them to nest on Isla Mujeres after they've been tagged. People who come here usually end up staying at least an hour, especially if they opt for the guided tour, which I recommend. The sanctuary is on a piece of land separated from the island by Bahía de Mujeres and Laguna Makax; you need a taxi to get there. Admission is $2.30; the shelter is open daily 9 a.m. to 5 p.m. For more information, call ☎ **998-877-0595.**

Sightseeing and shopping in Isla

Just beyond the lighthouse, at the southern end of the island, are the strikingly beautiful remains of a small **Maya temple,** believed to have been built to pay homage to the moon and fertility goddess, Ixchel. The location, on a lofty bluff overlooking the sea, is worth seeing and makes a great place for photos. It's believed that Maya women traveled here on annual pilgrimages to seek Ixchel's blessings of fertility. If you're at Garrafón National Park and want to walk, it's not too far. Turn right from Garrafón. When you see the lighthouse, turn toward it down the rocky path.

Exploring your inner self in Isla

Increasingly, Isla is becoming known as a great place to combine a relaxing beach vacation with various types of yoga practice and instruction. The impetus for this trend began at Na Balam hotel (☎ **998-877-0279;** Internet: www.nabalam.com), where yoga classes are offered under its large poolside palapa, complete with yoga mats and props. The classes, which take place from Monday to Friday beginning at 9 a.m., are free to guests, or $10 per class to visitors. Na Balam is also the site of frequent yoga instruction vacations, featuring respected yoga teachers, and a more extensive practice schedule.

The Fortress of Mundaca is about 2½ miles in the same direction as Garrafón, about half a mile to the left. The fortress was built by a slave trader who claimed to have been the pirate Mundaca Marecheaga. In the early 19th century, he arrived at Isla Mujeres and proceeded to set up a blissful paradise in a pretty, shady spot, while making money selling slaves to Cuba and Belize. According to island lore, he decided to settle down and build this hacienda after being captivated by the charms of an island girl. However, she reputedly spurned his affections and married another islander, leaving him heartbroken and alone on Isla Mujeres. Admission is $2, and the fortress is open daily from 10 a.m. to 6 p.m.

A visit to **Isla Contoy** should make the top of the list of things to do for those interested in natural attractions. This pristine uninhabited island, 19 miles by boat from Isla Mujeres, was set aside as a national wildlife reserve in 1981. The oddly shaped 3.8-mile-long island is covered in lush vegetation and harbors 70 species of birds, as well as a host of marine and animal life. Bird species that nest on the island include pelicans, brown boobies, frigates, egrets, terns, and cormorants. Flocks of flamingos arrive in April. June, July, and August are good months to spot turtles burying their eggs in the sand at night.

Most excursions here troll for fish (which will be your lunch), anchor en route for a snorkeling expedition, and skirt the island at a leisurely pace for close viewing of the birds without disturbing the habitat, and then pull ashore. While the captain prepares lunch, visitors can swim, sun, follow the nature trails, and visit the fine nature museum. For a while, the island was closed to visitors, but it has reopened following an agreement that fishermen and those bringing visitors will follow a set of rules for its use and safety. The trip from Isla Mujeres takes about 45 minutes one way, more if the waves are choppy. Because of the tight-knit boatmen's cooperative, prices for this excursion are the same everywhere: $40 for adults and $20 for children. You can buy a ticket at the **Sociedad Cooperativa Turística** located on Avenida Rueda Medina (next to Mexico Divers and Las Brisas restaurant), or at one of several travel agencies, such as **La Isleña,** on Morelos between Medina and Juárez (☎ **998-877-0578**). La Isleña is open daily from 7:30 a.m. to 9:30 p.m. and is a good source for tourist information. Contoy trips leave at 8:30 a.m. and return around 4 p.m. Cash is the only accepted form of payment.

Boat captains should respect the cooperative's regulations regarding ecological sensitivity, and boat safety, including the availability of life jackets for everyone on board. Snorkeling equipment is usually included in the price, but double-check that before heading out. On the island, there is a small government museum with bathroom facilities.

Let me put it simply — you'd never come to Isla for the shopping experience. **Shopping,** as everything else in Isla, is quite a casual affair, with only a few shops of any sophistication. More typically, you're bombarded by shop owners, especially on Hidalgo, selling the whole gamut of tourist kitsch including saltillo rugs, onyx, silver, Guatemalan clothing, blown glassware, masks, folk art, beach paraphernalia, and T-shirts in abundance. Prices are lower here than in Cancún or Cozumel, but with the overeager sellers, bargaining is necessary to avoid paying too much.

The one treasure you're likely to take back is a piece of fine jewelry — Isla is known for its excellent, duty-free prices on gemstones and hand-crafted work made to order. You can purchase diamonds, emeralds, sapphires, and rubies as loose stones and then have them mounted while you're off exploring the island. The superbly crafted gold, silver, and gems are available at very competitive prices in the workshops near the central plaza. The stones are also available in the rough. **Van Cleef & Arpels** (☎ **998-877-0331** or 998-877-0299) has a store here, with a broad selection of jewelry at competitive prices. Located at the corner of Morelos and Juárez streets, it's easily the largest store in Isla, open daily 9 a.m. to 9 p.m.; it accepts all major credit cards.

Isla Mujeres after dark

Those in a party mood by day's end may want to start out at the beach bar of the **Na Balam** hotel on Playa Norte, which hosts a crowd until around midnight. On Saturday and Sunday, live music plays between 4 and 7 p.m. **Las Palapas Chimbo's** restaurant on the beach becomes a jammin' dance joint with a live band from 9 p.m. until whenever. Farther along the same stretch of beach, **Buho's,** the restaurant/beach bar of the Cabañas María del Mar, has its moments as a popular, low-key hangout. **Pinguino** in the Hotel Posada del Mar offers a convivial late-night hangout, where a band plays nightly during high season from 9 p.m. to midnight. Near Matéos and Hidalgo, **KoKo Nuts** caters to a younger crowd, with alternative music for late-night dancing.

Fast Facts: Isla Mujeres

Area Code

The telephone area code is **998**. Note: It just changed in November 2001, from 9.

Baby Sitters

Baby-sitting services are less common on Isla than in Cancún, and many sitters speak only limited English. If available, rates range from $3 to $8 per hour.

Banks, ATMs, and Currency Exchange

Only one bank is in Isla, Banco Bital, and it's located directly across from the ferry docks at Av. Rueda Medina (☎ **998-877-0104** or 998-877-0005). It's open from 9 a.m. to 5 p.m. Monday through Saturday. Isla Mujeres has numerous *casas de cambios,* or money exchanges, which you can easily spot along the main streets. Most of the hotels listed here provide this service for their guests, although often at less favorable rates than the commercial enterprises.

Business Hours

Most offices maintain traditional Mexican hours of operation: from 10 a.m. to 2 p.m., and from 4 to 8 p.m. daily, while shops remain open throughout the day. Offices tend to be closed on Saturday and Sunday, while shops will be open on at least Saturday, and increasingly offer limited hours of operation on Sunday.

Emergencies

Police emergency, ☎ 060; **local police,** ☎ 998-877-0458; **Red Cross,** ☎ 998-877-0280.

Hospitals

The **Hospital de la Armada** (Naval Hospital) is on Avenida Rueda Medina at Ojon P. Blanco (☎ **998-877-0001**). It's half a mile south of the town center. It's not generally open to civilians, but they do take you in case of a life-threatening emergency. Otherwise, you're referred to the **Centro de Salud** on Avenida Guerrero, a block before the beginning of the Malecón (☎ **998-877-0117**).

Information

The **City Tourist Office** (☎/Fax: **998-877-0767** or 998-877-0307) is located on Avenida Rueda Medina, in front of the pier. It's open from Monday to Friday 8 a.m. to 8 p.m. and Saturday and Sunday 8 a.m. to 2 p.m. Also look for *Islander,* a free publication with history, local information, advertisements, and event listings (if any).

Internet Access

Compulsla, Abasolo 11, between Medina and Juárez streets (☎ **998-877-0898**), offers Internet access for $4 per hour from Monday to Friday 8 a.m. to 10 p.m., and Saturday 9 a.m. to 4 p.m.

Maps

Islander, a free publication with history, local information, advertisements, and event listings (if any) also has maps of the island included in it. The City Tourist office, located across from the ferry pier, is the best source of other maps and area information.

Pharmacy

Isla Mujeres Farmacía (☎ **998-877-0178**) has the best selection of prescription and over-the-counter medicines. It's located on Calle Benito Juárez, between Morelos and Bravo, across from Van Cleef & Arpels.

Post Office

The post office (☎ **998-877-0085**), or *correo,* is located on calle Guerrero no. 12, at the corner with López Matéos, near the market. It's open from Monday to Friday 9 a.m. to 4 p.m.

Safety

Isla Mujeres enjoys a very low crime rate. Most crime or encounters with the police are linked to pickpocket crimes, so use common sense and never leave your belongings unattended at the beach.

Taxes

A 10% IVA (value-added) tax is charged on goods and services, and it's generally included in the posted price.

Taxis

Call for a taxi at ☎ **998-877-0066.**

Telephone

You can find Ladatel phones accepting coins and prepaid phone cards at the plaza and throughout town.

Time Zone

Isla Mujeres operates on Central Standard Time, although Mexico's observance of Daylight Savings Time varies somewhat from that in the United States.

Tourist Information

The Isla Mujeres Tourist Information office is located at Av. Rueda Medina 130, across from the Ferry docks (☎ **998-877-0307** or 998-877-0767; Fax: 998-877-0307; Internet: www.isla-mujeres.net).

Tourist Seasons

Isla Mujeres's tourist season (when hotel rates are higher) is a bit different from that of other places in Mexico. High season runs December through May, a month longer than in Cancún; some hotels raise their rates in August, and some hotels raise their rates beginning in mid-November. Low season is from June to mid-November.

Chapter 13

Cozumel

• •

In This Chapter

▶ Getting around the island

▶ Searching Cozumel for the best hotels and restaurants

▶ Beach-bumming, scuba diving, and other outdoor activities

▶ Shopping for the best duty-free deals

• •

C ozumel was a well-known diving spot before Cancún even existed, and it has ranked for years among the top-five dive destinations in the world. Tall reefs lining the island's southwest coast create towering walls that offer divers a fairytale landscape to explore. For nondivers, Cozumel has the beautiful waters of the Caribbean with all the accompanying watersports and seaside activities. Because the island is also a popular cruise-ship port, you find excellent duty-free shopping here. Cozumel definitely has a get-away-from-it-all feel — roads that don't go very far, lots of mopeds, few buses and trucks, and a certain sense of separation. The island is 12 miles from the mainland, and the name comes from the Maya word *Cuzamil,* meaning "Land of the Swallows."

Getting to Cozumel

Nothing could be simpler than arriving to the island and getting around the place. The airport is small and presents no surprises. The island layout is easy to understand. And if you rent a car, it's not like you have a lot of roads to choose from.

By air

In recent years, the number of international commercial flights in and out of the island has actually decreased while the number of charter flights has increased. You may want to inquire about buying a ticket from one of the travel packagers, such as Funjet or Apple. (See Chapter 5 for more information.) Some packagers work with a lot of Cozumel's hotels — even some of the small ones in town; others allow you to buy a ticket without making it part of a package.

At present, **AeroMexico** flies to and from Atlanta, and Continental flies to and from Houston and Newark. **Aerocozumel,** a Mexicana affiliate, has numerous flights to and from Cancún. **Mexicana** flies from Mexico City (other international Flights connect through Mexico City).

Knowing what to expect when you arrive

Cozumel's airport is small enough to eliminate any chance for confusion. When you walk into the main building, the lines for immigration are right in front of you. You need proof of citizenship and a picture ID. Showing a passport is always the easiest thing. On the plane, you're given an immigration form to fill out. Most people miss the fact that they have to sign it on the back in two different places. Doing so prevents hold-ups in the line.

When you receive your **Mexican tourist permit (FMT)** put it in a safe place. You're supposed to keep this permit with you at all times — you may be required to show it if you run into any sort of trouble. You also need to turn it in upon departure, or you may be unable to leave without out a replacement.

Then you go through Customs. They ask you to push a button, which randomly triggers on either a green light or a red light. If it's green, you go right through. If it's red, they may look into your bags. Are you feeling lucky?

Getting from the airport to your hotel

Cozumel's **airport** is immediately inland from the island's only town, San Miguel. If you're picking up a rental car, the counters are along a short hallway to the left of the airport exit. Both **Avis** (☎ **987-872-0099**) and **Executive** (☎ **987-872-1308**) have staff there. Otherwise, you'll want to buy a ticket for a cab. A counter at the exit reads **"Transportes Terrestres."** This company provides transportation to all the hotels in air-conditioned Suburbans. To hotels downtown, the fare is $5 per person; to hotels along the north shore, it's $8, and to hotels along the south shore, it's $9 and up.

By sea

Cozumel is a large island across from Playa del Carmen, 12 miles off the Yucatán coast. Passenger ferries travel to and from Playa del Carmen, and a car/passenger ferry makes the longer trip to and from Puerto Morelos. See Chapter 14 for more on both Playa del Carmen and Puerto Morelos.

Taking the passenger ferry from Playa del Carmen

If you're crossing without a vehicle, take the Playa del Carmen ferry; it's cheaper and more convenient. **Water Jet Service** (☎ **987-872-1508**

Cozumel Island

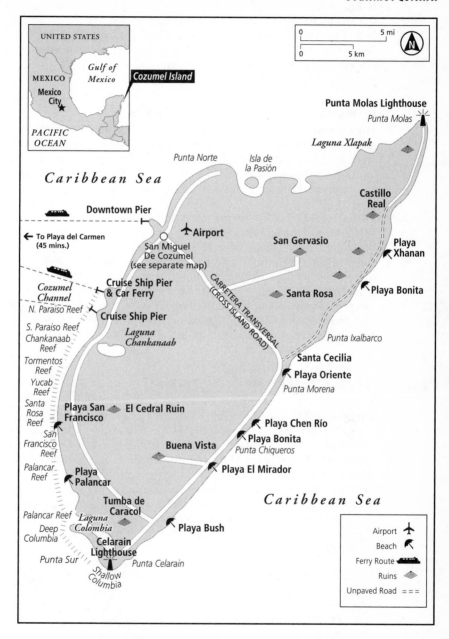

UNITED STATES

Gulf of Mexico Cozumel Island

MEXICO

Mexico City ★

PACIFIC OCEAN

0   5 mi
0   5 km

Punta Molas Lighthouse
Punta Molas

Laguna Xlapak

Punta Norte   *Isla de la Pasión*

C a r i b b e a n   S e a

Castillo Real

Downtown Pier

✈ **Airport**

San Gervasio

Playa Xhanan

← **To Playa del Carmen (45 mins.)**

San Miguel De Cozumel (see separate map)

Cozumel Channel

Cruise Ship Pier & Car Ferry

CARRETERA TRANSVERSAL (CROSS ISLAND ROAD)

Santa Rosa

Playa Bonita

N. Paraíso Reef

Cruise Ship Pier

S. Paraíso Reef

Chankanaab Reef

Laguna Chankanaab

Punta Ixalbarco

Tormentos Reef

Santa Cecilia

Playa Oriente

Yucab Reef

Punta Morena

Santa Rosa Reef

Playa San Francisco **El Cedral Ruin**

San Francisco Reef

Playa Chen Río

Playa Bonita

Buena Vista

Punta Chiqueros

Palancar Reef

Playa Palancar

Playa El Mirador

Tumba de Caracol

C a r i b b e a n   S e a

Palancar Reef *Laguna Colombia*

Deep Columbia

Playa Bush

Celarain Lighthouse

Punta Sur *Punta Celarain*

Shallow Columbia

Airport ✈
Beach ✦
Ferry Route ⛴
Ruins ▒
Unpaved Road = = =

or 987-872-1588) operates ferries between Playa and Cozumel. You'll arrive in Cozumel at the Muelle Fiscal dock, one block from the town's main square. The trip takes either 25 or 45 minutes, depending on the boat. It costs $9 one way, and the boats are enclosed and air-conditioned. In Playa del Carmen, the ferry dock is 1½ blocks from the main square and the bus station. Departures are almost hourly from 5 a.m. to midnight. Schedules are subject to change, so check the departure time at the docks, especially the time of the last returning ferry if that's the one you intend to use. Storage for luggage and such is available at the Cozumel dock for $2 per day.

Taking the car ferry from Puerto Morelos

The car ferry to Cozumel from Puerto Morelos (20 miles north of Playa del Carmen) takes longer, costs a lot, and is inconvenient. Plan accordingly. The crossing takes 2½ hours. The ferry arrives in Cozumel at the International Pier just south of town, near La Ceiba Hotel. The fare is $55 for a car, $100 for a van, and $5 per extra passenger.

Note: *To take a vehicle on the ferry, always arrive at least three hours in advance of the ferry's departure to purchase a ticket and to get in line.* The schedule is usually daily at 5:30 a.m., 10:30 a.m., and 4 p.m., but it's a good idea to call the terminal in **Puerto Morelos** (☎ **998-871-0008**) to double-check. On Sundays, the last trips are sometimes canceled. Cargo takes precedence over private cars. Officials suggest that camper drivers stay overnight in the parking lot to be first in line for tickets. The return trips to Puerto Morelos depart at 8 a.m., 1:30 p.m., and 7 p.m. daily. In Cozumel, you can call ☎ **987-872-0950** to verify the schedule.

Getting around Cozumel

The island of Cozumel is 45km (28 miles) long and 18km (11 miles) wide. A road runs along the along its western shore. Where the road passes along the waterfront of the island's only town, it's known as **Avenida Rafael Melgar.** Outside of town, it has several names: North of town it's called **Santa Pilar** or **San Juan,** south of town it's called **Costera Sur.** It eventually reaches the southern tip of the island (Punta Sur). Another road cuts across the island to the undeveloped east coast. It's called **Carretera Transversal.** When it gets to the ocean, it turns south and goes all the way to southern tip where it meets the Costera Sur road.

The town of San Miguel is on the west coast. Despite an increase in development over the last 20 years, it's still a small town. Running parallel to the coast (north-south) are other *avenidas* numbered in multiples of five — 5, 10, 15, and so on — that increase as you go inland. **Avenida Juárez** crosses these avenidas starting at the passenger-ferry dock, passing the main square, and heading inland, where it eventually becomes the Carretera Transversal. It divides San Miguel into northern

San Miguel de Cozumel

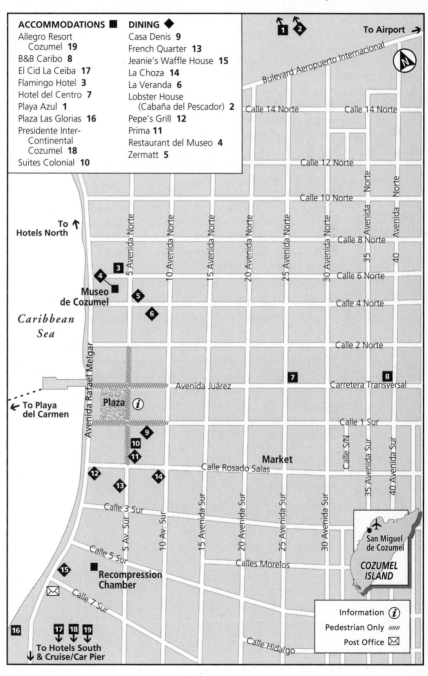

ACCOMMODATIONS ■   **DINING** ◆
Allegro Resort
    Cozumel **19**
B&B Caribo **8**
El Cid La Ceiba **17**
Flamingo Hotel **3**
Hotel del Centro **7**
Playa Azul **1**
Plaza Las Glorias **16**
Presidente Inter-
    Continental
    Cozumel **18**
Suites Colonial **10**

Casa Denis **9**
French Quarter **13**
Jeanie's Waffle House **15**
La Choza **14**
La Veranda **6**
Lobster House
    (Cabaña del Pescador) **2**
Pepe's Grill **12**
Prima **11**
Restaurant del Museo **4**
Zermatt **5**

To Airport →

Bulevard Aeropuerto Internacional

Calle 14 Norte   Calle 14 Norte

Calle 12 Norte

Calle 10 Norte

To ↑
Hotels North

5 Avenida Norte
10 Avenida Norte
15 Avenida Norte
20 Avenida Norte
25 Avenida Norte
30 Avenida Norte
35 Avenida Norte
40 Avenida Norte

Calle 8 Norte

Calle 6 Norte

Museo
de Cozumel

Calle 4 Norte

*Caribbean
Sea*

Calle 2 Norte

Avenida Rafael Melgar

Avenida Juárez   Carretera Transversal

← To Playa
del Carmen

Plaza ⓘ

Calle 1 Sur

Calle S/N
35 Avenida Sur
40 Avenida Sur

Market

Calle Rosado Salas

Calle 3 Sur

5 Av. Sur
10 Av. Sur
15 Avenida Sur
20 Avenida Sur
25 Avenida Sur
30 Avenida Sur

Calle 5 Sur

Recompression
Chamber

Calles Morelos

San Miguel
de Cozumel

**COZUMEL
ISLAND**

Calle 7 Sur

To Hotels South
& Cruise/Car Pier

Calle Hidalgo

Information ⓘ
Pedestrian Only /////
Post Office ✉

and southern halves. North of Juárez, the avenues are labeled Norte (Av. 5 Norte), and south, they're labeled Sur. The streets (*calles*) that run east and west, parallel to Avenida Juárez, are also numbered: north of Juárez, they're even numbers 2, 4, 6, and so on; south, they're odd numbers 1, 3, 5, and so on, with the one exception of Calle Rosado Salas, which runs between calles 1 and 3.

When driving around town, keep in mind that the avenidas running north-south have the right of way, and traffic doesn't slow down or stop (except when intersecting Juárez). You often won't see a stop sign.

Here is a brief rundown of your transportation choices in Cozumel:

- ✔ **Taking taxis.** Cozumel has a wealth of taxis and a strong taxi-driver union. Fares are standardized — so don't attempt to bargain. Sample fares for two people (expect an additional charge for extra passengers) include island tour, $60; from town to southern hotel zone, $5 to $18; from town to northern hotels, $3 to $5; from town to Chankanaab National Park (see "Visiting the nature parks," later in this chapter), $7; and in and around town, $2 to $4.

- ✔ **Renting cars.** Driving around the island is easy. The only paved roads are those described in the previous section, and these roads take you to just about all the worthwhile places on the island. There's no point in leaving the pavement unless you're just feeling adventurous. Rental rates vary according to demand. An economy car can go for as little as $30 in low season and for as much as $60 in high season. The local agency numbers are Avis (☎ 987-872-0219); Budget (☎ 987-872-5177); Dollar (☎ 987-872-1196); Executive (☎ 987-872-1308); Hertz (☎ 987-872-5979); and National (☎ 987-872-3263).

- ✔ **Renting mopeds.** Moped rentals are available all over town and at the big hotels. They cost anywhere from $15 to $30 for 24 hours, depending upon the season. If you decide to use this mode of transport, be careful. Riding a moped made a lot more sense when Cozumel had less traffic; now, thanks to Cozumel's numerous, pushy motorists, it's a risky proposition. Moped accidents easily rank as the highest cause of injury in Cozumel. Before renting a moped, give it a careful inspection to see that all the gizmos are in good shape — horn, light, starter, seat, mirror — and be sure to note any existing damage to the moped on the rental agreement. I've been given mopeds that had unbalanced tires and would wobble as they went, but I was able to replace them with no questions asked. Riding a moped without a helmet outside of town is illegal (subject to a $25 fine).

- ✔ **Walking around on foot.** The town of San Miguel is small enough for walking, which is helpful when pub crawling. Few places are far enough away to warrant a cab ride.

Fast Facts: Cozumel

American Express

The local representative is Fiesta Cozumel (Calle 11 No. 598; ☎ 987-872-0725).

Area Code

The telephone area code is **987.**

Banks, ATMs, and Currency Exchange

The island has several banks and *casas de cambio* (currency exchange offices), as well as ATM machines. Most places accept U.S. dollars, but you usually get a better deal paying in pesos.

Business Hours

Most offices maintain traditional Mexican hours of operation (9 a.m. to 2 p.m. and 4 to 8 p.m. daily), but shops remain open throughout the day. Offices tend to close on Saturday and Sunday, but shops are open on Saturday, at least, and increasingly offer limited hours of operation on Sunday.

Climate

From June to November, strong winds and some rain can prevail over the Yucatán. In Cozumel, wind conditions in November and December can make diving dangerous. June to September is the rainy season. Temperature during the day in the summer is 80°F to 90°F; in winter, it's 75°F to 80°F.

Diving

If you intend to dive, bring proof of your diver's certification. Underwater currents can be strong here, and many of the reef drops are quite steep, making them excellent sites for experienced divers but too challenging for novice divers.

Information

The State Tourism Office (☎/Fax: 987-872-7563) is located on the second floor of the Plaza del Sol commercial building, facing the central plaza, and is open Monday to Friday 9 a.m. to 3 p.m. and 6 to 8 p.m.

Internet Access

A number of cybercafes are on and around the main square. One of the most reliable is **Modutel** (Av. Juárez No. 15, at the intersection with Av. 10). Hours are 10 a.m. to 8 p.m. If you can't find an unoccupied machine at this place or in the vicinity, you can always go to **Coffee Net,** on the north side of the main square. It's larger and keeps longer hours than most, but it's also more expensive.

Police

Dial **060.** Remember that you're unlikely to find an English-speaking operator at the police station.

Post Office

The post office *(correo)* (Av. Rafael Melgar at Calle 7 Sur, at the southern edge of town; ☎ 987-872-0106) is open Monday to Friday 9 a.m. to 6 p.m. and Saturday 9 a.m. to noon.

Recompression Chamber

Four recompression chambers *(cámaras de recompresión)* are in Cozumel. **Buceo Médico,** staffed 24 hours, is on Calle 5 Sur, 1 block off Avenida Rafael Melgar between Melgar and Avenida 5 Sur (☎ 987-872-2387, 987-872-1430). Another one is the **Hyperbaric Center of Cozumel** (Calle 4 Norte, between avenidas 5 and 10; ☎ 987-872-3070).

Taxes

A 15% IVA (value-added tax) on goods and services is charged, and it's generally included in the posted price.

Taxis

Fares on the island are fixed with little variation and generally are not open to negotiation. Taxis charge extra for more than two passengers. Call ☎ 987-872-0236 for taxi pickup.

Telephone

Avoid the phone booths that have signs in English advising you to call home using a special 800 number — these booths are absolute rip-offs and can cost as much as U.S.$20 per minute. The least expensive way to call is by using a Telmex (LADATEL) prepaid phone card, available at most pharmacies and mini-supers, using the official Telmex (Lada) public phones. Remember, in Mexico, you need to dial 001 prior to a number to reach the United States, and you need to preface long-distance calls within Mexico by dialing 01.

Staying in Cozumel

All of Cozumel's hotels are on the western coast of the island, which faces mainland Mexico. This side is also where the island's only town, San Miguel, is located. This coast is sheltered from the open water and has little surf, which makes it perfect for swimming. The hotels and B&Bs in town tend to be the most economical properties on the island. Staying in town can be both entertaining and convenient, although the hotels in this area tend to be smaller and older. If you choose to stay here, a number of stores, dive shops, travel agencies, restaurants, and nightspots are within easy walking distance. To get to a beach, you need to take a taxi. A few small beaches are nearby for you to enjoy.

But if the most you want to do is hang out around the pool with the occasional dip into the Caribbean, you'll want one of the beach hotels either north or south of town. For the most part, the beaches on the southern coast are nicer than the ones on the northern coast, but most of the southern hotels are farther out, making it more expensive to go back and forth between your hotel and town.

All the northern hotels are lined up in close proximity on the coast side of the road next to the golf course and a short distance from town and the airport. The hotels to the south of town are closer to the popular Chankanaab National Park and tend to be more spread out. Some are on the inland side of the road, and some are on the ocean side, making for a difference in price. The properties farthest away from town are mostly all-inclusives; the beaches at the southern end of the island tend to be the best.

Finding the place that's right for you

If you're vacationing with your family and want to economize, consider all-inclusive hotels or condo/villa rentals. Both types of lodging allow you to cut costs, but they make for different vacations. If your main goal is to be bone idle and to not work on anything harder than your tan while the kids romp in the pool, then go with an all-inclusive. But if you enjoy striking out on your own and adapting to new surroundings, try a rental.

Choosing to stay at an all-inclusive — if you reserve through one of the large packagers such as Apple Vacations or Fun Jet (see Chapter 5) — means you pay one lump price for air transport, lodging, food, and drink. All you have to pay for is the taxi to and from the airport and for whatever tours and incidentals you decide to purchase.

Vacation packages to Cozumel, unlike those to other parts of the Mexican Caribbean, cannot include ground transportation because of an agreement reached between the island's taxi drivers union and the local authorities requiring all transportation between the airport and the hotels to be in union taxis.

A few things to remember about all-inclusive hotels:

- ✔ They operate on narrow profit margins and large volume, so they're usually close to full-capacity. This fact can make it hard to avoid crowds for a little peace and quiet.
- ✔ On the other hand, they have plenty of activities for both adults and kids to do.
- ✔ They make for an easy vacation in which most things, such as entertainment and food, require a minimum of effort on your part.
- ✔ You tend to be isolated and not get much of a feel for the island or the people.

Renting a condo or an apartment can save you money by avoiding eating out. This way, you also get more privacy. But you'll most likely want to rent a car for trips to the grocery store and for other errands, which you need to remember when budgeting. For most first-time visitors to the island, you're probably better off staying at a hotel so that you don't have to get your bearings immediately and you can enjoy getting acquainted with the island at a more relaxing pace.

Checking out Cozumel's best hotels

The prices I quote here are for rack rates (the full rate without discounts) for two people spending one night in a double room. You can usually do better, especially if you're purchasing a package that includes airfare. (See Chapter 6 for tips on avoiding paying rack rates.) Prices quoted here include the 12% room tax. All hotels have air-conditioning unless otherwise indicated.

Because Cozumel is such a big destination for divers, all the large hotels and many small ones offer dive packages. I don't mention this fact in the reviews, but you should ask about them if you plan to do a lot of diving. All the large waterfront hotels have dive shops on the premises and a pier, so I don't mention these amenities in my reviews.

But if you prefer staying at a particular hotel while using a different dive operator, no one is going to say anything. Any dive boat can pull up to any hotel pier to pick up customers. Most dive shops don't pick up from the hotels north of town, so it's best to dive with the in-house operator at these hotels.

For info about renting a villa or condo, try **Cozumel Vacation Villas and Condos** (Av. 10 Sur 124, 77600 Cozumel, Q. Roo; ☎ **800-224-5551** in the U.S., or 987-872-0729; Internet: www.cvvmexico.com), which offers accommodations by the week.

Allegro Resort Cozumel

$$$$ **South of town**

This all-inclusive has many sister hotels across the way on the mainland, but this one enjoys something the others don't: the placid water of Cozumel's protected coast. It also has a nice beach and plenty of beach front. The rooms are in large two-story, Polynesian-style thatched buildings surrounding a large pool. You have a choice of two double beds or one king. Rooms are normal to large with standard bathrooms. The hotel gets a mix of families and couples and offers its guests a wide range of activities and water equipment. A quieter pool, which is a little removed from the main activities, enables you to enjoy some relative calm. This hotel is a good choice for families who want only to be on the beach. Taking a taxi to town from here can be expensive; the hotel is at the far southern end of the island. The hotel has three restaurants: The main one is international food served on a buffet, and the two others (one Mexican, one Italian) are open only for dinner. You can also take advantage of a poolside snackbar.

Carretera Costera Sur km 16.5 ☎ *800-858-2258 in the U.S. and Canada, or 987-872-9770. Fax: 987-872-9729. Internet: www.allegroresorts.com. 300 units. Rack rates: High season $262–$300 double; low season $248–$262 double. Rates include all food, beverages, and nonmotorized watersports equipment. AE, MC, V.*

B&B Caribo

$ **In town**

The American owners of this B&B go out of their way to make you feel right at home. The rates are a good deal; they include air-conditioning, breakfast, and several little extras. Six neatly decorated rooms come with cool tile floors, painted furniture, and big bottles of purified drinking water; these units share a guest kitchen. The six apartments (minimum one-week stay) have small kitchens. Most rooms have a double bed and a twin bed. The inn also has a number of common rooms and a rooftop terrace. Breakfasts are full, and the cooking is good. You can also take advantage of a television and computer room with e-mail service. To find the Caribo from the plaza, walk 6½ blocks inland on Juárez to the smartly painted blue-and-white house on the left.

Av. Juárez No. 799. ☎ *987-872-3195. Internet:* www.visit-caribo.com. *12 units. Rack rates: High season $50 double; $60 apartment; low season $40 double; $50 apartment. Rates include full breakfast. AE, MC, V.*

El Cid La Ceiba

$$$–$$$$ South of town

Located on the beach side of the road, La Ceiba is great for snorkeling and shore diving — a submerged airplane is just offshore. It's a popular hotel with divers as it offers unlimited tanks for shore diving and was voted one of the world's top 15 dive resorts in *Rodale's Scuba Diving* magazine. All rooms have oceanviews, balconies, and two doubles or one king bed. Bathrooms are roomy and well lit, with granite countertops and strong water pressure. Superior rooms are larger than standard and have more furniture. Some suites are available for limited periods and only to guests who make direct reservations, not to groups. The emphasis here is on watersports, particularly scuba diving, and if it's your passion, be sure to ask about the special dive packages when you call for reservations. (Ask for the Frommer's discount.) Diving is available right from the hotel beach. For those post-dive evenings, choose between two restaurants, as well as a bar. Other diversions include a lighted tennis court, a small exercise room with sauna, a whirlpool, and watersports-equipment rentals.

Costera Sur, km 4.5. ☎ *800-435-3240 in the U.S., or 987-872-0844. Fax: 987-872-0065. Internet:* www.elcid.com. *98 units. Free parking. Rack rates: High season $152–$187 double; low season $105–$126 double. AE, MC, V.*

Flamingo Hotel

$ In town

A small hotel just off Avenida Rafael Melgar, the Flamingo offers three stories of attractive, comfortable rooms around a small, plant-filled inner courtyard. Highlights include an inviting rooftop terrace and a comfortable bar/coffee bar that serves breakfast. Second- and third-story rooms, which have air-conditioning and TV, cost more. Rooms are large, with two double beds, white-tile floors, medium-size bathrooms, and ceiling fans. A penthouse suite comes with a full kitchen and sleeps up to six. The English-speaking staff is helpful and friendly. To find it, walk three blocks north on Melgar from the plaza and turn right on Calle 6; the hotel is on the left.

Calle 6 Norte No. 81. ☎ *800-806-1601 in the U.S., or* ☎*/Fax: 987-872-1264. Internet:* www.hotelflamingo.com. *22 units. Rack rates: High season $55–$77 double; low season $36–$45 double. AE, MC, V.*

Hotel del Centro

$ In town

Although this surprisingly stylish hotel is five long blocks from the water-front, it's a bargain if you want a pool. The rooms are small but modern, air-conditioned, and extra-clean. They come with two double beds or one king (which costs $10 less). A small courtyard with an oval pool makes for a lovely place to relax. From the plaza, head straight down Juárez; when you get to Ave. 25, it's on your left.

Av. Juárez 501. ☎ *987-872-5471. Fax: 987-872-0299. E-mail:* hcentro@cozumel. com.mz. *14 units. Rack rates: High season $60–$70 double; low season $50–$60 double. No credit cards.*

Playa Azul

$$$$ North of town

This quiet hotel is perhaps the most relaxing of the island's beachfront properties. It has a small beach with shade palapas that is one of the best on this side of the island. Service is attentive and personal. Almost all the rooms come with balconies and views of the ocean. The rooms in the original section are all suites — large suites with very large bathrooms painted in cool white and decorated with a taste for simplicity (no tele-visions). The new wing mostly has standard rooms that are comfortable and large and decorated with light tropical colors and furniture. All rooms come with either a king bed or two double beds; suites also offer two convertible single sofas in the separate living-room area. There's also a restaurant, two bars, a small pool, and a nearby golf course that guests can access. On the beach is a watersports-equipment rental pavilion, and a game room with pool table, TV, and videos is located above the lobby. This is an especially good hotel for golfers because guests receive unlim-ited golf priviledges and don't pay greens fees.

Carretera San Juan, km 4. ☎ *987-872-0199 or 987-872-0043. Fax: 987-872-0110. Internet:* www.playa-azul.com. *50 units. Free parking. Rack rates: High season $210 double, $280 suite; low season $150 double, $180 suite. AE, MC, V.*

Plaza Las Glorias

$$$–$$$$ South of town

This all-suite, five-story hotel combines the top-notch amenities of the expensive hotels farther out with the convenience of being five blocks from town. For people who must have a beach, this hotel is the wrong choice. Don't dismiss it out of hand, though; a smart terraced sunning area sits just above the water — and when you're ready for a swim, just climb down the ladder for easy access to the sea. The split-level rooms are large and have separate sitting areas. The furniture and beds are com-fortable, and the bathrooms are large, with stone countertops and tub/shower combinations. Bed choices include two doubles, two twins, or one king. All rooms face the water and have a balcony or a terrace. The dive shop is very professional.

Av. Rafael Melgar, km 1.5. ☎ *800-342-AMIGO in the U.S. and Canada, or 987-872-2000. Fax: 987-872-1937. Internet:* www.sidek.com.mx. *174 units. Free parking. Rack rates: High season $280 double; low season $150 double. AE, MC, V.*

Presidente Inter-Continental Cozumel

$$$$$ South of town

This hotel is Cozumel's finest in terms of location, quality of beachfront, on-site amenities, and service. Palatial in scale and modern in style, the Presidente spreads across a long stretch of coast with only distant hotels for neighbors. Rooms come in four categories — superior, deluxe, deluxe oceanfront, and deluxe beachfront — distributed among four buildings (two to five stories tall). Superior rooms come with a view of the garden; deluxe rooms come with a view of the ocean. Most deluxe and superior rooms are spacious with large, well-lit bathrooms. Deluxe oceanfront rooms (on the second floor) and beachfront rooms (at ground level, with direct access to the beach) are even larger and have spacious balconies or patios. Most rooms come with a choice of one king bed or two double beds and are furnished with an understated, modern taste. A long stretch of sandy beach dotted with palapas and palm trees fronts the entire hotel, as does a large pool, wading pool, and a dive shop/watersports-equipment rental booth. The hotel has two restaurants and a bar, plus 24-hour room service. A special in-room dining option with a serenading trio is available for beachfront rooms. Two lighted tennis courts, a fully equipped gym, and a moped-rental service for getting around the island are also on-site. A children's activities center makes this hotel a good choice for families.

Costera Sur, km 6. ☎ *800-327-0200 in the U.S., or 987-872-0322. Fax: 987-872-1360. Internet:* www.cozumel.intercontinental.com. *253 units. Free parking. Rack rates: High season $385–$450 double; low season $336–$400 double. Discounts and packages available. AE, DC, MC, V.*

Suites Colonial

$ In town

Around the corner from the main square, on a pedestrian-only street, you'll find this pleasant four-story hotel. Standard rooms, called "studios," are large and have large bathrooms and attractive red-tile floors, but they could be better lit. They come with air-conditioning, a small fridge, and one double and one twin bed. The suites come with air-conditioning, too, and hold two double beds, a kitchenette, and a sitting and dining area. The hotel supplies free coffee and sweet bread in the morning. Note that the phone number listed also takes reservations for another hotel, Casa Mexicana (not reviewed in this book), so when you call, specify the Colonial.

Av. 5 Sur 9. ☎ *987-872-9080. Fax: 987-872-9073. Internet:* www.casamexicana cozumel.com. *28 units. Rack rates: High season $65 studio, $68 suite; low season $50–$57 studio, $58–$63 suite. Rates include continental breakfast. AE, MC, V.*

Dining in Cozumel

For such a small town on such a small island, Cozumel offers a wide variety of restaurants where you can choose from extensive menus. As in most Mexican beach resorts, even the finest restaurants are casual when it comes to dress. Men seldom wear jackets, although women are occasionally seen in dressier resort wear.

You should know that taxi drivers may attempt to take you to restaurants that pay them commissions. They may tell you the restaurant you want to go to is closed or that the quality has declined. And taxis aren't the only ones who do it. I strongly suspect that cruise ship staff steer their passengers toward certain restaurants because I always see them eating at the same places.

Tips run about 15%, and most wait-staff really depend on these tips for their income, so be generous if the service warrants. Please see Appendix B for more information on Mexican cuisine.

If you're in the mood for just a little bread or pastry to go with your coffee, try **Zermatt** (☎ **987-872-1384**), a terrific little bakery on Avenida 5, at Calle 4 Norte.

Casa Denis
$ **In town   YUCATECAN/MEXICAN**

This yellow wooden house, one of the few remaining houses built in the old island style, is a great homestyle Mexican restaurant. Small tables are scattered outside on the pedestrian-only street. A few tables are in back, on the shady patio. You can make a light meal from empanadas filled with potatoes, cheese, or fish. Better yet, try one of the Yucatecan specialties such as *pollo pibil, panuchos,* or *tacos de cochinita pibil.*

Calle 1 Sur 267 (just off the main plaza). ☎ *987-872-0067. Reservations not accepted. Breakfast $3–$5; main courses $7–$11. No credit cards. Open: Mon–Sat 7 a.m.–11 p.m.; Sun 5–11 p.m.*

French Quarter
$$$ **In town   LOUISIANA/SOUTHERN**

In a pleasant upstairs open-air setting, the French Quarter serves Southern and Creole classics. The jambalaya and étouffée are delicious. The menu also lists such specialties as blackened fish, and the owner goes to great lengths to get the freshest lump crabmeat, which usually appears in one form or another as a daily special. The filet mignon with red-onion marmalade is a real charmer. The restaurant has an air-conditioned dining room and a bar area downstairs. The French Quarter is on Av. 5, one and a half blocks south of the town square.

Av. 5 Sur 18.. ☎ 987-872-6321. Reservations recommended in high season. Main courses $10–$25. AE, MC, V. Open: Daily 4–11 p.m.

Jeanie's Waffle House
$ In town   BREAKFAST/DESSERTS

The specialty here is crisp, light waffles served in a variety of ways, including waffles *ranchero* with eggs and salsa, waffles Benedict with eggs and hollandaise sauce, and waffles with whipped cream and chocolate. Hash browns, homemade breads, and great coffee are other reasons to drop in for breakfast, which is served until 3 p.m.

Av. Rafael Melgar between calles 5 and 7 Sur. ☎ 987-872-4145. Reservations not accepted. Breakfast: $4–$7. No credit cards. Open: Mon–Sat 6 a.m.–9 p.m.; Sun 6 a.m. to noon.

La Choza
$$ In town   YUCATECAN/MEXICAN

Local residents consider this one of the best Mexican restaurants in town. Platters of poblano chiles stuffed with shrimp, *mole poblano,* and *pollo en relleno negro* (chicken stuffed with a preparation of scorched chilies) are among the specialties. The table sauces and guacamole are great, and the daily specials are a good bet. This open-air restaurant has well-spaced tables under a tall thatched roof. From the ferry pier, walk two blocks inland on Juárez, turn right on Av. 10, and walk another two blocks. The restaurant is on the corner.

Rosado Salas 198 (at Av. 10 Sur). ☎ 987-872-0958. Reservations not accepted. Breakfast $4; main courses $8–$14. AE, MC, V. Open: Daily 7:30 a.m.–11 p.m.

La Veranda
$$$ In town   SEAFOOD/INTERNATIONAL

This restaurant is the perfect place to go if you're getting tired of fried fish or fish with *achiote* sauce (a type of chile paste), or if you just want something different. The highly inventive menu emphasizes tropical ingredients and fuses West Indian with European cooking styles. Every dish I tried was delicious and artfully presented. The spiced mussel soup had a delicious broth scented with white wine. The Veranda mango fish included a mango sauce that was both light and satisfying. And the Palancar coconut shrimp consisted of shrimp boiled in a coconut sauce to which the chef added little bits of raw (not sweet) coconut. The indoor and outdoor dining areas are airy and quite pleasant. You can hear soft jazz and the whirring of ceiling fans in the background. The tables are well separated and attractively set.

Calle 4 Norte (between av. 5 and 10). ☎ 987-872-4132. Reservations recommended in high season. Main courses: $14–$20. MC, V. Open: Daily 4:30 to midnight.

Lobster House (Cabaña del Pescador)
$$$$ **North of town** **LOBSTER**

The thought I often have when I eat a prepared lobster dish is that the cook could have simply boiled the lobster to achieve a better effect. The owner of this restaurant seems to agree. The only item on the menu is lobster boiled with a hint of spices and served with melted butter, accompanied by sides of rice, vegetables, and bread. The weight of the lobster tail you select determines the price, with side dishes included. The glow of candles and soft lights amidst dark woodwork creates intimate spaces in the cozy dining rooms, which are bordered by gardens, fountains, and a small duck pond. The owner, Fernando, will even send you next door to his brother's excellent Mexican seafood restaurant, El Guacamayo, if you must have something other than lobster.

Carretera Santa Pilar, km 4 (across from Playa Azul Hotel). No phone. Reservations not accepted. Main courses: $15–$30, lobsters sold by weight. No credit cards. Open: Daily 6–10:30 p.m.

Pepe's Grill
$$$ **In town** **STEAKS/SEAFOOD**

The chefs at Pepe's were the first on the island (and up and down the mainland coast) to popularize grilled food. They seem fascinated with fire; what they don't grill in the kitchen, they flambé at your table. The most popular items are the prime rib, filet mignon, and lobster. For something out of the ordinary, try the shrimp Bahamas, which is shrimp flambéed with a little banana and pineapple in a curry sauce with a hint of white wine. Pepe's is a second-story restaurant with one large air-conditioned dining room under a massive beamed ceiling. The lighting is soft, and a guitar trio plays background music. Large windows look out over the town's harbor. The children's menu offers breaded shrimp and broiled chicken. For dessert, Pepe's offers a few more flaming specialties: bananas Foster, crêpes suzette, and café Maya (coffee, vanilla ice cream, and three liquors).

Av. Rafael Melgar at Calle Rosado Salas. ☎ 987-872-0213. Reservations recommended. Main courses: $18–$35; children's menu $7. AE, MC, V. Open: Daily 5–11:30 p.m.

Prima

$$ **In town** NORTHERN ITALIAN

One of the few good Italian restaurants in Mexico, everything is fresh — the pastas, vegetables, and sourdough pizzas. Owner Albert Domínguez grows most of the vegetables in his local hydroponic garden. The menu changes daily and specializes in northern Italian seafood dishes. It may include shrimp scampi, fettuccine with pesto, or lobster and crab ravioli with cream sauce. The fettuccine Alfredo is wonderful, the salads are crisp, and the steaks are USDA choice. Pizzas are cooked in a wood-burning oven. Desserts include Key lime pie and tiramisu. Dining is upstairs on the breezy terrace.

Calle Rosado Salas No. 109A (corner with Av. 5) ☎ *987-872-4242. Reservations recommended. Pizzas: $5–$10; pastas $8–$10; steaks $15–$20. AE, MC, V. Open: Daily 4–11 p.m.*

Restaurant del Museo

$ **In town** AMERICAN/MEXICAN

The most pleasant place in San Miguel to have breakfast or lunch (weather permitting) is at this rooftop cafe above the island's museum. It offers a serene view of the water, removed from the traffic noise below and sheltered from the sun above. The tables and chairs are comfortable and the food reliable. Your choices are limited to the mainstays of American and Mexican breakfast and lunch dishes such as eggs and bacon, huevos à la mexicana, sandwiches, enchiladas, and guacamole — all well prepared with a slight Mexican accent. It's three blocks north of the ferry pier.

Av. Rafael Melgar (corner of Calle 6). ☎ *987-872-0838. Breakfast $4–$5; lunch main courses $5–$9. No credit cards. Open: Daily 7 a.m.–2 p.m.*

Having Fun on the Beach and in the Water

For **diving and snorkeling,** you have plenty of dive shops to choose from, including those recommended in this section. For **island tours, ruins tours** on and off the island, **glass-bottom boat tours, fiesta nights, fishing,** and other activities, go to a travel agency such as **InterMar Cozumel Viajes,** Calle 2 Norte 101-B, between avenidas 5 and 10 (☎ **987-872-1098;** Fax: 987-872-0895; e-mail: intermar@cozumel. com.mx). It's not far from the main plaza.

One of the advantages of vacationing in Cozumel is that you can indulge in a true island experience and still be just a short hop from mainland Mexico and some of it's remarkable sites. **Playa del Carmen** on the mainland is a convenient 45-minute ferry ride away. Travel agencies on the island can set you up with a tour to see the major ruins on the mainland, such as **Tulum** or **Chichén-Itzá,** or one of the nature parks such as **Xel-Ha** and **Xcaret** (check out Chapter 14).

Cozumel also has its own ruins, but they can't compare with the major ruins sites on the mainland. Some believe that during pre-Hispanic times, each Mayan woman traveled the 12 miles by boat to the island at least once in her life to worship the goddess of fertility, Ixchel. More than 40 sites containing shrines remain around the island today, and archaeologists still uncover the small dolls that were customarily offered in the fertility ceremony.

Scoring quality beach time

Although most of Cozumel's shoreline is rocky, the island has some nice beaches. The beaches here have advantages over the mainland because the island's western shore is protected — you get the optimum combination of placid water without the seaweed that you find in the sheltered areas along the mainland. On the unprotected eastern shore, the water is rougher and not suitable for swimming; however, if you only want to catch some rays and avoid the crowds, you're likely to have some of the eastern shore's small beaches and coves all to yourself. This side of the island sees few people except on Sundays, when the locals have picnics here.

Along both the east and the west coasts are signs advertising this or that beach club. A "beach club" in Cozumel usually means a *palapa* (thatched roof) hut open to the public serving soft drinks, beer, and fried fish. Some of them also rent water gear. **Nachi Cocom** is more elaborate than the other beach clubs. It's on the western shore about 8 miles south of town. It features a swimming pool, a good restaurant, and watersports-equipment rental. Other beach clubs include **Paradise Cafe** on the southern tip of the island across from Punta Sur Nature Park and **Playa Bonita, Chen Rio,** and **Punta Morena** on the eastern side. **Playa San Francisco** and **Playa Palancar** are broad, sandy beaches that are popular on the island. They're about 14 miles south of town. One of the biggest attractions is the **Chankanaab National Park,** which has a great beach with beach chairs if you don't mind crowds. You can find a lonelier beach at the **Punta Sur Ecological Reserve.** Both places charge admission and have activities you may enjoy; for more details see the upcoming section "Visiting the nature parks."

Going deep: Scuba diving

Cozumel is the *numero uno* dive destination in the Western Hemisphere. Don't forget to bring your dive card and dive log. The dive shops on the island rent scuba gear, but they won't take you out on the boat until they see some documentation. If you have a medical condition, bring a letter signed by a doctor stating that you're cleared to dive. A two-tank, morning dive costs around $60; some shops are now offering an additional one-tank, afternoon dive for $9 for folks who took the morning dives. A lot of divers save money by buying a hotel and dive package with or without air transportation and food. These packages usually include two dives a day with the standard day off at the end.

Diving in Cozumel is drift diving, which can be a little disconcerting for novices. The current that sweeps along Cozumel's reefs, pulling nutrients into them and making them as large as they are, also dictates how you dive here. The problem is that it pulls at different speeds at different depths and in different places. When it's pulling strong, it can quickly scatter a dive group, which is why you need a dive master experienced with the local conditions who can pick the best place for diving, given the current conditions.

Fortunately, Cozumel has a lot of reefs to choose from. Here are just a few:

- **Palancar Reef:** Famous for its caves and canyons, plentiful fish, and a wide variety of sea coral

- **Santa Rosa Wall:** Monstrous reef famous for its depth, sea life, coral, and sponges

- **San Francisco Reef:** Features a shallower drop-off wall than many reefs and fascinating sea life

- **Yucab Reef:** Highlights include beautiful coral

Finding a dive shop in town is even easier than finding a jewelry store. Of Cozumel's more than 50 dive operators, two that I can recommend are the following: Bill Horn's **Aqua Safari,** on Avenida Rafael Melgar at Calle 5 (☎ **987-872-0101;** Fax: 987-872-0661; Internet: www.aquasafari. com), which is a PADI five-star instructor center. I also recommend **Dive House,** on the main plaza (☎ **987-872-1953;** Fax: 987-872-0368), which offers PADI, NAUI, and SSI instruction.

Underwater Yucatán offers two twists on diving — **cenote diving** and **snorkeling.** On the mainland, the peninsula's underground *cenotes* (say-*noh*-tehs), or sinkholes, which were sacred to the Maya, lead to a vast system of underground caverns. Here, the gently flowing water is so clear that divers appear to be floating on air through the *cenotes* and caves that look just like those on dry land, complete with stalactites and stalagmites.

The experienced cave divers of **Yucatech Expeditions** (☎/Fax: **987-872-5659;** e-mail: yucatech@cozumel.czm.com.mx) offer a trip five times a week. *Cenotes* are 30 to 45 minutes from Playa del Carmen, and a dive in each *cenote* lasts around 45 minutes. (Divers usually do two or three.) Dives are within the daylight zone, about 130 feet into the caverns and no more than 60 feet deep. Company owner Germán Yañez Mendoza inspects diving credentials carefully, and divers must meet his list of requirements before cave diving is permitted. He also offers the equivalent of a resort course in cave diving and a full cave-diving course. For information and prices, call or drop by the office at Avenida 15 No. 144, between Calle 1 Sur and Rosado Salas. Several other *cenote* dive operators on the mainland are closer to the *cenotes,* especially in Akumal and near Tulum.

Enjoying snorkeling

Anyone who can swim can snorkel. Rental of the snorkel (breathing tube), goggles, and flippers should cost only about $5 to $10 for half a day, and you can probably have a good time snorkeling in front of the hotel. But what's more fun is to take a trip to snorkel Paradise Reef and a couple of other good locations. One shop that specializes in snorkeling trips is the **Kuzamil Snorkeling Center** (☎ **987-872-4637** or 987-872-0539). It's located at the far end of town at Av. 50. bis 565 Int. 1, between 5 Sur and Hidalgo, Colonia Adolfo López Matéos. It's better to make arrangements over the phone or through a local travel agency rather than visiting the office. A full-day snorkel trip costs $65 per person; $50 for children younger than 12. It includes the boat, the guide, a buffet lunch, and snorkel equipment, and it visits four reefs. You can also take half-day trips.

Visiting the nature parks

Chankanaab National Park is the pride of many island residents. Chankanaab means "little sea," which refers to a beautiful land-locked pool connected to the sea through an underground tunnel — a sort of miniature ocean. Snorkeling in this natural aquarium is not permitted, but the park has a lovely beach for sunbathing and good snorkeling just a few yards off shore. Arrive early, to stake out a chair and palapa before the cruise-ship crowd arrives. Likewise, the snorkeling is best before noon. You can also watch a sea lion show for $5 per person; it uses rescued sea lions that had been captured illegally. Tickets are available through any travel agency in town. And don't miss the scarlet macaws, beautiful birds that were confiscated from captors and are in a reproduction-and-release program. The park has bathrooms, lockers, a gift shop, several snack huts, a restaurant, and a palapa for renting snorkeling gear.

Surrounding the lagoon is a botanical garden with shady paths and 351 species of tropical and subtropical plants from 22 countries, as well as 451 species from Cozumel. Several Maya structures have been re-created within the gardens to give visitors an idea of Maya life in a jungle setting. The park has a small natural history museum as well. Admission to the park costs $10. Hours are 8 a.m. to 5 p.m. daily. The park is south of town, just past the Fiesta Americana Hotel. Taxis are always available.

Punta Sur Ecological Reserve (admission $15) is a large area encompassing the southern tip of the island, including the large Columbia Lagoon. The only practical way of going there is to rent a car or scooter; there is no taxi stand, and, usually, few people. This area is an ecological reserve, not a park, so don't expect much infrastructure. The reserve has an information center, several observation towers, and a snack bar. In addition, guides point out things of interest about the habitat on the four boat rides per day around the Colombia Lagoon (bring bug spray). Punta Sur has some interesting snorkeling (bring your own gear) and lovely beaches kept as natural as possible. Regular hours are 9 a.m. to 5 p.m. A special program (☎ 987-872-2940 for info) allows visitors to observe turtle nests in season, and you can participate as a volunteer in the evenings during the nesting season.

Cruising the seas

Travel agencies and hotels can arrange boat trips, a popular pastime on Cozumel. Your options include evening cruises, cocktail cruises, glass-bottom boats, and more. Do inquire whether the trip will be filled with cruise-ship passengers, because trips that cater to the cruise-ship crowds can be packed. Tour operators are usually pretty open about this subject, but you may want to double-check. Departures before 10 a.m. are a good bet if you prefer smaller crowds.

One rather novel boat trip is a ride in a submarine, offered by **Atlantis Submarines** (☎ 987-872-5671). The sub can hold 48 people. It operates almost 3km (2 miles) south of town in front of the Casa del Mar hotel and costs $72 per adult; $36 for kids. Call ahead or inquire at one of the travel agents in town. This submarine ride is a far superior experience to the **Sub See Explorer** offered by **Aqua World,** which is really a glorified glass-bottom boat. To inquire into any of these cruises go to a travel agency such as **InterMar Cozumel Viajes** (Calle 2 Norte, No. 101-B, between avenidas 5 and 10; ☎ 987-872-1098; Fax: 987-872-0895; e-mail: intermar@cozumel.com.mx). The agency isn't far from the main plaza.

Catching the big one

The best months for fishing offshore Cozumel are from April to September, when the catch includes blue and white marlin, sailfish, tarpon, swordfish, *dorado,* wahoo, tuna, and red snapper. Fishing excursions costs $450 for six people for the whole day, or $80 to $85 per person for four people for a half day. One travel agency that specializes in fishing (deep-sea and fly-fishing) is **Aquarius Travel Fishing**

(Calle 3 Sur No. 2, between Avenida Rafael Melgar and Avenida 5; ☎ 987-872-1092; e-mail: gabdiaz@hotmail.com).

Swimming with dolphins

Dolphin Discovery offers visitors the experience of swimming with dolphins for $119 per person. Contact Dolphin Discovery (☎ 987-872-6605; www.dolphindiscovery.com) for information and reservations. The dolphin site is located in the **Chankanaab National Park.** You can incorporate your swim with the other activities that the park offers. See above for details.

Keeping Your Feet on Dry Land

If you want some time off from all the strenuous sunbathing and paddling around the pool, Cozumel offers a number of activities to interest you. Some local Maya ruins make for a short, pleasant outing, or you can do a day-trip to one of the major Maya sites on the mainland. Several companies offer bus tours to places like Chichén Itzá or Tulum. Or how about a round of golf? Or perhaps some shopping. The following sections offer a few ideas to keep you busy.

Hitting the links

Cozumel has a new 18-hole course designed by Jack Nicklaus. It's at the **Cozumel Country Club** (☎ 987-872-9570), just north of San Miguel. Greens fees are $144, including tax. You can reserve tee times three days in advance. A few hotels have special memberships with discounts for guests and advance tee times, especially Hotel Playa Azul and El Cid La Ceiba (both hotels reviewed earlier in this chapter).

"Jungle" tours a dubious choice

One ranch south of town contracts with the local travel agencies to offer visitors a four-hour horseback tour of the island's interior jungle during which you see some very minor ruins and are told a few things about the fauna of the island. Even in the best of times, this ride can't be called spectacular. Most of the terrain is flat, and the jungle is more scrublike than the term *jungle* indicates. The same can be said for some "jungle Jeep tours" and "jungle ATV tours." If you're interested in any of these ho-hum trips, look up the folks at the InterMar Cozumel Viajes travel agency. (See the listing under the "Cruising the seas" section, earlier in this chapter.)

Seeing the sites

Companies offer a couple of tours of the island, but to be frank, the best part of Cozumel isn't on land; it's what's in the water. If you're starting to look like a prune from all the time in the water or you simply want to try something different, travel agencies can book you on a group tour of the island for around $40. Prices vary a bit depending on whether the tour includes lunch and a stop for snorkeling and swimming at Chankanaab Park. If you're only interested in Chankanaab, go by yourself and save money. Taxi drivers charge $60 for four-hour tours of the island, which most people would consider only mildly amusing depending on the personality of the taxi driver.

Exploring Maya ruins on Cozumel

One of the most popular island excursions is to **San Gervasio** (100 B.C.–A.D. 1600). Follow the paved transversal road. You see the well-marked turn-off about halfway between town and the eastern coast. Stop at the entrance gate and pay the $1 road-use fee. Go straight ahead over the pothole-laden road to the ruins (about 3km; 2 miles farther) and pay the $5 fee to enter; still and video camera permits cost $5 each. A small tourist center at the entrance sells cold drinks and snacks.

When it comes to Cozumel's Maya remains, getting there is most of the fun — do it for the mystique and for the trip, not for the size or scale of the ruins. The buildings, though preserved, are crudely made and would not be much of an attraction if they were not the island's principal ruins. More significant than beautiful, this site was once an important ceremonial center where the Maya gathered, coming even from the mainland. The important deity was Ixchel, the goddess of weaving, women, childbirth, pilgrims, the moon, and medicine. Ixchel was the wife of Itzamná, the sun god, and as such, preeminent among all Maya gods.

Tour guides charge $10 for a tour for one to six people. A better option is to find a copy of the green booklet *San Gervasio,* sold at local checkout counters or bookstores, and tour the site on your own. Seeing it takes 30 minutes. Taxi drivers offer a tour to the ruins for about $25; the driver will wait for you outside the ruins.

Day-tripping off to the mainland

Going to the nearby seaside village of **Playa del Carmen** and the **Xcaret** nature park on your own is as easy as a quick ferry ride from Cozumel. (For more details on Playa del Carmen and Xcaret, see

Chapter 14.) Cozumel travel agencies offer an Xcaret tour that includes the ferry fee, transportation to the park, and the park admission fee of $80 for adults, $50 for children. Given what the package includes, this price is reasonable.

Travel agencies can also arrange day-trips to the fascinating ruins of **Chichén-Itzá** either by air or by bus. The ruins of **Tulum,** overlooking the Caribbean, and **Cobá,** in a dense jungle setting, are closer to Cozumel, so they cost less to visit. Trips to Cobá and Tulum begin at 8 a.m. and return around 6 p.m. For more information on these sites, check out Chapter 15.

Looking at the island's natural history

In town, fronting the water, is a small museum, **Museo de la Isla de Cozumel,** on Avenida Rafael Melgar between calles 4 and 6 Norte (☎ 987-872-1475). It's more than just a nice place to spend a rainy hour. The first floor of the museum has an excellent exhibit displaying endangered species in the area, the origin of the island, and its present-day topography and plant and animal life, including an explanation of coral formation. The second-floor galleries feature the history of the town, artifacts from the island's pre-Hispanic sites, and colonial-era relics like cannons, swords, and ship paraphernalia. The museum is open daily from 9 a.m. to 6 p.m. Admission is $3; guided tours in English are free. A rooftop restaurant serves breakfast and lunch.

Shopping in Cozumel

If you like shopping for silver jewelry, you can spend a great deal of time examining the wares of all the jewelers along Melgar who cater to cruise-ship shoppers. Numerous duty-free stores sell items such as perfumes and designer wares. If you're interested in Mexican folk art, a number of stores now display a wide variety of interesting pieces. Check out the following shops, all of which are on Avenida Melgar (with the exception of Sante Fe): **Los Cinco Soles** (☎ 987-872-2040); **Indigo** (☎ 987-872-1076); **Talavera** (no phone); and **Santa Fe** (no phone), on Rosado Salas No. 58.

Prices for serapes (ponchos), T-shirts, and other souvenirs are less expensive on the side streets off Melgar.

Enjoying Cozumel's Nightlife

Cozumel is a town frequented by divers and other active visitors who play hard all day and wind down at night. The nightlife peaks in the early evening. The cruise-ship crowd offers an exception to this rule. On Sunday evenings, the place to be is the main square, which usually hosts a free concert and lots of people strolling about and visiting with friends. The nightlife scene is generally low key: People sit in outdoor cafes and enjoy the cool night breezes until the restaurants close. **Carlos 'n Charlie's** (☎ 987-872-0191), **Hard Rock Cafe** (☎ 987-872-5271), and a couple of other clubs are grouped together along Avenida Rafael Melgar on the north side of the main plaza. These spots are among the liveliest and most predictable places in town.

Part V
Exploring the Yucatán

The 5th Wave   By Rich Tennant

SHELLING ON MEXICO'S YUCATÁN COAST

© RICHTENNANT

"Oooo! Back up Robert. There must be a half dozen Lightening Whelks here."

In this part . . .

If you want to leave the hustle and bustle of Cancún and Cozumel behind, you've come to the right place. Chapter 14 covers the stretch of coastline dubbed the Riviera Maya, named for the yin-and-yang combination of luxurious modern resorts and ancient Maya ruins found throughout the region. From funky beach towns like Playa del Carmen to ecotheme parks like Tres Ríos to the getaway-from-it-all cabañas at Tulum, the Riviera Maya is where you can take a deep breath and absorb the essence of warm-weather Mexico.

This neck of the Yucatán Peninsula is also home to some of Mexico's most spectacular ruins, where pyramids, statues, and mysterious carvings provide tantalizing clues to ancient civilizations. In Chapter 15, I introduce you to the most impressive and easily accessible of these sites.

Chapter 14

Playa del Carmen and the Riviera Maya

. . . .

In This Chapter

▶ Chilling out in funky Playa del Carmen

▶ Searching out the best snorkeling and scuba diving

▶ Beach-bumming along the coast

▶ Enjoying the area's many eco-parks

. . . .

The Riviera Maya is a stretch of the Yucatán's Caribbean coast from just south of Cancún to the town of Tulum. It's a beautiful coastline that boasts a mix of "ecoparks," small resort towns, and all-inclusive resorts. A reef system protects this coast and offers many snorkeling and diving opportunities. Where gaps appear in the reef, you find good beaches — mainly at Playa del Carmen (the major town on the coast), Xpu-ha, and Tulum. The action of the surf washes away silt and seagrass and erodes rocks, leaving a sandy bottom. Where the reef is prominent, you can expect good snorkeling just offshore with lots of fish and other sea creatures. And this increasingly popular stretch of coastline bustles with development; every month it seems another new resort has opened somewhere along the coast.

Exploring the Riviera Maya

The Riviera Maya is an easy region to navigate. A four-lane highway travels from Cancún to Playa del Carmen, and a two-lane highway gets you from Playa del Carmen to Tulum. Though bus service is plentiful, I prefer to rent a car and set my own schedule. (For more on seeing the region by rental car, see "The Riviera Maya," later in this chapter.) Here's a brief rundown of the best towns and attractions:

> ✔ **Playa del Carmen:** Playa (as locals call it) is a small town on one of the best stretches of beach on the entire coast. It's perfect for enjoying the simple (and perhaps the best) pleasures of a seaside vacation — taking in the sun and the sea air while working your

toes into soft, white sand; cooling down with a swim in clear blue water; and strolling leisurely and aimlessly down the beach while listening to the wash of waves and feeling the light touch of tropical breezes on your skin.

✔ **Puerto Morelos:** So far, this town located 30 minutes south of Cancún has remained a sleepy little village with a few small hotels and rental houses. Locals refer to it as "Muerto Morelos" (Dead Morelos) during the off season for the lack of activity. It's a short distance from the bustle of Cancún and Playa del Carmen and can be considered a convenient escape from the crowds, perfect for a relaxed vacation of lying about the beach and reading a book (with perhaps the occasional foray into a water sport or two). The coast is sandy and well protected by an offshore reef, which means good snorkeling and diving nearby, but lots of seagrass on the beach and in the water.

✔ **Tres Ríos:** A few miles before you get to Playa, you see signs for this eco-park. This natural reserve has 150 acres where you can ride horseback, paddle a canoe or kayak, bike along jungle trails, or just hang out at the beach. This eco-park is the least developed of the three on this coast.

✔ **Xcaret:** Just south of Playa del Carmen is this large eco-park that draws people, mostly families from Cancún, Cozumel, and all points along this coast. Highlights include floating through an underground river (not for everybody), nightly shows, and lots of seaside activities.

✔ **Xpu-ha:** You won't find anything to see here but a long, wide stretch of perfect sandy beach. You can elect to stay here or stay elsewhere and make a day-trip out of it.

✔ **Akumal:** This small, modern, and ecologically-oriented community is built on the shores of two beautiful bays — Akumal and Half-Moon Bay. This community has been around long enough that it feels more relaxed than other places on the coast that are booming, such as Playa and Tulum. A lot of families vacation here.

✔ **Xel-ha:** A large, well-protected lagoon is the centerpiece for this lovely eco-park. It attracts crowds of snorkelers who come to view the fish in the calm, clear waters. The park also offers dolphin swims and a small grouping of ruins.

✔ **Tulum:** The town of Tulum (82 miles from Cancún and close by the ruins of the same name) has a hotel district of about 30 palapa hotels, stretching down a beautiful beach. The town itself has a half-dozen restaurants, a bank, and three cybercafes A few years ago, Tulum was mainly a destination for backpacker types, but with some of the most beautiful beaches on this coast and many improvements in hotel amenities, it's attracting a greater variety of visitors. Construction is booming, both in the town and along the coast. But you can enjoy the beach here in relative solitude

The Riviera Maya

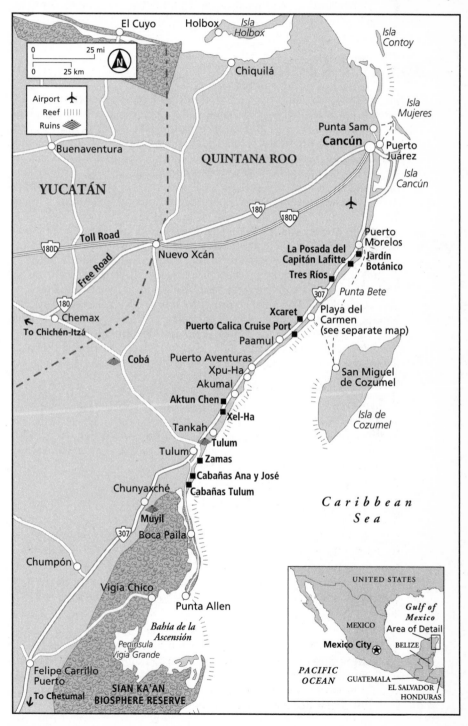

and quiet (unless your hotel is busy building additional rooms).
Of course, the flip side of peace and quiet is that Tulum doesn't
have the variety of restaurants that Playa and Cancún do.

Playa del Carmen

Playa started out attracting a lot of ex-hippie types who weren't interested in the mass tourism of Cancún. Many settled into the village building small, simple hotels and shops to supply the needs of like-minded
travelers. Over the years, it has changed, and though no longer having
the feel of a village, it still can provide that rare combination of simplicity (you can go just about anywhere on foot) and variety (with its many
one-of-a-kind hotels, restaurants, and shops). This appealing combination sets it apart from all the other destinations on this coast.

If solitude is what you're seeking, go elsewhere. Playa now draws crowds
of visitors with its lively street scene. South of town is a large development called Playacar, complete with golf course and a dozen large,
all-inclusive hotels. Farther south is a cruise-ship pier. People from
both places come to the town's beaches and shopping areas. Playa
has a casual feel. The local architecture has adopted elements of native
building — rustic clapboard walls, thatched roofs, lots of tropical foliage,
irregular shapes and angles, and a ramshackle, unplanned look. All
these features reflect its toned-down approach to tourism. In the last
few years, though, slicker architecture has appeared along with chain
restaurants and stores.

A strong European influence has made topless sunbathing (nominally
against the law in Mexico) a nonchalantly accepted practice anywhere
there's a beach. The beach grows and shrinks, from broad and sandy
to narrow with occasional rocks, depending on the currents and wind.
Even on a bad-weather day, it's a beauty.

Settling into Playa

Playa is one of those places that's easy to enjoy. Once you've reached
the end of the chain of taxis, airplanes, buses, and rental cars that it
took to bring you here, and you're finally in your hotel room, you can
simply switch to autopilot. Nothing could be simpler or more effortless
than settling into this town and enjoying what it has to offer. Here's the
skinny on how to arrive in Playa.

Getting from the Cancún airport to Playa

For getting through customs and such at the Cancún airport, see Chapter 9. If you're **driving**, follow the signs as you exit the airport. It feeds
you right on to Hwy. 307 (head south, or you're going to end up in
Cancún). The ride takes about 40 minutes.

Playa del Carmen

ACCOMMODATIONS ■
El Faro Hotel and Beach Club **6**
Hotel Desco **5**
Hotel Jungla Caribe **11**
Hotel Lunata **10**
Hotel Porto Real **2**
Iberostar Tucán **15**
Shangri-La Caribe **1**
Treetops **7**
Villa Catarina Rooms
  & Cabañas **3**

DINING ◆
El Sarape Grill **14**
La Casa del Aqua **12**
La Parilla **8**
Media Luna **4**
Tarraya Restaurant/Bar **13**
Yaxché **9**

As you approach Playa, the highway divides, and two extra lanes are added in each direction. Stay in the left lane; you're able to make a left turn at either of two traffic lights. If you don't stay left, you have to keep going until you find a turn-around.

The first traffic light is Avenida Constituyentes, which you should take for destinations in northern Playa. The second is Avenida Juárez, the artery that connects the highway to the town's main square and ferry pier.

A company called **Autobuses Riviera** offers **bus** service from the Cancún airport about 12 times a day. Cost is $7 one-way. **Taxi** fares from the Cancún airport are high — about $70 one-way. Playa has two **bus** stations. Buses coming from Cancún and places along the coast, such as Tulum, arrive at the Riviera station, at the corner of Juárez and Avenida 5, by the town square. Buses coming from destinations in the interior of the peninsula arrive at the new ADO station, on Avenida 20 between 12th and 14th streets. Last time I checked, no taxi stand was by the new bus station.

Taking the ferry from Cozumel

A much less common route to Playa is through the Cozumel airport and then transferring to the Cozumel ferry. (See Chapter 13 for schedules, prices, and other details.) The passenger-ferry dock in Playa is 1½ blocks from the main square and within walking distance of hotels. **Tricycle taxis** meet the ferry and can transport your luggage to any central hotel or to a taxi if your destination is farther away.

Getting around Playa

Locals know and use street names, but few street signs exist. The main street, **Avenida Juárez,** leads to the *zócalo* (town square) from Highway 307. As it does so, it crosses several numbered avenues that run parallel to the beach, all of which are multiples of 5. Avenida 5 is closest to the beach; it's closed to traffic from the zócalo to Calle 6 (and some blocks beyond, in the evening). On this avenue are many hotels, restaurants, and shops. Almost all the town is north and west of the zócalo. South of the ferry pier is the Playacar development, with a golf course, a small airstrip, private residences, and large resort hotels.

Fast Facts: Playa del Carmen

Area Code

The telephone area code for Playa del Carmen and Tulum is **984.**

Banks, ATMs, and Currency Exchange

Playa has several banks with automated teller machines, along with several money-exchange houses. Many of these offices are close to the pier and along Avenida 5 at Calle 8. Be aware that few ATMs are along the Riviera Maya. Your best bet is to handle any banking or money exchange in Playa — the only other ATM along the coast, in Tulum, may be out of service.

Business Hours

Most offices maintain traditional Mexican hours of operation (10 a.m. to 2 p.m. and from 4 p.m. to 8 p.m. daily), but shops remain open throughout the day. Offices tend to close on Saturday and Sunday. Shops are usually open on Saturday but still generally respect the tradition of closing on Sunday. During peak season, many shops remain open until 9 or even 10 p.m.

Internet Access

In Playa, the speediest connections are at the **Atomic Internet Café** on Calle 8 between avenidas 5 and 10, open daily 9 a.m. to 11 p.m. Playa also has a few other cybercafes. **Cyberia,** at the corner of Calle 4 and Avenida 15, wins the award for best name.

Doctor

Dr. E. Medina Peniche speaks English, and you can reach him around the clock at ☎ **987-873-0134** (answering service).

Pharmacy

The **Farmacia del Carmen** (☎ **987-873-2330**), on Avenida Juárez between avenidas 5 and 10, is open 24 hours.

Post Office

The post office is on Avenida Juárez, 3 blocks north of the plaza on the right after the Hotel Playa del Carmen and the launderette.

Taxes

A 15% IVA (value-added tax) is taxed on goods and services, and it's generally included in the posted price.

Telephone

Avoid the phone booths that have signs in English advising you to call home using a special 800 number — these booths are absolute rip-offs and can cost as much as $20 US per minute. The least expensive way to call is by using a Telmex (LADATEL) pre-paid phone card, available at most pharmacies and mini-supers, using the official Telmex (Lada) public phones. Remember, in Mexico, you need to dial 001 prior to a number to reach the United States, and you need to preface long-distance calls within Mexico by dialing 01.

Staying in Playa

For grown-ups, staying in one of the small hotels in Playa is much more fun than staying in one of the growing number of all-inclusive resorts along this coast. Don't hesitate to stay in a place that's not on the beach. Town life here is a big part of the fun, and staying on the beach in Playa has its disadvantages — the noise produced by a couple of the beach-side bars, for one thing. And if you choose accommodations off of the beach, you don't have to worry about not being able to find that perfect strip of sand. Beaches are public property in Mexico, and you can lay out your towel anywhere you like without anyone bothering you.

The following rates listed include the 12% hotel tax and assume double occupancy. High-season rates generally don't include the week between Christmas and New Year's, when rates go still higher. The last time I was in town, I didn't get a chance to review one of the new hotels that was about to open, but from what I saw, it looked attractive, hip, and bohemian. You may want to check it out: **Hotel Deseo** on Av. 5 and Calle 12 (☎ 984-879-3620, www.hoteldeseo.com). The rates run between $135 and $190, including taxes.

El Faro Hotel and Beach Club

$$$$ **Playa del Carmen**

The hotel fronts 75 meters of sandy beach in the middle of Playa del Carmen. Its grounds are graced by tall palms and manicured gardens. A small but stunning pool (heated in winter) has islands of palms inside and is bordered by cushioned lounges and a palapa bar. The rooms, most of which are in two-story buildings with white-and-cream stucco exteriors, have clay-tile floors, ceiling fans, and marble bathrooms. They hold one king, one queen, or two double beds. Most have a large balcony or terrace. Rates vary according to the dominant view — garden, sea, or beachfront — the size of the room, and the time of year. Five smaller "standard" rooms and three cabañas lack air-conditioning and are cheaper. Also on the property is a working lighthouse that serves as the honeymoon suite.

*Calle 10 Norte. ☎ **888-243-7413** from the U.S., or 984-873-0970. Fax: 984-873-0968. Internet: www.hotelelfaro.com. 29 units. Limited free guarded parking. Rack rates: High season $190–$240 deluxe with A/C, $110–$150 double without A/C; low season $150–$185 deluxe with A/C, $97–$134 double without A/C. Rates include full breakfast. AE, MC, V.*

Hotel Jungla Caribe
$$ Playa del Carmen

Located right in the heart of the Avenida 5 action, "La Jungla" is an imaginative place, with a highly stylized look that mixes neoclassical with Robinson Crusoe. Its character is perfectly in keeping with the quirkiness of the town. Owner Rolf Albrecht envisioned space and comfort for guests, so all but eight of the standard rooms are large, with gray-and-black marble floors, the occasional Roman column, and large bathrooms. Fifteen of the rooms are suites. Catwalks connect the "tower" section of suites to the hotel. An attractive pool is nestled in the courtyard beneath a giant *Ramón* tree. Eight small rooms lack air-conditioning and are priced lower than the rates listed here.

*Av. 5 Norte at Calle 8. ☎ and fax: **984-873-0650**. Internet: www.jungla-caribe.com. 25 units. Rack rates: High season $95 double, $110–$135 suite; low season 30% off high-season prices. AE, MC, V.*

Hotel Lunata
$$ Playa del Carmen

The Lunata offers a combination of location, comfort, attractiveness, and price that no other hotel in this category can beat. It's built in hacienda style, with cut stone and wrought iron, and decorated in contemporary Mexican colors. The rooms show a lot of polish, with good air-conditioning and nicely finished bathrooms. They also come with a TV, a small fridge, and a safe. The majority of rooms are deluxe, which are medium to large and come with a king or two doubles. A complimentary continental breakfast is served in the garden, and the third-story terrace makes a nice place to hang out. This hotel is right on Avenida 5; if you like to go to bed early, think of staying elsewhere.

*Av. 5 (between calles 6 and 8). ☎ **984-873-0884**. Fax 984-873-1240. Internet: www.lunata.com. 10 units. Free guarded parking. Rack rates: $50–$80 double, $70–$120 deluxe and jr. suite. Rates include continental breakfast. AE, MC, V.*

Hotel Porto Real
$$$ Playa del Carmen

The only all-inclusive in Playa, the Porto Real is on the beach a few blocks north of the town's social center. The location is great for its mainly adult clientele; children have less to do here than in the all-inclusives in Playacar. The majority of rooms are called junior suites. These suites come with a terrace or balcony, and most have an oceanview. They have a good amount of space and large bathrooms. Furniture and decorations are modern, tropical style. The hotel recently bought the property next door, which adds 61 standard rooms to its 200 junior suites. The standard rooms run a good bit less than the other, but the exact price depends on the packager or travel agent you work though. You can opt for the all-inclusive plan or standard plan without meals and drinks. On site are five restaurants, two pools, a couple of bars, a spa and a gym, and a tennis court. The rack rate quoted is for the room only, not the all-inclusive packager; for more accurate figures, call a travel agent.

Av. Constituyentes 1. ☎ *1-800-543-7556 U.S. and Canada or 984-871-7340. Internet:* www.realresorts.com.mx. *270 units. Rack rates: High season $275 jr suite; low season $205 jr. suite. AE, MC, V.*

Iberostar Tucán
$$$ Playacar

This all-inclusive hotel is a member of a large chain of resorts based in Spain. The Tucán is actually just one half of the resort; the other half is called Iberostar Quetzal. They're exactly the same, so don't be confused by the different names when talking to travel agents or packagers. Here, you're comparing apples to apples. Families make up the majority of the guests, and Iberostar makes sure to have plenty for children to do, including evening shows and a day-time kids club. The food is good and reliable. The hotel has three restaurants: a main buffet restaurant and two restaurants (Mexican and Italian) open only for dinner. It also has four pools: a large general pool, an activities pool, kids pool, and an adults-only pool, which will soon have a swim-up bar.

Lote Hotelero 2, Fracc. Playcar. ☎ *888-923-2722 in the U.S., or 984-877-2000. Internet:* www.iberostar.com. *350 units. Rack rates: High season $330 double; low season $230 double. Rates include all food and beverages, and watersports-equipment rental. AE, MC, V.*

Shangri-La Caribe
$$$–$$$$ Playa del Carmen

Most of the rooms in this property are in two-story, thatched bungalows spread out across a wide and beautiful beach. Accommodations have a patio (ground floor) or terrace (second floor), complete with hammock. Most come with two double beds, but a few have a king bed. Windows are screened, and a ceiling fan circulates the breeze. The 33 rooms farthest from the sea ("gardenview") have air-conditioning and are priced lower than the bungalows on the beach. Though you're on the outskirts of Playa, the feeling is one of being many miles from civilization. Book well in advance during high season. The turnoff to the hotel is on the north side of the city, by a Volkswagen dealership. Look for the Shangri-La Caribe sign. On the grounds are a couple of large pools and a poolside grill, as well as a dive shop.

Calle 38 and the beach. ☎ ***800-538-6802*** *in the U.S. or Canada, or 984-873-0611. Fax: 984-873-0500. Internet:* www.shangri-la.com.mx. *107 units. Free guarded parking. Rack rates: High season $180 gardenview, $200 oceanview double, $240 beachfront double; low season $130 gardenview $150 oceanview double, $190 beachfront double. Rates include breakfast and dinner. Book well in advance during high season. AE, MC, V.*

Treetops

$ **Playa del Carmen**

Treetops not only offers a good price, but good location, too: half a block from the beach, half a block from Avenida 5, which is just enough distance to filter out the noise. The rooms at Treetops encircle a pool, a small cenote, and patch of preserved jungle that shades the hotel and lends the proper tropical feel. Rooms are large and comfortable and have air-conditioning, fans, refrigerators, and either balconies or patios. Some of the upper rooms, especially the central suite, have the feel of a treehouse. Two other suites are large, with fully loaded kitchenettes and work well for groups of four.

Calle 8 s/n. ☎/*Fax:* ***984-873-0351.*** *Internet:* www.treetopshotel.com. *17 units. Rack rates: High season $45–$78 double; low season $35–$65 double. Rates include continental breakfast. MC, V.*

Villa Catarina Rooms and Cabañas

$ **Playa del Carmen**

Hammocks stretch out in front of each of the stylishly rustic rooms and *cabañas* at this property nestled in a grove of palms and fruit trees, just a block from the beach. Each of the clean, well-furnished rooms has one or two double beds on wooden bases with carpet or wood floors. Some rooms have a small loft for reading and relaxing; others have palapa roofs or terraces. Furnishings and Mexican folk-art decorations add a great touch that's uncommon for hotels in this price range. Bathrooms are detailed with colorful tiles, and some of the larger rooms have sitting areas. Good cross-ventilation through well-screened windows keeps the rooms relatively cool. Complimentary coffee is available every morning.

Calle Privada Norte between av. 12 and 14. ☎ ***984-873-2098.*** *Fax: 984-873-2097. 14 units. High season $65–$85 double; low season $45–$60 double. MC, V.*

Dining in Playa

Restaurants in Playa constantly open and close. None of the following restaurants accept reservations — which isn't a problem, because you never have trouble getting a table. If you want to try some *comida del pueblo* (people's food) I can recommend a taco restaurant, **El Sarape Grill,** on Avenida Juárez between avenidas 20 and 25.

La Casa del Agua

$$–$$$ **Playa del Carmen**   EUROPEAN/MEXICAN

This new arrival to Playa offers some of the best of both Old and New Worlds. What I tried was delicious — chicken in a wonderfully scented sauce of fine herbs accompanied by fettuccine, and a well-made tortilla soup listed as *sopa mexicana.* A number of cool and light dishes are appetizing for lunch or an afternoon meal; for example, an avocado stuffed with shrimp and flavored with a subtle horseradish sauce on a bed of alfalfa sprouts and julienned carrots — a good mix of tastes and textures. The dining area is upstairs under a large and airy palapa roof.

Av. 5 at Calle 2. ☎ 984-803-0232. Main courses: $9–$15. AE, MC, V. Open: Daily 2 p.m. to midnight.

La Parrilla

$$ **Playa del Carmen**   MEXICAN/GRILL

One of the most popular restaurants in town, this place has an open dining area where the aroma of grilling fajitas permeates the air. The chicken fajitas make for a larger serving. Grilled lobster is also on the menu. The cooks do a good job with Mexican standards, such as tortilla soup, enchiladas, and quesadillas. Mariachis show up around 8 p.m.; if you want to avoid them and dine in relative tranquillity, get a table on the upper terrace in back.

Av. 5 at Calle 8. ☎ 984-873-0687. Reservations not accepted. Main courses: $8–18. AE, MC, V. Open: Daily noon–1 a.m.

Media Luna

$$ **Playa del Carmen**   VEGETARIAN/SEAFOOD

The owner-chef here has come up with an outstanding, eclectic menu that favors grilled seafood, sautés, and pasta dishes with inventive combinations of ingredients. Everything I had was quite fresh and prepared beautifully, taking inspiration from various culinary traditions — Italian, Mexican, and Japanese. Keep an eye on the daily specials. The open-air restaurant also makes sandwiches and salads, black bean quesadillas, and crêpes. The decor is primitive-tropical chic.

Av. 5, between calles 12 and 14. ☎ 984-873-0526. Main courses: $8–$14; sandwich with a salad $4–$8; breakfast $4–$8. No credit cards. Open: Daily 7:30 a.m.– 11:30 p.m.

Tarraya Restaurant/Bar

$ **Playa del Carmen SEAFOOD/BREAKFAST**

"The restaurant that was born with the town," proclaims the sign outside of this establishment. This restaurant is also the one locals recommend as the best for seafood. It's right on the beach, and the water practically laps at the foundations. Because the owners are fishermen, the fish is so fresh that it's practically still wiggling. The wood hut doesn't look like much, but you can have your fish prepared in several ways here. If you haven't tried the Yucatecan specialty *tik-n-xic* fish (named for locally caught fish — like grouper or mahi-mahi — prepared in a spicy bar-b-que style sauce), this restaurant is a good place to do so. Tarraya is on the beach opposite the basketball court. It's also now open for breakfast with a set menu that includes hot cakes, French toast, and eggs any style.

Calle 2 Norte at the beach. ☎ *984-873-2040. Main courses: $4–$9; whole fish $8 per kilo; breakfast is $2.50–$5. No credit cards. Open: Daily 7 a.m.–9 p.m.*

Yaxché

$$–$$$ **Playa del Carmen MAYA/YUCATECAN**

The menu here makes use of many native foods and spices to produce a style of cooking different from what you usually get when ordering Yucatecan food. You find such things as a cream of *chaya* (a native leafy vegetable) or xcatic chile stuffed with cochinita. I also like the classic fruit salad, done Mexican style with lime juice and dried powdered chile. The menu is varied and includes a lot of seafood dishes, and the ones I had were fresh and well prepared.

Calle 8 between Av. 5 and 10. ☎ *984-873-2502. Main courses: $8–$20. AE, MC, V. Open: Daily noon to midnight.*

Having fun on and off the beach

Time spent in Playa can be as active or as relaxing as you want it to be. You can easily arrange a trip to see the ruins or spend the day at Xcaret. And, as is the case with just about anywhere on this coast, you can always line up a snorkel or scuba trip, which leaves the evening free for strolling about Playa and taking in the town's amusing street scene.

Getting quality beach time

Playa is Spanish for beach and in this town, life *is* a playa. Stroll down the beach to find you're favorite spot. I like swimming at the beach that's between the Porto Real and the Shangri-La Caribe hotels. It's broad and flat. Playa has "beach clubs" where, for a small fee, you can get a variety of amenities, including beach furniture, shade, and bar service. They're a good deal if you plan on spending the day at the beach.

Diving and snorkeling

Tank-Ha Dive Center (☎ 984-873-0302; Fax 984-873-1355; www. tankha.com) offers dive trips to sites nearby. The owner, Alberto Leonard, came to Playa by way of Madrid. He can set you up for a dive offshore, or, if you're up for it, he arranges excursions to the cenotes down the coast. Snorkeling trips cost around $30 and include soft drinks and equipment. Two-tank dive trips are $65; resort courses with SSI and PADI instructors cost $75. If you're traveling down the coast on this same trip, it's probably best to hold off on the cenote diving until then. (See the section on Akumal, later in this chapter.)

Teeing off and playing tennis

If golf is your bag, an 18-hole championship **golf course** (☎ 984-873-0624), designed by Robert Von Hagge, is adjacent to the Continental Plaza Playacar. Greens fees are $120 (includes cart), caddies cost $20, club rental costs $20, and the price includes tax. The club also has two **tennis** courts. Two **tennis** courts are also available at the club at a rate of $8 per hour.

Day-tripping to Maya ruins and nature parks

One of the most popular bus tours from Playa is a day-trip to **Chichén-Itzá**. (See Chapter 15 for information on the ruins and the surrounding area.) The trip usually includes a couple of stops, including one for lunch and perhaps a swim. You usually get to the ruins shortly after noon and return about 5 or 6 p.m. In many cases, you can reserve a tour through your hotel, if not, you can do so at any of the local travel agencies.

You can also go to Chichén-Itzá by rental car. Choosing this approach lets you enjoy a morning at the beach before driving to the ruins in the heat of the afternoon. (Be sure to rent a car with air-conditioning.) Check into a hotel and perhaps go see the evening sound-and-light show and then get up early and see the ruins in the morning. When you do it this way, you avoid most of the bus tours, which arrive in the afternoon, and you see the ruins in the coolness of the morning. Driving to Chichén is fairly easy; the ruins are 2½ hours from Playa. For more details, see Chapter 15.

Another popular bus tour combines a half day at Tulum (described in Chapter 15) with a half day at the eco-park Xel-Ha (described later in this chapter) for swimming and snorkeling. This itinerary makes for a convenient, no-hassle trip with a nice combination of activities — you work up a sweat at the ruins and then cool off in the lagoon at Xel-ha. (Don't do it the other way around.)

The other most popular trip is to **Xcaret** (see the section on Xcaret, later in this chapter). If you want to set your own schedule, take a taxi there and back rather than buy admission and transportation as a package. However, some tours include dropping you back in Playa for lunch and taking you back to the park for the afternoon and evening. You can also take tours to **Cozumel,** but these trips are disappointing. You see exactly what the cruise-ship passengers see — lots of duty-free, souvenir, and jewelry shops. You're better off going by yourself on the ferry and spending at least a couple of nights there (see Chapter 13).

For information or to sign up for a tour, you can contact any travel agency in Playa. A reputable one, with smaller tours is Turquoise Reef Tours (☎ **984-879-3456**). It's on Calle 16 between Av. 5 and the beach. One of the large bus tour outfits is Caribbean Coast Travel (☎ **984-873-1689**). It's located at Av. 10 Norte 211, B-6.

Going shopping

Playa del Carmen offers lots of **shopping** choices. Most of the stores are along its popular Avenida 5, or just off to one side or the other. On this pedestrian-only street, you can find dozens of trendy shops selling imported batik (Balinese-style) clothing, Guatemalan clothing, premium tequilas, Cuban cigars, masks, pottery, hammocks, and a few T-shirts. Throw in a couple of tattoo parlors, and you complete the mix.

Living la vida loca: Playa's nightlife

It seems like everyone in Playa is out on Avenida 5 or on the square until 10 or 11 p.m. each night. Pleasant strolls, meals and drinks at street-side cafes, and visiting shops fill the early hours of the evening. Then music starts up at a few locations on the avenue, and some larger venues spring into life. Down by the ferry dock is a **Señor Frog's** (☎ **987-873-0930**), with its patented mix of thumping dance music, gelatin shots, and frat-house antics; it's on the beach at Calle 4. **Captain Tutiz** (no phone) is also on the beach. It's designed like a pirate ship and has a large bar area, a dance floor, and live entertainment nightly. And, of course, there's the perennial favorite beachside bar in Playa at the **Blue Parrot** (☎ **987-873-0083**).

The Riviera Maya

The largest towns on this coast from north to south are Puerto Morelos, Playa del Carmen (covered in the previous section), Puerto Aventuras, Akumal, and Tulum. The ecoparks are Tres Rios, Xcaret, Xel-ha, and Aktun Chen. A single road, Highway 307, runs the length of the Riviera Maya. From Cancún to Playa del Carmen (51km; 32 miles), it's a four-lane divided highway with speed limits up to 110 kmph (68 mph). A couple of traffic lights and several reduced-speed zones around the major turnoffs also appear. From Playa to Tulum (80km; 50 miles), the road becomes a smooth two-lane highway with wide shoulders. Speed limits are the same, but with more spots that require you to reduce your speed. It takes around 1½ hours to drive from the Cancún airport to Tulum. Lots of buses travel this stretch of highway, but I prefer renting a car because many buses only stop in the larger towns, or they leave you a half mile from the beach you're trying to get to. A car gives you more flexibility. Beyond Tulum is a large natural preserve called the Sian Ka'an, and from there all the way to Belize the coast is predominantly mangrove with only a few poor-quality beaches.

It's always a good idea when traveling this coast to have plenty of cash in pesos. Aside from Playa del Carmen, you don't find a lot of banks or cash machines, and in the smaller towns and resorts and gas stations, you often can't pay with a credit card. In Puerto Morelos, I've found one cash machine in the town, which is out of service on occasion, and another on the Highway at the turnoff junction. After Playa del Carmen, the next cash machines are in Tulum. There are three of them, making your chances good that you can get cash. One more thing to note: Sometimes power failures occur on this coast, and they can last a whole day; during one of these failures, you can't get cash or gasoline.

Puerto Morelos and Environs

For the most part, development has bypassed Puerto Morelos; not even the opening of four luxury spa resorts in the general vicinity has altered the sleepy character of the town. Offshore is a prominent reef, which has been declared a national park for its protection. Because of the reef, the beaches in Puerto Morelos have a lot of seagrass. But the water is as clear and calm as anywhere along the coast and offers good snorkeling, diving, and kayaking. If you want to get away from the crowds, you'll find this a cozy spot. And if you run through your reading material too quickly, visit the large English-language used bookstore on the main square, which is open during high season. Puerto Morelos is also the terminus for the car ferry to Cozumel.

Getting there

Drive south from Cancún on Highway 307. At the km 31 marker is a traffic light for the turnoff to Puerto Morelos. It's well marked. The town is 2 km (1½ miles) from the highway. Many buses going either from the Cancún bus station or the airport to Playa del Carmen stop in Puerto Morelos. A taxi ride costs about $50.

If you're driving to Puerto Morelos to take the car ferry to Cozumel, take a right when you get to the main plaza and keep going. (See Chapter 13 for more info.) You should double-check the ferry schedule by calling ☎ **998-871-0008.** Always arrive at least three hours before the ferry's departure to purchase a ticket and get in line. Taking a rental car to Cozumel makes no sense and is a waste of time and money. Take the ferry from Playa instead and rent a car when you get to the island.

Getting around

Puerto Morelos is so small that you can get around most of the town on foot, but you need a car to visit nearby attractions and beaches. Or you can hire a local taxi, which you can usually find around the main square. For trips farther away, you can take a bus. The best way to do catch a bus is to take a taxi to the highway; it takes you to where the buses stop to pick up passengers.

Staying in and around Puerto Morelos

Lodging in Puerto Morelos tends to be simple, except for the four nearby luxury spa resorts. These resorts target a well-heeled crowd, offering spa treatments, privacy, and personal service, all in a Caribbean setting. Rack rates for the least expensive rooms run $300 to $600 a night, but in the off-season, you may score a discount. I review the least expensive of the four — **Ceiba del Mar** — in this section.

Of the other three, **Paraiso de la Bonita** (☎ 800-327-0200; Internet: www. paraisodelabonitaresort.com) has the largest and most impressive spa, which specializes in French Thalassotherapy (seawater-based spa treatments). The rooms here are lovely and look out to a great stretch of beach. **Maroma** (☎ 866-454-9351; Internet: www.orient-express. com) has an even prettier beach, beautiful gardens, and a cozier feel. The rooms are tasteful and luxurious, though not as stunning as those at Paraiso de la Bonita; however, the common areas, especially the beachside restaurant and bar, are more welcoming. **Ikal del Mar** (☎ 888-230-7330; Internet: www.ikaldelmar.com) is smaller and still more private than Maroma. Accommodations are in large individual palapas tucked away in the jungle and connected by illuminated paths. The beach is rocky and not as good for swimming as the beaches at Paraiso and Maroma, but all three resorts have impressive outdoor pools. If someone were to give me a gift certificate (please make it out to David Baird) to any of these resorts, I'd choose Maroma, for its beauty, atmosphere, and the quality of its beach.

Amar Inn
$ Puerto Morelos

This hotel offers simple rooms on the beach, in a home-style setting. The cordial hostess, Ana Luisa Aguilar, is the daughter of Luis Aguilar, a Mexican singer and movie star of the 1940s and '50s. Besides running her little B&B, she keeps busy promoting environmental and equitable-development causes. She can line up snorkeling and fishing trips, as well as jungle tours for guests. Three palapas are in back, opposite the main house, and four upstairs rooms offer views of the beach. The décor has something indelibly, unselfconsciously Mexican about it. The palapas and one of the upstairs rooms have thatched roofs. Bedding choices include one or two doubles, one king-size, or five twin beds. A full Mexican breakfast is served in the garden. Rooms come with a fan and usually a fridge.

From the plaza, turn left; it's a half-mile farther, immediately after the Hotel Ojo de Agua.

Av. Javier Rojo Gómez, at Lázaro Cárdenas. ☎ *998-871-0026. E-mail:* amar_ inn@hotmail.com. *Rack rates: High season $65 double; low season $45 double. Rates include full breakfast. No credit cards.*

Ceiba del Mar
$$$$ Puerto Morelos

This new spa resort is on the coast a bit north of town. Turn left at the plaza and keep going north. It's a mile away; watch for signs. The Ceiba del Mar consists of eight three-story buildings, each with a rooftop terrace with Jacuzzi. The carefully tended white sand beach with thatched shade umbrellas is inviting, as is a seaside pool with Jacuzzi, bar, and a native-style steambath (*temascal*). The spa is quite complete and offers a long menu of treatments. The air-conditioned rooms are large, with either two doubles or one king-size bed, and have a terrace or balcony, and CD player, TV/VCR, and minibar. The large, well-appointed bathrooms have shower/tub combinations, marble countertops, and makeup mirrors. Suites are very large, with two bedrooms, two or three full bathrooms, and separate entryways. Emphasis is on personal service; for example, each morning, you get coffee and juice delivered to your room through a closed pass-through.

Av. Niños Héroes s/n, ☎ *877-545-6221 from the U.S. or 998-873-8060. Fax 998-872-8061. Internet:* www.ceibadelmar.com. *Rack rates: High season $426 deluxe, $708 two-bedroom suite; low season $330 deluxe, $538 two-bedroom suite. Rates include continental breakfast, full breakfast, and dinner. AE, MC, V.*

Hacienda Morelos
$ Puerto Morelos

This small hotel is on the water and offers pleasant rooms and good prices. Simple rooms are spacious and comfortable, and all have ocean-views. Most come with a kitchenette and two double beds, and eight have air-conditioning. The hotel has a small pool and a restaurant (Johnny Cairo's Bar and Grill; see the section "Where to Dine," later in this chapter). When you get to the town plaza, turn right, then left, and then right.

Av. Rafael Melgar 2 L. 5 ☎ *998-871-0448. 15 units. Rack rates: High season $75 double; low season $56 double. AE, MC. V.*

Hotel Ojo de Agua
$ Puerto Morelos

This seaside hotel has modern rooms. Two three-story buildings stand on the beach at a right angle to each other. Most rooms have balconies and glass sliding doors. They're simply furnished and very clean. Most rooms have two double beds or a double and a twin; those with one double bed go for $10 less. Twenty-four rooms have air-conditioning, and 24 have phones (not the same 24). "Studio" units have small kitchenettes. There's a medium size pool and a restaurant. Service is friendly. You can set up snorkeling and scuba trips with the hotel. Turn left when you get to the town plaza and keep going; look for the sign.

Supermanzana 2, lote 16 ☎ ***998-871-0027*** *or 998-871-0507. Fax 998-871-0202. Internet:* www.ojo-de-agua.com. *36 units. Rack rates: High season $45–$55 double, $60 studio; low season $30–$40 double, $50 studio. Weekly and monthly rates available. AE, MC, V.*

La Posada del Capitán Lafitte
$$$ South of Puerto Morelos

A large sign on the left side of Hwy. 307, eight miles south of Puerto Morelos, points you in the direction of La Posada del Capitán Lafitte. This lovely seaside retreat sits on a solitary stretch of sandy beach. Here, you can enjoy being isolated while still having all the amenities of a relaxing vacation. The one- and two-story white stucco bungalows, which hold one to four rooms each, stretch along a powdery white beach. They're smallish but comfortable, with tile floors, small, tiled bathrooms, either two double beds or one king-size bed, and an oceanfront porch. Twenty-nine bungalows have air-conditioning; the rest have fans. You can get coffee as early as 6:30 a.m. in the game room. A dive shop on the premises sees a lot of business because the clientele includes many divers. The hotel offers transportation to and from the Cancún airport for $50 per person (minimum of two passengers). Your room price includes both breakfast and dinner, plus there's a poolside grill and bar. Amenities include a medium-size pool, watersports equipment, and a TV/game room.

Carretera Cancún-Tulum (Hwy. 307) Km 62. ☎ ***800-538-6802*** *in the U.S. and Canada, or 984-873-0214. Internet:* www.mexicoholiday.com. *62 units. Free guarded parking. Rack rates: High season $210 double; low season $140 double. Rates include breakfast and dinner. MC, V.*

Dining in and around Puerto Morelos

In addition to the following restaurants, you can find a few more modest eateries. Especially popular is the pizzeria on the plaza, a local hangout.

Johnny Cairo's
$$ Puerto Morelos CONTEMPORARY

I don't know what to tell you about this restaurant except that you can count on two things: that the food will be good, and that the next time you go, everything will be totally different. The owner, a one-time

Ritz-Carlton chef, seems to get bored easily and is always ready to change things. His ilk is the bane of travel writers, but I can't punish him on that score. His food has been dependably good, and he is careful to get the freshest seafood. The restaurant is especially popular on Sunday afternoon, when it serves barbecue with all the traditional meats and sides. For the monthly full-moon party, the staff moves the entire restaurant down to the beach, builds a bonfire, and cooks an entirely different menu.

Hacienda Morelos hotel, Av. Rafael E. Melgar. ☎ *998-871-0449. Reservations accepted. Main courses: $5–17. No credit cards. Open: Tues–Sat from 6–10 p.m. and Sun 1–6 p.m.*

Los Pelícanos
$$ Puerto Morelos   SEAFOOD

To the right of the plaza, this oceanview restaurant is quite a pleasant place to dine. Select a table inside under the palapa or outside on the terrace (if there's no breeze, wear mosquito repellent in the evenings). The seafood menu has many offerings, mostly prepared in true Mexican fashion, such as ceviche and the *pescado a la veracruzana* (fish cooked with tomatoes, olives, onions and peppers). For those who don't want seafood, there's grilled chicken and steak.

On the main square by the sea. ☎ *998-871-0014. Main courses: $8–16; lobster $27. MC, V. Open: Daily 10 a.m. –11 p.m.*

Enjoying the great outdoors
Besides stretching out on the beach or by the pool and reading a favorite book, the main activities are snorkeling, diving, and kayaking. You can line up these things by asking at one of the local hotels, or you can visit the local dive shop **Sub Aqua Explorers (☎ 998-871-0078; Fax 998-871-0027)**, which is on the town square. It also arranges fishing trips. More than 15 dive sites are nearby, and many are close to shore. A two-tank dive costs around $60, and night dives cost $55. Two hours of fishing costs around $80, and snorkeling excursions run around $5.

Activities on dry land includes jungle tours such as the one offered by a local resident Goyo Morgan, which includes a swim in a *cenote* (sinkhole) and a visit to a local ranch ($40 for half-day tour). Also in the area are a couple of roadside amusements. One is a zoological park specializing in crocodiles called **Croco Cun (☎ 998-884-4782)**. It's on the east side of Hwy. 307 a couple of miles north of the Puerto Morelos turnoff. It's an interactive zoo with crocodiles in all stages of development, as well as animals of nearly all the species that range, crawl, or slither around the Yucatán. A visit to the new reptile house is fascinating, though it may make you think twice about venturing into the jungle. The rattlesnakes and boa constrictors are particularly intimidating, and the tarantulas are downright enormous. The guided tour lasts 1½ hours. Children enjoy the guides' enthusiasm and are entranced by the spider monkeys and wild pigs. Wear plenty of bug repellent. The restaurant sells refreshments. Croco Cun is open daily 8:30 a.m. to 5:30 p.m. As with other attractions of this sort along the coast, entrance fees are high: $15 adult, $9 children 6 to 12, free for children under 6.

Tres Ríos

About midway between Puerto Morelos and Playa del Carmen is **Tres Ríos** (☎ **998-887-8077** in Cancún; Internet: www.tres-rios.com), an eco-adventure park similar to Xcaret and Xel-ha. It's actually a nature reserve on more than 150 acres of land. Admission is $21 for adults and $17 for children ages 5 to 11, which includes canoe trips; the use of bikes, kayaks, and snorkeling equipment; and the use of hammocks and beach chairs after you tire yourself out. Extra charges apply for scuba diving, horseback riding, and extended guided tours through the preserve and its estuary. It's definitely less commercial than the other eco-theme parks and is essentially just a great natural area for participating in these activities. An all-inclusive option includes admission, diving, horseback riding, and all food and beverages for $74 for adults or $58 for children, ages 5 to 11; reservations are required. For an additional $11 per person, it includes transportation, if arranged at least 24 hours in advance. Tres Ríos also has bathroom facilities, showers, and a convenience store; however, the facilities are much less sophisticated than the area's other, more developed eco-theme parks. The park is open daily 9 a.m. to 5 p.m.

After Tres Ríos, you come to Playa del Carmen. The town is big enough that I cover it in the first section of this chapter.

Xcaret

Ten kilometers (6½ miles) south of Playa del Carmen (and 80km/50 miles south of Cancún) is the turnoff to Xcaret (pronounced ish-car-*et*), an "eco-archaeological" theme park that many call Mexico's answer to Disneyland, with all that the label implies. Attractions are varied and numerous, kids love it, and the jungle setting and palm-lined beaches are beautiful. But this "natural" park is highly engineered, down to the Mayan temple-style ticket booths. Admission and food prices are high, and crowds can be plentiful.

Pathways meander around bathing coves, the snorkeling lagoon, and the remains of a group of real Mayan temples. You have access to swimming beaches; limestone tunnels to snorkel through; a wild-bird breeding aviary; a *charro* (Mexican cowboy) exhibition; horseback riding; scuba diving; a botanical garden and nursery; a sea turtle nursery that releases the turtles after their first year; a pavilion showcasing regional butterflies; and a tropical aquarium, where visitors can touch underwater creatures such as manta rays, starfish, and octopi. One of the park's most popular attractions is the "Dolphinarium," where visitors (on a first-come, first-served basis) can swim with the dolphins for an extra charge of $90.

Another attraction is a replica of the ancient Mayan game, Pok-ta-pok. In this game, six "warriors" bounce around a 9-pound ball with their hips. The Seawalker, a type of watersport designed for nonswimmers, is another attraction. By donning a special suit and helmet with a connected air pump, you can walk on the ocean floor or examine a coral reef in a small bay.

The visitor center has lockers, first-aid assistance, and a gift shop. Visitors aren't allowed to bring in food or drinks, so you're limited to the rather high-priced restaurants on-site. No personal radios are allowed, and you must remove all suntan lotion if you swim in the lagoon to avoid poisoning the lagoon habitat.

Xcaret is open Monday to Saturday 8:30 a.m. to 8 p.m. and Sunday 8:30 a.m. to 5:30 p.m. The admission price of $49 per person entitles you to use the facilities, boats, life jackets, snorkeling equipment for the underwater tunnel and lagoon, and lounge chairs. Other attractions cost extra, such as snorkeling ($32), horseback riding ($49), scuba diving ($55 for certified divers; $75 for a resort course), and the dolphin swim ($90). Some equipment (such as beach chairs) may be scarce, so bring a beach towel and your own snorkeling gear just in case.

Xpu-Ha

Thirty km (18½ miles) south of Xcaret is the beautiful beach of Xpu-Ha. If you want quality beach time, this is the place. Xpu-Ha is a wide bay lined by a broad, beautiful sandy beach, perhaps the best beach on the entire coast. At each end of the bay is an all-inclusive resort (**Xpu-Ha Palace** and **Robinson Club**), and in the middle is another, the **Hotel Copacabana.** But the beach is long and wide enough that it usually feels empty — except on weekends, when people from up and down the coast come for the day. To get to the beach, turn off when you see

Up close and personal with the dolphins

Traveling south from Xcaret, you pass by Puerto Aventuras 26 km (16 miles) down the road. This marina community has a few restaurants and hotels and a lot of condos. The buildings are mostly modern glass blocks, not especially attractive, but you can go swimming with dolphins here. Make reservations with **Dolphin Discovery** (☎ **984-883-0779;** Internet: www.dolphindiscovery.com) and grab a bite to eat. The town always seems half-deserted when I'm there, and the people I do see are usually real-estate agents wanting to sell me a condo.

the Copacabana and take either the road that goes along the south side of the hotel or the next road after that. (The latter is labeled X-6.) Construction work is always changing the signs and road around, so I can't provide specific directions. But no one can close off access, because some restaurants and small hotels are on the beach.

If Xpu-Ha sounds like your idea of the perfect home base for a Riviera Maya vacation, then consider staying at either of these all-inclusives. The **Hotel Copacabana** (☎ **800-562-0197** in the U.S.; Internet: www. hotelcopacabana.com) is owned and operated by an Acapulco-based outfit. The design of the hotel preserves much of the native flora, with large parts of the central area up on stilts. The rooms are in three-story buildings. The hotel has a lovely pool and, of course, you have the beach beyond it. The **Xpu-Ha Palace** (☎ **866-385-0256** in the U.S.; no local number; Internet: www.xpuha-palace.com) is built on the site of a failed eco-park. The area is lovely. Rooms are in palapa-style bunga-lows. You can make reservations at either of these hotels through travel agents or packagers. The **Robinson Club** is marketed mainly to Germans, and you run the risk of being an outcast unless you speak German, so I don't recommend it.

The other option is to stay at one of the small, basic hotels on this beach. Rooms are quite simple: two twin or full beds, private bathroom, cement floors, and perhaps a ceiling fan. Most are rented on a first-come, first-served basis. Rates vary from $20 to $50 a night, depending upon how busy they are. The nicest establishment is **Villas del Caribe Xpu-Ha** (☎ **984-873-2194**), which lets you make a reservation. Rates run $35 to $50 for a double; no credit cards accepted. Another option is to stay in nearby Akumal (see the next section) and drive the short distance to the beach.

Akumal

Akumal is a small, ecologically oriented community built on the shores of two beautiful bays. This community has been around long enough that it feels more relaxed than the booming places on the coast, such as Playa and Tulum. It's popular with families who can rent a condo or a villa for a week and save money by doing their own cooking. Akumal's location makes it a perfect base camp for organizing expeditions for snorkeling, diving, beach-combing, or visiting the ruins. Otherwise, you may enjoy just stopping here for a few hours to take a dip and have a bite at one of the restaurants.

Getting there and getting around

Continue south on Highway 307 from Xpu-Ha for only 3km (1½ miles). You'll come to the turnoff that is marked with a sign that reads Playa Akumal. (Don't be confused by other turnoffs marked Villas Akumal or Akumal Aventuras or Akumal Beach Resort.) Less than 1km (½ mile) down the road is a white arch. Just beyond the arch is Akumal Bay; the road to the left of the arch takes you to shallow, rocky Half Moon Bay, lined with two- and three-story villas, and eventually to Yalku Lagoon, a small, perfectly placid lagoon, good for swimming.

Navigating Akumal is simple. At the white arch, you find a couple of convenience stores (including the Super Chomak, where you can buy groceries) and a good place to take your laundry. Passing through the arch, you come to Akumal Bay. To the right is the Club Akumal Caribe Hotel. If you go left and keep to the left, you arrive at Half Moon Bay after crossing some *monster* speed bumps. (Nobody speeds in this town.) The same road, after running the distance of the bay, ends at Yalku Lagoon.

Staying in Akumal

You can rent most of the condos and villas in Akumal for a week at a time. Here are a couple of agencies specializing in villas: **Akumal Vacations** (☎ **800-448-7137** in the U.S. Internet: www.akumalvacations.com) and **Caribbean Fantasy** (☎ **800-523-6618** in the U.S. Internet: www.caribbfan.com). You can also find a few hotels, which are a more flexible option because you can rent by the day.

Club Akumal Caribe/Hotel Villas Maya Club
$$–$$$ **Akumal**

The hotel rooms and garden bungalows of this hotel, set along the pristine and tranquil Akumal Bay, are both large and comfortable. The 40 Villas Maya bungalows are simply furnished and come with kitchenettes. The 21 rooms in the three-story beachfront hotel are more elaborately furnished. They come with refrigerators and a king or two queen beds. Both the bungalows and the rooms have air-conditioning, tile floors, and good-size bathrooms, but neither have phones or TVs. A large pool on the grounds, a children's activities program (during high season), two restaurants, and a bar round out the facilities. This hotel also leases villas and condos, such as the **Villas Flamingo** on Half Moon Bay. The villas have two or three bedrooms and large living, dining, and kitchen areas, as well as a lovely furnished patio just steps from the beach.

Carretera Cancún-Tulum (Hwy. 307) Km 104. ☎ *800-351-1622 in the U.S., 800-343-1440 in Canada, or 915-584-3552 for reservations; 987-875-9012 direct. Internet:* www.hotelakumalcaribe.com. *70 units. Free parking. Rack rates: High season $120 bungalow, $145 hotel room, $160–$420 villa/condo; low season $95 bungalow, $105 hotel room; $100–$300 villa/condo. Ask for special packages for low season. AE, MC, V. Cash only at the restaurants.*

Vista del Mar Hotel and Condos
$$ **Half Moon Bay**

This beachfront property is a great place to stay for several reasons. It offers hotel rooms at good prices and large, fully equipped condos that you don't have to rent by the week. The lovely, well-tended beach in front of the hotel has chairs and umbrellas. An on-site dive shop has an experienced staff. Hotel rooms contain a queen bed or a double and a twin. The 12 condos are large, and though they lack air-conditioning, they have ceiling fans and good cross-ventilation. They consist of a kitchen, a living area with TV, and two or three bedrooms and one or two bathrooms. All have balconies or terraces facing the sea and are equipped with hammocks. Several rooms come with whirlpool tubs.

Half Moon Bay. ☎ *877-425-8625 in the U.S. Fax 505-988-3882 in the U.S. Internet:* www.akumalinfo.com. *27 units. Free parking. Rack rates: High season $85 double; $175–$240 condo. Low season $56 double; $84–$125 condo. MC, V.*

Dining in Akumal

Akumal has about ten places to eat and a good grocery store (**Super Chomak**) by the archway. The **Turtle Bay Café and Bakery,** near the Akumal Dive Shop, is good for breakfast or a light lunch. A good dining spot for lunch or dinner is **La Buena Vida,** on Half Moon Bay.

Enjoying the great outdoors

On Akumal Bay are two dive shops with PADI-certified instructors. The older is the **Akumal Dive Shop** (☎ **984-875-9032;** Internet: www.akumal.com), one of the oldest and best dive shops on the coast. Offshore, you can visit almost 30 dive sites (from 9 to 24m or 30 to 80 feet deep). The shop also specializes in cenote diving at some of the less-visited sites. Both Akumal Dive Shop and **Akumal Dive Adventures** (☎ **984-875-9157**), the dive shop at the Vista del Mar hotel on Half Moon Bay, offer resort courses as well as complete certification.

A bit beyond Akumal is the turnoff for **Aktun Chen** cavern (☎ **998-892-0662** or 998-850-4190; Internet: www.aktunchen.com), a type of eco-park. This park, consisting of a spectacular 5,000-year-old grotto and an abundance of wildlife, marks the first time that above-the-ground cave systems in the Yucatán have been open to the public. The name means "cave with an underground river inside." The main cave containing three rivers is more than 600 yards long with a magnificent vault. Discreet illumination and easy walking paths make visiting the caves more comfortable, without appearing to alter the caves too much from their natural state. The caves contain large chambers with thousands of stalactites, stalagmites, and sculpted rock formations, along with a 40-foot-deep *cenote* (an underground, spring-fed cave) with clear blue water.

Aktun Chen was once underwater itself, and you can see fossilized shells and fish embedded in the limestone as you walk along the paths. Caves are an integral part of this region's geography and geology, and knowledgeable guides lead you through the site while providing explanations and offering mini history lessons on the Maya's association with these caves. Tours have no set times — guides are available to take you when you arrive — and groups are kept to a maximum of 20 people. The tour takes about an hour and requires a good amount of walking. The footing is generally good.

Nature trails surround the caves throughout the 988-acre park, where spotting deer, spider monkeys, iguanas, and wild turkeys is common. A small, informal restaurant, gift shop, and zoo with specimens of the local fauna are also on-site.

You can easily travel to Aktun Chen on your own. On Highway 307 (the road to Tulum), just past the turnoff for Akumal, a sign on the right side of the highway indicates the turnoff for Aktun Chen (at Km. 107, Cancún–Tulum road). From there, it's a 3- to 5-km (2- to 3-mile) drive west along a smooth but unpaved road. The park is open daily from 9 a.m. to 5 p.m. Admission is $17 for adults, $9 for children.

Xel-Ha

Thirteen kilometers (8 miles) south of Akumal, a beautiful lagoon called **Xel-ha** (shell-*hah*) is the centerpiece of a 10-acre ecological park where you can swim and snorkel in perfectly calm, clear water and view a variety of brilliantly colored tropical fish. The variety is less than what you find in the open water along the coastal reefs, but snorkeling here offers a much higher comfort level for those who feel anxious about waves and currents. The park entertains lots of visitors, mainly families.

Signs clearly mark the turnoff to Xel-ha (☎ **998-884-9422** in Cancún or 984-875-5000 in Playa; Internet: www.xelha.com.mx). One kilometer (½ mile) of paved road leads to the entrance.

After you arrive at the 10-acre park, you can rent snorkeling equipment and an underwater camera, but you may also bring your own. Food and beverage service, changing rooms, showers, and other facilities are available. Platforms allow nonsnorkelers to view the fish. When you swim, be careful to observe the "swim here" and "no swimming" signs. You can see the greatest variety of fish right near the ropes that divide the swimming areas from the nonswimming areas and near any groups of rocks.

In addition, the resort offers "snuba," a clever invention that combines snorkeling and scuba. Snuba is a shallow-water diving system that places conventional scuba tanks on secure rafts that float at surface level; the "snuba-diver" breathes normally through a mouthpiece, which is connected to a long air hose attached to the tank above. This setup enables a swimmer to go as deep as 20 feet below the surface and stay down for as long as an hour or more. It's a great transition to scuba, and many divers may enjoy it more because it frees you of the cumbersome tank and weights while allowing you to stay down without having to hold your breath. Rental costs $39 for approximately an hour.

Another attraction is the interactive dolphin swim — a one-hour interactive swim costs $90, or a 15-minute "educational swim" (more like a photo-op) with the dolphins priced at $35. Hour swims are available at 11 a.m., noon, 1 p.m., and 3 p.m. Make reservations at least 24 hours in advance (☎ 998-887-6840) for one of the four daily times: 9:30 a.m., 12:30 p.m., 2 p.m., and 3:15 p.m.

Xel-Ha is open daily 8:30 a.m. to 5 p.m. Parking is free. Admission for adults is $25 on weekdays, $19 on weekends; for children age 5 to 11, it's $13 on weekdays, $10 on weekends; children under 5 enter free. Admission includes use of inner tubes, life vest, and shuttle train to the river. An all-inclusive option includes snorkeling equipment rental, locker rental, towels, food, and beverages for $52 for adults and $30 for children (no weekend discounts). The park accepts American Express, MasterCard, and Visa.

If you're driving, just south of the Xel-Ha, turn off on the west side of the highway, don't miss the ruins of **ancient Xel-Ha.** You're likely to be the only one there as you walk over limestone rocks and through the tangle of trees, vines, and palms. There's a huge, deep, dark *cenote* to one side, a temple palace with tumbled-down columns, a jaguar group, and a conserved temple group. A covered palapa on one pyramid guards a partially preserved mural. Admission is $2.50.

Xel-Ha is also close to the ruins at **Tulum** (see Chapter 15) and makes a good place for a dip after you finish climbing the Mayan ruins.

On the way to Tulum

Only a couple of kms past Xel-ha, you see a sign on your right advertising **Hidden Worlds Cenotes** center (☎ 984-877-8535; Internet: www.hiddenworlds.com.mx), which offers an excellent opportunity to snorkel or dive in a couple of nearby caverns. If you've been considering snorkeling or diving in a cenote to see what it's like, this spot is the perfect place to do so. The site is really close by a dive shop, and it's a good one. The water is crystalline (and a bit cold) and the rock formations impressive, which all makes for a fun stop. The snorkel tour costs $25.

After you pass Hidden Worlds, the next couple of turnoffs to the left lead to Soliman and Tankah bays. On Punta Soliman Bay is a good beach restaurant called **Oscar y Lalo's,** where you can rent kayaks and snorkel equipment and paddle out to the reefs for some snorkeling. Approximately 3km (2 miles) farther is the turnoff for Tankah. Pull in here, and you come to a cenote by a lovely bay, which has good snorkeling in the bay. The palapa restaurant next to the cenote serves grilled food. A couple of small hotels are on this bay. One has a dive shop and is called the **Tankah Dive Inn** (☎ 984-874-2188 Internet:

www.tankahdiveinn.com). Rates vary from $80 to $100 for a double. It has only five rooms, and the couple who manage it are personable and welcoming.

Tulum

About 15 km (10 miles) south of Xel-ha is the walled Maya city of Tulum, a large post-Classic site overlooking the Caribbean in a dramatic setting. (See Chapter 15 for a description.) You also find the small town of present-day Tulum and on the coast a long stretch of beautiful beach dotted with small cabaña hotels. The only electricity here is what's generated by each hotel. Tulum is a good choice for those who like to splash around in the water and lie on the beach far away from the resort scene. The town has a half-dozen restaurants, three cybercafes, a bank, and three cash machines.

Getting there and getting around

The town of Tulum (130km; 81miles from Cancún) lies directly on the highway a little beyond the entrance to the ruins. But before you get to the town, you come to a highway intersection with a traffic light. The road to the left leads to the hotel zone.

There is really nothing more to Tulum than what fronts the highway and about two blocks on either side of the road. It's a small town. To get to the hotels on the beach, turn east at the highway intersection. Go 3 km (2 miles), and you'll run into a "T" junction. The best cabaña hotels are to the right. The pavement quickly turns into sand, and on both sides of the road, you start seeing cabañas. If you were to stay on this road, you would eventually enter the **Sian Ka'an Biosphere Reserve.** The road can be really bad at times. If, from the main highway (Hwy. 307) you were to head west at the intersection, you would reach the ruins at Cobá (see Chapter 15).

Staying in Tulum

You can stay either on the beach at one of the cabaña hotels in the hotel zone, or in town. The seven or eight hotels in town are cheaper than all but the most basic of beach accommodations, but they aren't as much fun. They offer basic lodging for $20 to $50 a night. I really like staying in the cabaña hotels. You have more than 20 to choose from, and they run the gamut from minimal lodging requirements to refined luxury.

Most of the cheap cabañas are on the coast closest to the ruins. I would warn against these cabañas; I've heard from several sources that travelers have had their possessions stolen. South are the majority of the cabañas, including some moderately priced places.

Cabañas Ana y José
$$–$$$ Punta Allen Peninsula

These cabañas offer a tranquil escape that feels worlds away from the rest of civilization and provide sufficient creature comforts to make for a relaxing stay. The beach in front of the hotel is pure white sand. The rock-walled cabañas closest to the water (called "oceanfront") are a little larger than the others and come with two double beds. I also like the attractive second-floor "vista al mar" rooms, which have tall palapa roofs. The standard rooms are much like the others but don't face the sea. The hotel has one suite. There is 24-hour electricity for lights and ceiling fans but no TV. All rooms have tile or wood floors, one or two double beds, and patios or balconies. The hotel, located 4 miles from the Tulum ruins, can have a rental car waiting for you at the Cancún airport. Reservations are a must in high season, and around Christmas and the New Year, the rates are a little higher than normal high-season prices.

Carretera Punta Allen Km 7. ☎ *987-887-5470. Fax: 987-887-5469. Internet:* www. anayjose.com. *15 units. Free parking. Rack rates: High season $100–$140 double; low season $90–$130 double. MC, V.*

Cabañas Tulum
$ Punta Allen Peninsula

Next door to Ana y José's is a row of bungalows facing the same beautiful ocean and beach. This place offers basic accommodations. Rooms are simple yet attractive and large, though poorly lit. The large bathrooms are tiled. All rooms have two double beds (most with new mattresses), screens on the windows, a table, one electric light, and a porch facing the beach. Electricity is available from 7 to 11 a.m. and 6 to 11 p.m. Billiard and Ping-Pong tables provide entertainment. The cabañas are often full between December 15 and Easter, and in July and August.

Carretera Punta Allen Km 7. ☎ *984-879-7395. Fax 984-871-2092. Internet:* www. hotelstulum.com. *32 units. $50–$70 double. No credit cards.*

Zamas
$$ Punta Allen Peninsula

Zamas is a grouping of stylish beach cabañas located on a rocky point on the coast just south of Tulum. Each cabaña comes with a small porch area and hammocks, a thatched roof, a large bathroom, and electricity. Mosquito netting hangs over each bed. What the cabañas don't have are ceiling fans, which they generally don't need. In this respect, the hotel's location is enviable in that it almost always has a breeze. Rooms come with a variety of bed combinations and are ranked in three categories: gardenview, oceanview, and beachfront. Note that the rooms also don't have A/C, TV, or phones. (Even the hotel doesn't have a phone! You have to call a number in the United States to make reservations.) The hotel's restaurant has great food.

Carr. Punta Allen, Km. 5. ☎ *800-538-6802 in the U.S. or Canada for reservations. Internet:* www.zamas.com. *16 units. Rack rates: High season $125 oceanview double, $80–$105 double; low season $90 oceanview double, $50–$80 double. No credit cards.*

Dining in Tulum

A few restaurants in the town of Tulum have reasonable prices and good food. **Charlie's** (☎ 987-871-2136), my favorite for Mexican food, and **Don Cafeto's** (☎ 987-871-2207) are two safe bets. Both places are on the main street. There's a good, authentic-Italian restaurant called **Il Giardino di Toni e Simone** (☎ 044-987-804-1316, a cell phone; closed Wed) one block off the highway. Look for a large building-supply store called ROCA — the restaurant is on the opposite side of the road one block away. A couple of roadside places that grill chicken and serve it with rice and beans are also in town. Two good restaurants are on the coast — the one at **Zamas** (good seafood!) and the one at **Cabañas Ana y José.** (See the previous section for information on both these places.)

Enjoying the great outdoors

In the Tulum area, the main thing to do is to visit the **Tulum ruins.** Staying here gives you the advantage of seeing them early in the morning before it gets hot and before the large tour buses (and attendant crowds) arrive. If you have a car, you can also visit the nearby ruins of **Cobá.** For more on these two ruins sites, see Chapter 15.

You can arrange an interesting day-trip to visit the mammoth **Sian Ka'an Biopreserve.** You're guaranteed seeing several species of wildlife and learn some interesting things about the plant life in the zone. Most tours include a boat ride around the large lagoon in the park and perhaps through one of the canals that connect it to small lakes. In Tulum, contact **Sian Ka'an Tours** (☎ 984-871-2363; e-mail: siankaan_tours@ hotmail.com); the tour office is on the east side of the road, one block south of the highway intersection. This outfit offers a general-interest day tour and a sunset tour.

Chapter 15

A Taste of the Maya: Nearby Ruins

• •

In This Chapter

▶ Choosing which ruins to visit

▶ Getting there and back

▶ Exploring the ruins

▶ Understanding the ancient Maya

• •

*F*rom top to bottom and from coast to coast, the Yucatán is littered with the ruined cities and settlements of the ancient Maya. At its peak, the area must have been super-populated, for even today it seems that you can hardly trek out into the forest without tripping over some yet undiscovered site.

Of course, most of these smaller ruins aren't of interest to the casual observer because they're mere mounds of earth and stone overgrown by forest; they tell you nothing about the past. It's only with excavation and reconstruction that you can get an idea of what this ancient civilization was all about, and, even then, seeing these cities reconstructed generally begs more questions than answers. But they're fascinating sights with dramatic architecture, and exotic surroundings. If you can tear yourself away for a day from the comforts of beach life, you may enjoy a visit to one or more of these places.

All of the Yucatán is *"tierra caliente"* (the hotlands), so be prepared. Take sun protection and remember that you'll be walking and perhaps climbing at these sites, so you need comfortable shoes or sandals and a bottle of water. And try to see the sights as early in the day as possible. At Cobá, you need mosquito repellent.

Deciding Which Ruins to Visit

From Cancún or anywhere else along the Caribbean coast, four major ruins are within easy reach and worth visiting. Each is remarkably different from the others, offering a lot of variety. But don't try to see more than one or two; leave the rest for another trip. You can easily overdo the ruins, and they're best appreciated when viewed with fresh eyes.

- ✔ **Chichén Itzá:** No, it doesn't rhyme with "chicken pizza;" the accents are on the last syllables (chee *chin* eat-*zah*). Without a doubt, this complex is the marquee ruins site of the Yucatán. You can marvel at many things here, but the most famous sights are the much-photographed pyramid known as **El Castillo;** the mysterious and ancient-looking **sacrificial cenote** (a cenote is a natural well or sinkhole found only in the Yucatán), which is 180 feet across and 60 feet down to the water; and the great **ballcourt** adorned with graphic depictions of players literally losing their heads. Chichén Itzá is in the heart of the Yucatán, two hours by car from Cancún. Many day tours by bus leave from Cancún, Playa del Carmen, and most of the big resorts. Or you can rent your own car and stay overnight in the area.

- ✔ **Tulum:** Built later than Chichén Itzá and on a much smaller scale, these ruins represent the only major coastal ruins in this part of the Yucatán. The setting is gorgeous: Picture a stylish Maya pyramid crowning a tall cliff jutting out over the turquoise waters of the Caribbean, and you've got the idea. Below this pyramid is a pretty little beach, so take your swimsuit. To me, the buildings in Tulum are less grand than those of the other three sites, but the other three don't have the Caribbean settting. Tulum is 1½ hours south of Cancún.

- ✔ **Cobá:** Older than Chichén Itzá and much larger than Tulum, Cobá was the dominant city of the eastern Yucatán before A.D. 1000. The site is large and spread out. Two lakes border the ruins, and the tropical forest grows thickly between the different temple groups. Rising high above the forest canopy are tall, steep classic Mayan pyramids. Of the four sites, this one is the least reconstructed, and so disappoints those who expect another Chichén Itzá. Appreciating it requires a greater exercise of the imagination. Cobá is a little more than a half-hour inland from Tulum.

- ✔ **Ek Balam:** Off the beaten track (but not for long) are these impressive ruins where some startling recent discoveries are making waves in the archaeological world. See Ek Balam now before it becomes a major attraction. Highlights include a ceremonial doorway representing the gaping mouth of the Maya underworld god, Itzamná. The site also has the tallest pyramid in the upper Yucatán. Not hard to get to, Ek Balam is off the same toll highway leading to Chichén Itzá — one exit earlier and about 14 km north.

The Yucatán Peninsula's Major Ruins

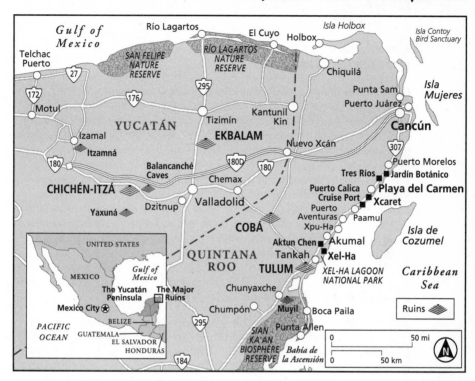

 If you're going to one of these sights on your own, try to schedule your trip on a Sunday when admission is free. (You still have to pay for parking.) But if you plan to go by bus tour where the admission is only one among many things included in the price, such as lunch and entertainment, you usually don't get a discount for a Sunday visit.

Chichén Itzá

Many people coming to the Yucatán for the first time will feel the need to see these ruins, if only so as not to have to explain to their friends and neighbors how it was that they traveled this far without seeing them. While it's true that Chichén Itzá is plenty hyped, it does live up to its reputation. But if ruins aren't your cup of tea and the beach is, you should have the courage of your convictions and be ready to tell any people who ask that it's none of their business what you did on your vacation. I do this as a matter of principle.

For the rest of you who plan to see these ruins, the question you should ask yourselves is whether you want to overnight here. The advantage is that you can catch the sound-and-light show at night and then see the ruins in the early morning when it's cooler and before most of the tour buses arrive. The drawback is that you need to rent a car or take regular bus service.

Getting there

Chichén Itzá is on the old main Highway 180 in the interior of the peninsula. To get there by car, use the new *autopista* (toll highway) and take the exit for Chichén Itzá and the village of Pisté. The road leads you right into the village of Pisté from the north. It ends at the old Highway 180; turn left here. Signs point the way.

Any number of bus tours depart from Cancún and Playa del Carmen. These tours usually stop a few times before getting to the ruins for lunch, a snack, or a swim. You arrive at the ruins usually around noon or shortly thereafter, and you're back in Cancún or Playa del Carmen by nightfall. Regular bus service is trickier and more frequent from Cancún than from Playa del Carmen.

Where to stay

The expensive hotels in Chichén all occupy beautiful grounds, are close to the ruins, and have good food. All have toll-free reservations numbers, which I recommend. Some of these hotels do a lot of business with tour operators — they can be empty one day and full the next. The inexpensive hotels are in the village of Pisté, 2 km (1 mile) away.

Hacienda Chichén
$$$ At the ruins

The smallest and most private of the hotels at the ruins is also the quietest and the least likely to have bus tour groups. This was the hacienda that served as the headquarters for the Carnegie Institute's excavations in 1923. Several bungalows, built to house the staff, have been modernized and are now the guest rooms. Each is simply and comfortably furnished (with a dehumidifier and ceiling fan in addition to air-conditioning) and is a short distance from the others. Each bungalow has a private porch from which you can enjoy the beautiful grounds. Standard rooms come with two twin or two double beds. Suites are larger and have larger bathrooms and double or queen beds. The main building was part of the original hacienda and holds the restaurant, which offers dining on the terrace by the pool or inside in air-conditioning.

Zona Arqueológica. ☎ *800-624-8451 in the U.S or 985-851-0045. Internet:* www.yucatanadventure.com.mx. *28 units. Free guarded parking. Rack rates: $117 double; $140 suite. AE, DC, MC, V.*

Chichén Itzá Ruins

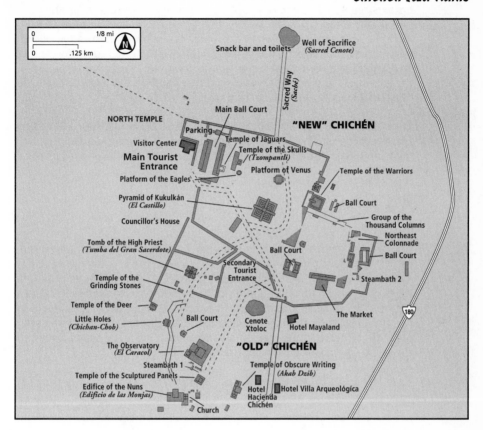

Hotel Dolores Alba

$ Old Highway east of the ruins

This little motel is perfect if you come by car. It's a bargain for what you get: two pools (one is an "ecological" pool with a stone bottom and nonchlorinated water), palapas and hammocks around the place, and large, comfortable, air-conditioned rooms. The restaurant serves good meals at moderate prices. You also get free transportation to the ruins and the Caves of Balankanché during visiting hours, though you will have to take a taxi back. The hotel is on the highway 2.5 km (1½ miles) east of the ruins.

Carretera Mérida–Cancún. Km. 122 ☎ *985-858-1555. Internet:* www.dolores alba.com. *40 units. Free parking. Rack rates: $35 double. No credit cards.*

Hotel Mayaland

$$$$ At the ruins

The main doorway frames El Caracol (the observatory) in a stunning view — that's how close this hotel is to the ruins. If a drawback exists, it's that the hotel books large bus tours, but this isn't so bad because the hotel is on a large piece of property that uses space liberally. The main building is long and three stories high. The rooms are large, with comfortable beds and large tiled bathrooms. Bungalows, scattered about the rest of the grounds, are built native style, with thatched roofs and stucco walls; they're a good deal larger than the rooms. The grounds, including three pools, are gorgeous, with huge trees and lush foliage — the hotel has had 75 years to get them that way.

Zona Arqueológica. ☎ *800-235-4079 in the U.S., or 998-887-0870 for reservations office in Cancún or 985-851-0127 direct to the hotel. 101 units. Free guarded parking. Rack rates: High season $150 double, $200 bungalow. 10% low-season discount. AE, MC, V.*

Pirámide Inn
$ Pisté

A mile west from the ruins, in the village of Pisté, this hotel has simple rooms, most with two double beds (a few with three twins or one king). The bathrooms are nice, with counter space and tub/shower combinations. The air-conditioning is quiet and effective. Hot water comes on between 5 and 10 a.m. and 5 and 10 p.m. A well-kept pool and a *temascal* (a native form of steambath) occupy a small part of the landscaped grounds, which include the remains of a Maya wall. Try to get a room in the back. The hotel is right on the highway.

Calle 15 No. 30. ☎ *985-851-0115. Fax: 985-851-0114. Internet:* www.piramide inn.com. *44 units. $47 double. MC, V.*

Where to dine

Cafetería Ruinas
$ At the ruins   INTERNATIONAL

Though this cafeteria has the monopoly on food at the ruins, it actually does a good job with such basic meals as enchiladas, pizza, and baked chicken. It even offers some Yucatecan dishes. Eggs and burgers are cooked to order, and the coffee is good. You can also get fruit smoothies and vegetarian dishes. Sit outside at the tables farthest from the crowd, and relax.

In the visitor center. ☎ *985-851-0111. Reservations not accepted. Breakfast: $4; sandwiches $4–$5; main courses $4–$8. AE, MC, V. Open: Daily 9 a.m.–6 p.m.*

Fiesta
$ Pisté   YUCATECAN/MEXICAN

Though relatively inexpensive, the food here is dependable and good. You can dine inside or out, but make a point of going for supper or early lunch when the tours buses are gone. The buffet is quite complete, and the menu has many Yucatecan classics. Fiesta is on the west end of town.

Highway 180 in Pisté. ☎ _985-851-0038. Reservations not accepted. Main courses $4–$6; buffet $8.50 (served from 12:30 to 5 p.m.). No credit cards. Open: Daily 7 a.m.–9 p.m._

Exploring Chichén Itzá

When you think of a Maya pyramid, chances are that it's the main pyramid at Chichén Itzá that springs to mind. It's called **El Castillo** and it's dedicated to the feathered serpent god Kukulkán. No doubt you have seen pictures of it everywhere — in guidebooks, on posters, and on Web sites. The funny thing is that El Castillo shouldn't be the poster child for Maya architecture. It doesn't look like most Maya pyramids, and experts know for certain that the god Kukulkán was not originally worshipped in the Maya heartland but came here from Central Mexico (where he was known as Quetzalcoatl). Also, many architectural features of this city are strikingly similar to the Toltec city of Tula, in Central Mexico.

The burning question about Chichén Itzá (Chichén, for short) is, "Who really ran the show here?" Experts know that they called themselves the "Itzá," and the name of the city means "Well of the Itzá." It's pretty certain that the ones following orders here — the laborers, peasants, and artisans — were native Maya. The head honchos were perhaps either invading Toltecs who later intermarried with the Maya, or the Putún Maya, a merchant people from the Gulf coast who were receptive to foreign influences and more cosmopolitan than their Yucatán neighbors. Or maybe it was a combination of both. More digging at the site is necessary to answer this question, and that event doesn't look likely anytime soon.

Chichén Itzá occupies 6.5 square kilometers (4 sq. miles), and it takes most of a day to see all the ruins. Hours for the site are 8 a.m. to 5 p.m. daily. Service areas are open 8 a.m. to 10 p.m. Admission is $11, free for children under 12, and free for all on Sundays and holidays. A video camera permit costs $4. Parking is extra. Chichén Itzá's **sound-and-light** show is worth seeing and is included in the cost of admission. For more information, see "More cool things to see and do," later in this section.

The large, modern visitor center, at the main entrance where you pay the admission charge, is beside the parking lot and consists of a museum, an auditorium, a restaurant, a bookstore, and bathrooms. You can see the site on your own or with a licensed guide who speaks English or Spanish. Guides usually wait at the entrance and charge around $40 for one to six people. Although the guides frown on it, there's nothing wrong with approaching a group of people who speak the same language and asking whether they want to share a guide. Be wary of the history-spouting guides — some of it is just plain out-of-date — but the architectural details they point out are enlightening. Chichén Itzá has two parts: the northern (new) zone, which shows distinct Toltec influence, and the southern (old) zone, with mostly Puuc architecture.

El Castillo pyramid

Once you pass the entrance gates, **El Castillo pyramid** will be in front of you. At 23 meters (75 feet) tall, the pyramid a giant numbers game tied to the old Pre-Columbian calendars: Four stairways have 91 steps each, which adds up to 364; when you add the top platform where they meet, the total is 365, the number of days in a year. On each side of these stairways are 9 terraces, making a total of 18 per side, which is the number of months in their solar calendar. Each face has 52 panels, equaling the 52 years that represented the magical cycle for all pre-Hispanic civilizations. This time period is how long it would take for the solar and the religious calendars to coincide.

Consider the pyramid's mysterious alignment. It's positioned so that twice a year, on the **spring** and **fall equinoxes** (March 21 and September 21), the corner edges of the pyramid cast shadows on the sides of the north stairway; these shadows resemble the geometric patterns on the body of a snake such as the diamondback. At the bottom of each side of the north stairway is a serpent's head carved in stone, so the shadow effect was probably intentional. As the sun rises, the shadows, representing the body of the snake, move slowly downward, making the "serpent" appear to descend into the ground. To be honest, watching the shadow effects is more of an intellectual curiosity than a dramatic sight, especially for those raised on the high excitement Indiana Jones movies. I don't think it's worth fighting the crowds that come to witness it. In truth, experts don't know what the pyramid may have looked like originally, because all the surfaces of this pyramid, including the stairways, were covered with a thick coat of smooth stucco and painted bright colors, perhaps in patterns.

Toltec tall tales

An intriguing myth from Central Mexico that some scholars use to argue was that the Toltecs founded Chichén. The short version goes like this: The god Quetzalcoatl (Feathered Serpent) was tricked by his brother, the god Tezcatlipoca (Smoking Mirror), and shamed into leaving. He fled to the Gulf coast of Mexico and there ascended into the east toward Venus, the morning star. According to these scholars, this myth represents a shorthand account of a Toltec religious civil war fought between the followers of these two gods. The losers, under the leadership of a priest-king, who naturally assumed the name of Quetzalcoatl, were pushed east to the Gulf of Mexico and from there moved to the Yucatán where they managed to build a new city at Chichén Itzá and reestablish the cult of the feathered serpent.

El Castillo was an enlargement of an earlier pyramid. The Maya frequently did this kind of thing. Archeologists have carved a narrow stairway into the pyramid at the western edge of the north staircase. It leads inside to the temple of the original structure, to a sacrificial altar-throne — a red jaguar encrusted with jade. The stairway is open from 11 a.m. to 3 p.m.; the inside is cramped, humid, and uncomfortable. A visit as close to the opening time as possible is best. Photos of the jaguar figure are forbidden.

Juego de Pelota (the main ball court)

Among all the peoples of pre-Columbian Mexico, there existed a popular game that was part ritual, part sport. Historians only know of it as "the ball game" or "pok-ta-pok" in Mayan. Ball courts have been found as far north as New Mexico and as far south as Honduras and everywhere in between. The **main court** at Chichén is one of at least nine in this city and is much larger and better preserved than any ball court found elsewhere. You find it immediately northwest of El Castillo. Carved on both walls of the ball court are scenes showing Maya figures dressed as ball players and decked out in heavy protective padding. The carved scene also shows a headless player kneeling with blood shooting from his neck; another player holding the head looks on.

Players on two teams tried to knock a hard rubber ball through one of the two stone rings placed high on either wall, using only their elbows, knees, and hips (no hands). According to legend, the losing players paid for defeat with their lives. However, some experts say the victors were the only appropriate sacrifices for the gods. One can only guess what the incentive for winning might be in that case. Either way, the game must have been riveting, heightened by the wonderful acoustics of the ball court.

Other highlights of Chichén Itzá

Temples are at both ends of the ball court. The **North Temple** has sculptured pillars and more sculptures inside, as well as badly ruined murals. The acoustics of the ball court are so good that from the North Temple, a person speaking can be heard clearly at the opposite end, about 136 meters (450 feet) away.

Follow the dirt road (actually an ancient *sacbé*, or causeway) that heads north from the Platform of Venus; after 5 minutes, you come to *Cenote de los Sacrificios* **(Sacrificial Cenote),** the great natural well that may have given Chichén Itzá its name. This well was used for ceremonial purposes, not for drinking water — according to legend, sacrificial victims were drowned in this pool to honor the rain god Chaac. Research done early in the 20th century showed that bones of both children and adults were found in the well.

Edward Thompson, who was the American consul in Mérida, purchased the ruins of Chichén early in the 20th century and explored the cenote with dredges and divers. His explorations exposed a fortune in gold and jade. Most of the riches wound up in Harvard's Peabody Museum of Archaeology and Ethnology — a matter that continues to be of concern to Mexican archeologists. Excavations in the 1960s unearthed more treasure, and studies of the recovered objects detail offerings from throughout the Yucatán and even farther away.

Due east of El Castillo is the *Templo de los Guerreros* **(Temple of the Warriors),** named for the carvings of warriors marching along its walls. It's also called the Group of the Thousand Columns for the rows of broken pillars that flank it. During the recent restoration, hundreds more of the columns were rescued from the rubble and put in place, setting off the temple more magnificently than ever. A figure of Chaac-Mool sits at the top of the temple, surrounded by impressive columns carved to look like enormous feathered serpents. South of the temple was a square building that archaeologists called the **Market** (*mercado*); a colonnade surrounds its central court. Beyond the temple and the market in the jungle are mounds of rubble, parts of which are being reconstructed.

Construction of the *El Caracol* **(the Observatory),** a complex building with a circular tower, was carried out over centuries; the additions and modifications reflected the Maya's careful observation of celestial movements and their need for increasingly exact measurements. Through slits in the tower's walls, astronomers could observe the cardinal directions and the approach of the all-important spring and autumn equinoxes, as well as the summer solstice. The temple's name, which means "snail," comes from a spiral staircase within the structure.

On the east side of El Caracol, a path leads north into the bush to the **Cenote Xtoloc,** a natural limestone well that provided the city's daily water supply. If you see any lizards sunning there, they may well be *xtoloc,* the lizard for which this cenote is named.

More cool things to see and do

From cave visits to laser shows, Chichén and the surrounding area hold even more interest for travelers.

✔ **"Head" on over to** *Tzompantli* **(the Temple of the Skulls).** To the right of the ball court is the Temple of the Skulls, an obvious borrowing from the post-Classic cities of central Mexico. Notice the rows of skulls carved into the stone platform. When a sacrificial victim's head was cut off, it was impaled on a pole and displayed in a tidy row with others. Also carved into the stone are pictures of eagles tearing hearts from human victims. The word *Tzompantli* is not Mayan but comes from Central Mexico. Reconstruction using scattered fragments may add a level to this platform and change the look of this structure by the time you visit.

✔ **Stay for the evening sound-and-light show.** The kind of severe geometry characteristic of Maya archicture really lends itself to this kind of spectacle; besides, you already paid for the show when you bought you ticket. The show, held at 7 or 8 p.m. depending on the season, is in Spanish, but headsets are available for rent ($4.50) in several languages so that you can enjoy the dramatic narrative.

✔ **Visit *Chichén Viejo* (Old Chichén).** For a look at more of Chichén's oldest buildings, constructed well before the time of Toltec influence, follow signs from the Edifice of the Nuns southwest into the bush to Old Chichén, about 1 km (½ mile) away. Be prepared for this trek with long trousers, insect repellent, and a local guide. The attractions here are the *Templo de los Inscripciones Iniciales* **(Temple of the First Inscriptions),** with the oldest inscriptions discovered at Chichén; and the restored *Templo de los Dinteles* **(Temple of the Lintels),** a fine Puuc building.

✔ **Explore the cave of Balankanché.** You see signs for this cave about 5½ km (3½ miles) from Chichén Itzá on the old highway to Cancún. The entire excursion takes about a half hour, but the walk inside is hot and humid. The highlight is a round chamber with a central column the size of a large tree trunk. You come up the same way you go down. The cave became a hideaway during the War of the Castes. You can still see traces of carving and incense burning, as well as an underground stream that served as the sanctuary's water supply. Outside, take time to meander through the botanical gardens, where most of the plants and trees are labeled with their common and scientific names.The caves are open daily. Admission is $6, free for children 6 to 12. Children younger than age 6 are not admitted. Use of a video camera costs $4 (free if you've already bought a video permit in Chichén the same day). Tours in English are at 11 a.m., 1 p.m., and 3 p.m.; and, in Spanish, at 9 a.m., noon, 2 p.m., and 4 p.m. Double-check these hours at the main entrance to the Chichén ruins.

✔ **Check out Cenotes Dzitnup & Sammulá.** The Cenote Dzitnup (also known as Cenote Xkekén) is along the same Highway 180 as Balankanché, about 20 miles further toward Cancún. It's worth a side trip, especially if you have time for a dip. Watch for the signs. When you get there, you descend a short flight of rather perilous stone steps, and at the bottom, inside a beautiful cavern, is a natural pool of water so clear and blue that it seems plucked from a dream. If you decide to swim, be sure that you don't have creams or other chemicals on your skin — they damage the habitat of the small fish and other organisms living there. Also, no alcohol, food, or smoking is allowed in the cavern. Admission is $2. The cenote is open daily 7 a.m. to 7 p.m. About 100 yards down the road on the opposite side is another recently discovered cenote, Sammulá, where you can also swim. Admission is $2.

Fast Facts: Chichén Itzá

Area Code

The telephone area code for Chichén and the neighboring village of Pisté is **985**.

Banks, ATMs, and Currency Exchange

You can find ATMs and banks in the nearby town of Valladolid, which you pass on your way to Chichén if you take the old Highway 180.

Medical

You can find a small first-aid station in the visitor center at the ruins.

Taxes

A 15% IVA (value-added tax) on goods and services is usually included in the posted price.

Tulum: Fortress City

Tulum was a Mayan fortress-city built over the most rugged part of the coast. In looking at the layout and scope of the city, it becomes clear that the builders of this citadel were interested in two things uppermost: trade and defense. And they picked the perfect spot for their city. It is a beautiful site facing out over the Caribbean. On the city's other three sides they constructed stout walls with watchtowers and fortified areas. The stonework used to build the ceremonial centers is of poorer quality than in other sites such as Chichén or Cobá, as if the temples were constructed in haste.

Tulum is also the name of the laid-back coastal town adjacent to the ruins, where you find beautiful and mostly isolated beaches, as well as a string of interesting hotels. For more on Tulum the town, see Chapter 14.

The city's origins date from the ninth century, which was the end of the Classic period and the beginning of Maya civilization's decline. The large cities to the south were abandoned, and smaller city-states rose to fill the void. Tulum was one of these city-states. Its original name was "Zama," meaning dawn, a good name because it obviously faces east toward the rising sun. It came to prominence in the 13th century as a seaport, controlling maritime commerce along this section of the coast, and remained inhabited well after the arrival of the Spanish. The primary god here was the diving god, depicted on several buildings as an upside-down figure above doorways. Seen at the Palace at Sayil and Cobá, this curious, almost comical figure is also known as the bee god.

The most imposing building in Tulum is a large stone structure above the cliff called the **Castillo** (castle). Actually a temple as well as a fortress, it was once covered with stucco and painted. In front of the Castillo are several unrestored palace-like buildings with partial remains of the old stucco covering. On the **beach** below, where the Maya once came ashore, visitors swim and sunbathe, combining a visit to the ruins with a dip in the Caribbean.

Tulum Ruins

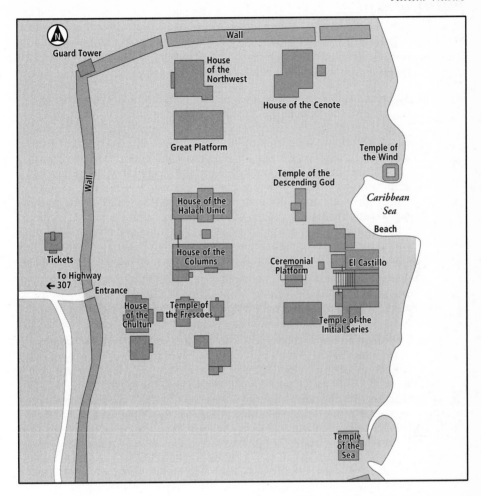

The **Temple of the Frescoes,** directly in front of the Castillo, contains interesting 13th-century wall paintings, though entry is no longer permitted. Distinctly Maya, they represent the rain god Chaac and Ixchel, the goddess of weaving, women, the moon, and medicine. On the cornice of this temple is a relief of the head of the rain god. If you pause a slight distance from the building, you see the eyes, nose, mouth, and chin. Notice the remains of the red-painted stucco — at one time, all the buildings at Tulum were painted bright red.

Much of what historians know of Tulum at the time of the Spanish Conquest comes from the writings of Diego de Landa, third bishop of the Yucatán. He wrote that Tulum was a small city inhabited by about 600 people who lived in platform dwellings along a street and who supervised the trade from Honduras to the Yucatán. Though it was a walled city, most of the inhabitants probably lived outside the walls, leaving the interior for the residences of governors and priests and ceremonial structures. Tulum survived about 70 years after the Conquest, when it was finally abandoned. Because of the great number of visitors this site receives, you can no longer to climb the ruins and are asked to remain behind roped-off areas to view them.

The ruins are open to visitors from 7 a.m. to 5 p.m. in the winter and from 8 a.m. to 6 p.m. in the summer. If you can, go early before the crowds start showing up around 9:30 a.m. The entrance to the ruins is about a 5-minute walk from the archaeological site. You find artisans' stands, a bookstore, a museum, a restaurant, several large bathrooms, and a ticket booth. After walking through the center, visitors pay the admission fee to the ruins ($4; free on Sunday), another fee ($1.50) if you choose to ride an open-air shuttle to the ruins, and, if you're driving, another fee ($3) to park. A video camera permit costs $4. Licensed guides have a stand next to the path to the ruins and charge $20 for a 45-minute tour in English, French, or Spanish for up to 4 persons. They can point out many architectural details that you may otherwise miss.

Cobá ("Water Stirred by Wind")

The Maya built many intriguing cities in the Yucatán, but few grander than Cobá ("water stirred by wind"). Much of the 67 sq. km (42 sq. mile) site, on the shores of two lakes, is unexcavated. A 96 km (60-mile) long *sacbé* (a pre-Hispanic raised road or causeway) through the jungle — remains of which are still visible — linked Cobá to Yaxuná, once a large, important Maya center 48km (30 miles) south of Chichén-Itzá. It's the Maya's longest known *sacbé,* and at least 50 shorter ones lead from here. Cobá flourished from A.D. 632 (the oldest carved date found here) until after the founding of Chichén-Itzá, around 800. Then Cobá slowly faded in importance and population until it was finally abandoned. Scholars believe Cobá was an important trade link between the Yucatán Caribbean coast and inland cities.

You can line up a bus tour to Cobá from Cancún or Playa del Carmen. (See Chapters 11 and 14 for details.) If you're driving, follow Highway 307 down the coast to Tulum. After you pass the entrance to those ruins but before you enter the town, you see a highway intersection with a traffic light. Turn right and follow this road for 40 minutes to reach the ruins. Always be on your guard for the ever-present speed bumps known as *topes*. They sometimes appear without warning. A couple of small restaurants are in the town, with another one in the Hotel Villa Arqueológica.

Once at the site, keep your bearings — getting lost on the maze of dirt roads in the jungle is easy, and *be sure* to bring bug spray. Branching off from every labeled path are unofficial narrow paths into the jungle, used by locals as shortcuts through the ruins.

Cobá Ruins

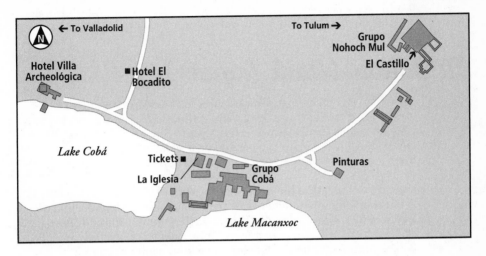

The **Grupo Cobá** boasts a large, impressive pyramid, *La Iglesia* **(Temple of the Church),** which you can find if you take the path bearing right after the entrance. Walking to it, notice the unexcavated mounds on the left. Though the urge to climb the temple is great, the view is better from El Castillo in the Nohoch Mul group farther back.

From here, return to the main path and turn right. You pass a sign pointing right to the ruined *juego de pelota* (ball court), but the path is obscure.

Continuing straight ahead on this path for 5 to 10 minutes, you come to a fork in the road. To the left and right are jungle-covered, unexcavated pyramids, and at one point, you see a raised portion crossing the pathway, which is the visible **remains of the *sacbé*** to Yaxuná. Throughout the area, intricately carved stelae stand by pathways or lie forlornly in the jungle underbrush. Although protected by crude thatched roofs, most are weatherworn enough that they're indiscernible.

The left fork leads to the **Nohoch Mul Group,** which contains **El Castillo.** With the exception of Structure 2 in Calakmul, this pyramid is the tallest in the Yucatán (rising even higher than the great El Castillo at Chichén-Itzá and the Pyramid of the Magician at Uxmal). So far, visitors are still permitted to climb to the top. From this magnificent lofty perch, you can see unexcavated jungle-covered pyramidal structures poking up through the forest all around.

The right fork (more or less straight on) goes to the **Conjunto Las Pinturas.** Here, the main attraction is the **Pyramid of the Painted Lintel,** a small structure with traces of its original bright colors above the door. You can climb up to get a close look. Though maps of Cobá show ruins around two lakes, only two groups of ruins have truly been excavated.

Admission is $4, free for children younger than age 12; Sunday and holidays, it's free to everyone. Parking is $1. A video camera permit costs $4. The site is open daily 8 a.m. to 5 p.m., sometimes longer.

Ek Balam (Dark Jaguar)

More than any of the better-known sites, Ek Balam excites a sense of mystery and awe at the scale of Maya civilization and the utter ruin to which it came. There are no bus tours yet to these ruins, but travel agencies in Cancún and Playa can get you on a smaller tour in a van. These tours are held sporadically, so you have to depend somewhat on luck.

If you're driving, take the new *autopista* (toll highway) from Cancún as if you were going to Chichén. Exit the highway at the intersection of Highway 295. The sign reads "Valladolid Tizimín." Turn right (north) as if you're headed for Tizimín. In 8 miles, you see a small sign for Ek Balam pointing to the right. Follow a narrow, winding road through a small village.

Built between 100 B.C. and A.D. 1200, the smaller buildings at Ek Balam are architecturally unique — especially the perfectly restored **Caracol.** However, the larger buildings in the main group have been reconstructed beautifully. Flanked by two smaller pyramids, the imposing central pyramid is 157m (517 ft.) long and 61m (200 ft.) wide. At more than 30m (100 ft.) high, it's easily taller than the highest pyramids in Chichén Itzá and Cobá.

On the left side of the main stairway, archaeologists recently uncovered a large, perfectly preserved stucco and stone figure of the gaping mouth of the god Itzamná forming a doorway. They had not yet excavated to see whether the doorway actually led somewhere or whether it was purely ornamental. From crumbled stucco on the other side of the pyramid, they believe the structure originally had a matching doorway. Around it are several beautifully detailed human figures.

If you climb to the top of the pyramid, in the middle distance you can see unrestored ruins looming to the north. To the southeast, you can spot the tallest structures at **Cobá,** 48km (30 miles) away. Also plainly visible are the **raised causeways** of the Maya — the sacbé appear as raised lines in the forest vegetation.

The entrance fee is $2.50, plus $4 for each video camera. The site is open daily 8 a.m. to 5 p.m. Admission is free on Sunday.

Part VI
The Part of Tens

The 5th Wave   By Rich Tennant

"Well, if you're not drinking Tequila with your breakfast burrito, then why is your cereal bowl rimmed in salt?"

In this part . . .

These three chapters are the *For Dummies* Top Ten lists, which cover in brief paragraphs the best, worst, and lesser-known charms of a Mexican vacation. I give you the ten best ways to avoid looking like a *gringo*. I also explain the most common myths and misconceptions about Mexico. For example, if you think all Mexican food is fiery hot, keep reading. And, speaking of Mexican food, I share my top-ten picks for the most deliciously Mexican dishes in this region.

Chapter 16

Ten Ways to Avoid Looking Like a Gringo

In This Chapter

▶ Figuring out how to look like a seasoned traveler to Mexico

▶ Preventing problems by knowing the local customs

*H*ow savvy of a traveler are you? If you follow the seasoned advice, "When in Rome . . .", you'll want to know a bit more about the customs and culture of Mexico before heading south of the border. This chapter offers tips and insights designed to clue you in to a few of the nuances of the Mexican way of life. Before you know it, you'll look a little more like a local.

Wake Up and Ask for the Coffee . . . Correctly

In Mexico, whenever you ask for cream for your coffee, you're served milk, or occasionally, evaporated milk, but never "cream," which is of a very heavy consistency in Mexico — you'd have to spoon it into your coffee. Simply request, *"Leche para el café, por favor"* (Milk for the coffee, please).

Practice Your Check Etiquette

In Mexico, it's considered rude for a waiter to bring your check before you've asked for it — after all, he wouldn't want to appear to be unwelcoming or to be rushing you. Always remember to ask, *"La cuenta, por favor"* (Check, please) when you're ready to leave.

Be on the Lookout for the Bus

Use care in crossing the streets, especially in view of public buses, which seem to regularly race one another in an attempt to reach more potential passengers. Their speed, combined with their sheer size, results in several fatalities each year. You'd rather be alive than right, right?

Go to the Pharmacy for Advice

When feeling under the weather, most Mexicans visit their local pharmacist before checking with a doctor — these professionals are used to dispensing advice, and the recommended remedy, even if it's a prescription medication back home. Pharmacies in Mexico generally don't require prescriptions (except in the case of more tightly controlled substances), so visitors routinely stock up on items such as Rogaine, Viagra, Retin-A, and birth control pills because of their accessibility and relatively low price.

Beware the Jewelry Scams

In Mexico, the difference between silver jewelry and silver-*colored* jewelry is a big one. When buying jewelry or other items made of silver, first look for the ".925" stamp, an alleged measure of the silver content of the piece. However, even if a stamp is visible, be aware that most of the silver-colored jewelry sold by strolling beach vendors is actually made from *alpaca,* a lesser quality metal with a heavy copper content. Established stores are your best bets for quality silver purchases.

In the Yucatán, you may also run into vendors trying to pass off plastic for Black Coral — a popular jewelry item in these parts. Black Coral is an endangered and protected species — you cannot even take it into the United States without a certificate of origin to establish that it was harvested from an area where Black Coral is being "raised" for specific harvest purposes. Furthermore, authentic Black Coral is extremely expensive. So if the item you want is too cheap to be true coral, it's probably plastic. And if you didn't buy it from a certified jeweler that deals with proper Black Coral harvesters, you're promoting the extinction of a rare kind of coral that took millions of years to create.

Know the Truth about the "Flower Girls"

At night, strolling and dining couples are invariably approached by children selling individual roses for the "nice couple" or *"la señorita"* (the young lady). The sharpest vendors hand you the rose, and once you take it, ask for anywhere between 10 and 20 pesos ($1 to $2) in exchange.

If you don't feel like buying the rose, don't take it to begin with; after it's in your hands, it's too late. These children are generally "managed" by adult operators, known as *Marías*. If you truly feel sorry for them or want to help the children, bring them toys or clothes on your next trip. Buying flowers from them simply assures their continued place on the streets — and the money mostly goes to their "manager."

Say Hello Like a Local

Despite the "macho" image of Mexico's men, when it comes to exchanging greetings, there's little reserve — in Mexico, everybody greets each other effusively. Men friends commonly share a big bear hug punctuated by a slap or two on the back. Men kiss women on the cheek once. Women kiss each other on the cheek once as well. Long-time friends hug and hold both hands for several seconds. Friends and acquaintances — and even people who have just met — exchange kisses and hugs when saying good-bye as well.

Distinguish between a Catcall and a Compliment

In Mexico, light-skinned, light-haired people are referred to as *güero* or *güera,* so if you're blonde and female, be prepared for lots of "güera, güerita" as you walk by. Understand that it's intended more as a compliment — though at times it may sound as if it's a sleazy catcall.

Recognize the Sign of the Cross

Confirming the deeply ingrained Catholic background of the Mexican culture, people often cross themselves as they walk or ride in front of a church as a sign of respect.

Mind the Macho Manner

Mexicans love to party and mingle, but Mexican men are known for being very jealous and protective of their women. Whenever you're at a nightclub, make sure that you check that the Mexican beauty you strike up a conversation with is not there with a boyfriend, husband, or other male companion. In large groups, your best bet is to start up a conversation with the guys in the group and let them introduce you to the girls.

Chapter 17

Top Ten (or So) Myths and Misconceptions about Mexico

● ●

In This Chapter

▶ Getting the geography straight

▶ Dissecting the stereotypical preconceptions

▶ Solving food and drink misconceptions

● ●

*I*f you've never visited Mexico, you may have some preconceptions about what you're likely to find here. Perhaps you think that the geography — apart from the beaches — is an arid landscape with a uniformly hot climate. Or you may think that you should only drink tequila as a shot — doused with lime and salt.

This chapter explains some of the most common misconceptions about this vast country and its rich culture. Read on — and the next time someone starts talking about how you can't drink the water in Mexico, you can set them straight!

Don't Drink the Water

In the past, visitors often returned home from Mexico with stomach illnesses (a condition known in Mexico as *turista* and colloquially in the United States as "Montezuma's revenge"), but this type of vacation souvenir is a rarity today. Massive investments in an improved infrastructure and a general increase in standards of cleanliness and hygiene have practically wiped out the problem. However, you can easily play it safe and drink bottled water. In addition, ice served in tourist establishments is purified. For more on how to prevent turista, see Chapter 7.

Mexicans Who Don't Speak English Are Hard of Hearing

At least it *appears* that many visitors buy into this statement. Some travelers seem to believe that a native Spanish speaker will somehow get over his or her inability to understand English if the English-speaking individual talks *even louder*. Many Mexicans understand at least some English, especially those in popular tourist areas.

Try this tip — and I guarantee it will work: Instead of panicking and starting to yell in order to get your point across, ask nicely for help, and an English-speaking local will come to assist you. (Better yet, try a few of the handy Spanish phrases listed in Appendix B to start a conversation.)

Another thing to keep in mind: Should you voice any negative comments about Mexico or Mexicans, don't assume that no one around you can understand your comments — you may find yourself in an embarrassing situation.

Mexico Is the Land of Sombreros and Siestas

The common image of a Mexican napping under his sombrero exists in some minds, but this stereotype is mostly made of myth. Today, Mexico is a mix of contemporary business professionals and traditional agrarian populations. The afternoon break — from 2 to 4 p.m. — is still a wonderful tradition, but rather than being a time for siesta, it's the time when families come together for their main meal of the day. The more familiar you become with Mexico, the more you find that the people are overwhelmingly hard-working, hospitable, and honest.

All Mexican Food Is Spicy

Not all Mexican food is spicy — although Mexican food does include some of the most intriguingly flavored foods I've ever enjoyed. Although spicy sauces are likely to be in the vicinity of the food you're served, the truth is that many delicious Mexican dishes don't include chile peppers among their ingredients. (See Chapter 18 for a list of some of my favorite regional dishes.)

Mexico Has No Drinking or Drug Laws

When on vacation, many travelers tend to let loose — and some tend to overindulge. Because of the welcoming and casual nature of Mexico, many visitors believe that the sale of alcoholic beverages — or illegal drugs — is unregulated. This belief is simply not true. The legal drinking age in Mexico is 18, and technically, you're not allowed to drink openly in public. However, if you're not acting intoxicated, you can generally enjoy a beer or even a cocktail while you stroll around town.

As with most things in Mexico, it's not so much what you do but how you do it. Although you can drink on public beaches, you can't be inebriated in public, so once again, beware of how much you drink and how well you can handle your alcohol intake. White-clad police patrolling Mexico's beaches are a common sight.

With regard to drugs, let me get straight to the point: They're illegal, and carrying even a small amount of marijuana can earn you a very unpleasant trip to jail. So keep your trip free of undesired encounters with the law and don't carry, buy, or use any kind of drugs. Remember that Mexican law states that you're guilty until proven innocent.

A Jeep Rental Is Really $10 a Day

One of the most common lures a timeshare salesperson uses is the "Rent a Jeep for $10 per day" enticement. Sure, it's true that the Jeep is only $10, but only after you spend up to half a day listening to an often high-pressured sales pitch. You decide — what's your vacation time really worth? And always remember: *If it looks too good to be true. . . .*

If in Trouble, Pay a Mordida

The concept of paying off someone for a favor or to overlook a transgression is as clichéd as the image of the sleeping Mexican under his sombrero. Although the idea of paying a mordida (translated literally as "little bite") may have been rooted in truth for a long time, in Mexico's new political era, an active campaign is underway to keep dishonesty to a minimum and to clean house of corrupt public servants. Many old-school traffic cops will still take a bribe when offered; however, officers belonging to the new generation of federal policemen are tested for honesty, and the penalties for corrupt behavior are severe — as are the penalties for those civilians inducing corruption by offering bribes to police officers. My suggestion is don't offer a "tip" or mordida to ease your way out of trouble; the best course of action is to just act politely and see what the problem is.

You Can Go Everywhere Wearing Just Your Swimsuit

You may be in a seaside resort, but keep in mind that it's also a home and place of business for many Mexicans. Wearing swim trunks or a *pareo* (sarong) skirt wrapped around your bikini while you're on your way to the beach is fine, but I recommend that you put on a shirt or a sundress when you plan to explore the town or when you take a tour that involves riding around in a bus. You can still go casual, but Mexicans frown upon tourists who can't tell the difference between beach and town — especially true when it comes to going into any church wearing inappropriate clothing.

If you want to blend in, just take a few minutes to see what the locals wear around town. Usually, walking shorts and T-shirts are fine everywhere. One more thing: Topless sunbathing is neither customary nor legal in Mexico — so avoid problems with the law and keep your top on.

Mexico Is a Desert, and It's Hot Everywhere

It's not true that Mexico is arid year-round: The geography of Mexico includes pine forests, and occasional snowfalls hit some of the country's higher elevations. Although the Yucatán beach resorts covered in this book do enjoy sultry climates, bringing along a sweater or light jacket for cool evenings is always wise, especially during winter months.

Chapter 18

Top Ten Most Delicious Yucatecan Dishes

● ●

In This Chapter

▶ Discovering the region's most notable specialties and sauces

▶ Indulging in uniquely Mexican beverages

● ●

Some like it hot . . . and then there's Mexican food! But true Mexican cuisine is noted more for its unique way of combining flavors — sweet and hot, chocolate and chiles — than for its fire appeal.

This chapter explains some of the most flavorful and traditional Mexican dishes popular in the Yucatán region that you're likely to see on a menu here — go ahead and be adventurous! Let your taste buds have a vacation from the foods you know and explore the favored flavors of Mexico.

Pescado Tikik-Chik

You're in a Mexican beach resort, so you're almost certain to indulge in the fresh fish and seafood. One of the most traditional and tasty ways to prepare fish is to grill it after it's marinated in a flavorful sauce. The name of this preparation — and the spices in the sauce — vary by region. Along the Yucatán coast, the Mexican-Caribbean variation of this fish is called *tikik-chik* or *tikin-chik* and is prepared by marinating the fish in a sauce of Worcestershire, lime juice, sour-orange juice, mild red-pepper paste, and *achiote* — annatto seed paste. The fish is then sandwiched between two tikin palm fronds and cooked slowly over a wood fire. Yum!

Pibil

Pibil is a thick, rich sauce used to prepare either pork or chicken. The traditional cooking method calls for the meat to be first marinated in this sauce made from *achiote* (annatto seed paste) plus a mixture of bitter orange juice, onions, tomatoes, habanero peppers, and the herb *epazote.* The meat is then wrapped in banana leaves and cooked in an underground pit, called a *pib.*

Cochinita Pibil is shredded pork in *pibil* sauce, traditionally served in tacos (corn tortillas). Typical garnishes include *Xnipec* (minced purple onions and habanero peppers in sour orange juice) or pickled onions (a milder version of *Xnipec,* prepared without habanero peppers).

Tamales

Tamales served in the Yucatán area are quite different from the ones typically found in the United States, which tend to be compact and greasy. Here, these tasty bundles of corn dough are cooked in several different ways, but all of them are wrapped in banana leaves, rather than the corn husks that are used in the central and northern regions of Mexico. They come with a variety of fillings, but usually include pork or chicken.

One popular variety is the *Vaporcitos* (translated as "little steamed ones"), steamed tamales filled with either chicken or corn in a red sauce made with annatto seed paste, tomatoes, oregano, onions, and garlic. Other tamales are baked rather than steamed; these types are called *chachaquas.* A popular variation is the *Tamal Pibipollo,* which is a huge chicken-filled tamale wrapped in banana leaves and cooked in an underground pit (*pib*). These tamales look charred due to their method of cooking, but when you open the leaves (which you don't eat), you cut into a fluffy, cake-like tamale filled with juicy chicken. The bean-filled version of this pit-baked tamale is called *Tamal de Espelóns* (espelóns are tiny black beans). *Colados* are tamales where the dough is cooked by simmering it in chicken broth and then wrapped in banana leaves and steamed.

Panuchos

The Yucatán's favorite snack, the *panucho,* is a must to try when you visit these lands. Panuchos are pan-fried corn tortillas, which puff up and are then slit and filled with refried beans and shredded pork or chicken. The tortilla is then topped with lettuce and accompanied by pickled onions.

Salbutes

One of the most traditional dishes in Yucatecan cuisine, s*albutes* are usually served as a snack or appetizer. A Mayan version of an enchilada, they're made from a corn tortilla dipped in a pumpkin seed puree, which is stuffed with hard-boiled eggs, topped with more puree, and served warm with a mild tomato sauce.

Huevos Motuleños

Mexican food lovers and connoisseurs would frown if I said that *huevos motuleños* are the Yucatán's version of the traditional Mexican *huevos rancheros*. Instead, I'll say that, though they share the same basic principles of assembly, *motuleños* are in a class of their own. This layered dish consists of refried beans spread on a plate topped by a pan-fried corn tortilla, topped by a fried egg, followed by a lightly spiced tomato sauce, another fried tortilla, and then more sauce. The whole creation is finished off with chopped ham, peas, and fried plantain slices.

Ceviche

Ceviche is one of Mexico's more traditional ways to enjoy fish and seafood. Ceviche is usually made of fish, but it may also be made from seafood, including shrimp, octopus, crab, and even conch (the last is a Cancún specialty). The fresh fish — or seafood — is marinated in lime and vinegar and mixed with chopped tomatoes, onions, and — depending on the region — cucumbers and carrots.

Puchero

The traditional Sunday dish in the Yucatán, *puchero* is a tasty three-meat (chicken, pork, and beef) stew with mashed vegetables and cooked plantains. People in the Yucatán say that Sundays aren't complete unless they have puchero.

Liquados

Not quite a meal, yet more than a beverage, *liquados* are blended drinks of fresh fruit, ice, and either water or milk. Popular flavors include mango, banana, pineapple, or watermelon. You can also make up your own combination of tropical fruit flavors. They're delicious, especially in the sultry heat.

Café de Olla

The popularity and tradition of drinking coffee is nothing new to Mexico, so to experience a taste of the past, try the traditional Mexican version called *café de olla*. The espresso-strength coffee is prepared in an earthenware pot and spiced with cinnamon, cloves, and raw brown sugar. It's certain to wake you up!

Appendix A

Quick Concierge

● ●

Abbreviations

Common address abbreviations include *Apdo.* (post office box), *Av.* or *Ave.* (*avenida;* avenue), *Blvd.* (*boulevard*), *c/* (*calle;* street), *Calz.* (*calzada;* boulevard), *Dept.* (apartments), and *s/n* (*sin numero* or without a number).

The "C" on faucets stands for *caliente* (hot), and "F" stands for *fría* (cold). "PB" (*planta baja*) means ground floor, and most buildings count the next floor up as the first floor (1).

American Express

All major resort destinations have local American Express representatives. For a detailed list of all representatives, visit the AmEx Web site at www.american express.com/mexico/. For credit card and traveler's checks information, call ☎ 800-504-0400 toll-free inside Mexico. The office that services the destinations covered in this guide is located in Cancún (Av. Tulum 408; ☎ 998-884-6942).

ATMs

Automated teller machines are widely available in the major resort towns, although you find fewer in smaller destinations. They're a great option to get cash at an excellent exchange rate. To find the closest ATM, visit these Web sites for the most popular networks: Plus (www.visa.com/pd/atm) and Cirrus (www.mastercard.com/atm). (See Chapter 6 for further details.)

Business Hours

In general, businesses in resort destinations are open daily between 9 a.m. and 8 p.m.; although many close between 2 and 4 p.m. Smaller businesses also tend to close on Sundays. The larger resort destinations have extended business hours — many shops stay open until 9 p.m. Bank hours are Monday to Friday 8:30 or 9 a.m. to anywhere between 3 and 7 p.m. Increasingly, banks are offering Saturday hours in at least one branch.

Credit Cards

Most stores, restaurants, and hotels accept credit cards. However, smaller destinations along the Riviera Maya, such as Tulum, where telephone lines aren't always available to process the authorization for the charge, may not be so credit-card friendly. The same goes for smaller, family-run shops and restaurants. You can withdraw cash from your credit card at most ATMs, but make sure that you know your PIN and you've cleared the card for foreign withdrawals with your bank. For credit-card emergencies, call the following numbers: **American Express** ☎ 001-880-221-7282, **MasterCard** ☎ 001-880-307-7309, and **Visa** ☎ 001-880-336-8472. These numbers connect you to the U.S. toll-free numbers to report lost or stolen credit cards; however, the call is not toll-free from Mexico.

Currency

The currency in Mexico is the Mexican peso. Paper currency comes in denominations of 20, 50, 100, 200, and 500 pesos. Coins come in denominations of 1, 2, 5, 10, 20 pesos, and 50 centavos (100 centavos equal 1 peso). The currency-exchange rate is about ten pesos to one U.S. dollar.

Customs

All travelers to Mexico are required to present proof of citizenship, such as a valid passport, an original birth certificate with a raised seal, or naturalization papers, and also need to have a Mexican tourist card (FMT), which is free of charge and can be attained through travel agencies and airlines and at all boarder-crossing points going into Mexico. For more information, see Chapter 7.

Doctors/Dentists

Every embassy and consulate can recommend local doctors and dentists with good training and modern equipment; some of the doctors and dentists even speak English. See the list of embassies and consulates under the "Embassies/Consulates," section later in this appendix. Hotels with a large foreign clientele can often recommend English-speaking doctors as well.

Drug Laws

To be blunt, don't use or possess illegal drugs in Mexico. Mexican officials have no tolerance for drug users, and jail is their solution. If you go to jail, you have very little hope of getting out until the sentence (usually a long one) is completed, or heavy fines or bribes are paid. Remember, in Mexico, the legal system assumes that you're guilty until proven innocent. (*Note:* It isn't uncommon to be befriended by a fellow user, only to be turned in by that "friend," who then collects a bounty.) Bring prescription drugs in their original containers. If possible, pack a copy of the original prescription with the generic name of the drug. U.S. Customs officials are also on the lookout for diet drugs that are sold in Mexico but illegal in the United States. Possession of these drugs may land you in a U.S. jail. If you buy antibiotics over the counter (which you can do in Mexico) — say, for a sinus infection — and still have some left, you probably won't be hassled by U.S. Customs.

Electricity

The electrical system in Mexico is 110 volts AC (60 cycles), as it is in the United States and Canada, but in reality, it may cycle more slowly and overheat your appliances. To compensate, select a medium or low speed for hair dryers. Many older hotels still have electrical outlets for flat, two-prong plugs; you'll need an adapter for any modern electrical apparatus that has three prongs or an enlarged end on one of the two prongs. Many first-class and deluxe hotels have the three-holed outlets (*trifásicos* in Spanish). Hotels that don't have these outlets may have adapters to loan, but to be sure, carry your own.

Embassies/Consulates

Embassies and consulates can provide valuable lists of doctors and lawyers, as well as regulations concerning marriages in Mexico. Contrary to popular belief, your embassy cannot get you out of a Mexican jail, provide postal or banking services, or fly you home when you run out of money. However, consular officers can provide you with advice on most matters and problems. Most countries have a representative embassy in Mexico City, and many have consular offices or representatives in the provinces.

The embassy of the **United States** is in Mexico City (Paseo de la Reforma 305; ☎ 55-5209-9100). Its hours are Monday to Friday 8:30 a.m. to 5:30 p.m. You can visit the embassy's Web site at www.usembassy-mexico.gov for a list of street addresses for the U.S. consulates inside Mexico. U.S. consular agencies are in Cancún (☎ 998-883-0272) and in Cozumel (☎ 987-872-4574).

The embassy of **Australia** is in Mexico City at Rubén Darío 55, Polanco (☎ 55-5531-5225; Fax: 55-5531-9552). It's open Monday to Friday 9 a.m. to 1 p.m.

The Embassy of **Canada** is also in Mexico City (Schiller 529, in Polanco; ☎ 55-5724-7900).

It's open Monday through Friday 9 a.m. to 1 p.m. and 2 to 5 p.m. (At other times, the name of an officer on duty is posted on the embassy door.) Visit the Web site at www.canada.org.mx for a complete list of the addresses of the consular agencies in Mexico. In Cancún, the Canadian Consulate is at Plaza Caracol 3rd floor, (☎ 998-883-3360; e-mail: cancun@canada.org.mx). It's open Monday through Friday 9 a.m to 5 p.m.

The embassy of **New Zealand** in Mexico City is at José Luis Lagrange 103, 10th floor, Col. Los Morales Polanco (☎ 5-5283-9460; Fax: 5-5283-9460; E-mail: kiwimexico@compuserve.com.mx).

The Embassy of the **United Kingdom** is at Río Lerma 71, Col. Cuauhtemoc (☎ 55-5207-2089, 55-5207-7672) in Mexico City. The embassy's Web site, which you can visit at www.embajadabritanica.com.mx, has an updated list of honorary consuls in Mexico. Honorary British consuls are in Acapulco (☎ 744-484-1735), Cancún (☎ 998-881-0100), and Huatulco (☎ 958-587-1742) — leave a message.

The Embassy of **Ireland** is located in Mexico City on Blvd. Cerrada Avila Camacho 76, 3rd floor, Col. Lomas de Chapultepec (☎ 55-5520-5803).

The embassy of **South Africa** is also in Mexico City on Andres Bello, 109th floor, Col. Polanco (☎ 55-5282-9260).

Emergencies

In case of emergency, always contact your embassy or consulate. For police emergencies, you must dial ☎ **060,** which will connect you to the local police department. Remember that in most cases, the person answering the phone doesn't speak English. The 24-hour tourist help line from Mexico City is ☎ 800-903-9200 or 55-5250-0151. A tourist legal assistance office *(Procuraduría del Turista)* is located in Mexico City (☎ 55-5625-8153, 55-5625-8154). Although the

phones are frequently busy, they do offer 24-hour service, and an English-speaking person is always available.

Health

No special immunizations are required. As is often true when traveling anywhere in the world, intestinal problems are the most common afflictions experienced by travelers. Drink only bottled water and stay away from uncooked foods, especially fruits and vegetables. Antibiotics and antidiarrheal medications are readily available in all drugstores.

Hotlines

The **Mexico Hotline** (☎ 800-44-MEXICO) is an excellent source for general information; you can request brochures on the country and get answers to the most commonly asked questions. While in Mexico, contact the 24-hour tourist help line, **Infotur** (☎ 800-903-9200), for information regarding hotels, restaurants, attractions, hospitals with English-speaking staff, and so on.

Information

The best source of information is the tourist help line **Infotur** (☎ 800-903-9200); however, it's important that you have a general idea of the information you're requesting — the approximate name of the hotel or restaurant, the name or subject matter of the museum, and so on. You can also find telephone-number information inside Mexico by dialing ☎ 040; however, it's very common to find that the telephone numbers are not listed under the known name of the establishment. A reminder: Very few information operators speak English.

Internet Access

In large cities and resort areas, a growing number of 5-star hotels offer business centers with Internet access. You can also find cybercafes in destinations that are popular with expatriates and business travelers. Even in remote spots, Internet access is common now — it's often their best way of communicating with the outside world. If you plan to check your e-mail while in Mexico, register for a Web-based e-mail address, such as those from Hotmail or Yahoo!

Language

The official language in Mexico is Spanish, but you'll find that a fair number of Mexicans who live and work in resort areas speak some English. Mexicans are very patient when it comes to foreigners trying to speak Spanish. See Appendix B for commonly used terms in Spanish.

Legal Aid

International Legal Defense Counsel (111 S. 15th St., 24th floor, Packard Building, Philadelphia, PA 19102; ☎ 215-977-9982) is a law firm specializing in legal difficulties of Americans abroad. Also, see "Embassies/ Consulates" and "Emergencies," earlier in this appendix.

Liquor Laws

The legal drinking age in Mexico is 18; however, it's extremely rare that anyone is asked for identification or denied purchase. Grocery stores sell everything from beer and wine to national and imported liquors. You can buy liquor 24 hours a day, but during major elections and a few official holidays, dry laws often are enacted as long as 24 hours beforehand. The laws apply to foreign tourists as well as local residents, even though it's not uncommon to find a few hotels and nightclubs that manage to obtain special permits to sell alcohol. Mexican authorities are beginning to target drunk drivers more aggressively. It's a good idea to drive defensively.

Drinking in the street is not legal, but many tourists do it. Use your better judgment and try to avoid carrying on while sporting beer bottles and cans — you're not only exposing yourself to the eyes of the authorities, but most Mexicans consider public intoxication tacky behavior.

Mail

Postage for a postcard or letter is 59¢, and the item may arrive at its destination anywhere between one to six weeks after you send it off. A registered letter costs $1.90. Sending a package can be quite expensive — the Mexican postal service charges $8 per kilo (2.20 pounds) — and unreliable; it takes between two and six weeks, if it arrives at all. Packages are frequently lost within the Mexican postal system, although the situation has improved in recent years. Federal Express, DHL, UPS, or other reputable, international-mail services are the best option.

Newspapers/Magazines

Mexico's English-language newspaper, the *News,* is published in Mexico City and distributed nationally. Newspaper kiosks in larger Mexican cities carry a selection of English-language magazines. Most resort towns have their own local publications in English, which provide helpful hints and fun reading tailored to visitors. In Cancún, you can find a wealth of information in *Cancún Tips,* a monthly publication in two formats: a small guide, and a larger, glossy magazine.

Pharmacies

Farmacias will sell you just about anything you want, with or without a prescription. Most pharmacies are open Monday to Saturday 8 a.m. to 8 p.m. Generally, one or two 24-hour pharmacies are located in the major resort areas. Pharmacies take turns staying open during off-hours, so if you're in a smaller town and you need to buy medicine after normal hours, ask for the *farmacia de turno* (pharmacist on duty).

Police

It's quite common to find that the majority of police forces in tourist areas are very protective of international visitors. Several cities, including Cancún, have gone so far as to set up a special corps of English-speaking tourist police to assist with directions, guidance,

and more. In case of a police emergency, dial
☎ **060** to contact the local police department, keeping in mind that, unless you're
dealing with tourist police, the force is
unlikely to speak English.

Restrooms

Public restrooms are usually more of an
adventure than a service — you can never
tell whether they'll be clean or toilet paper
will be available. Public restrooms usually
charge anywhere between 2 and 5 pesos
(20 to 50 cents), which gives you access
and a few squares of toilet paper.

Safety

Most resort areas in Mexico are very safe;
however, it's better to be prepared than sorry.
A few points to keep in mind: Before you
leave home, prepare for the theft or loss of
your travel documents by making two photo-
copies of them. Keep each copy and the original documents in separate places. Lock your
passport and valuables in the hotel safety-
deposit box. Keep credit-card company
phone numbers and the numbers of traveler's
checks somewhere other than your purse or
wallet. Don't dress or behave in a conspicu-
ous manner. When visiting crowded places,
be aware of your wallet or purse at all times.
Leave your best jewelry at home — who
wants jewelry tan lines anyway?

Taxes

Most of Mexico has a 15% value-added tax
(IVA) on goods and services, and it's supposed to be included in the posted price.
This tax is 10% in Cancún and Cozumel, as
they're considered "port zones" and qualify
for a reduction of duties. Mexico charges all
visitors an entry tax of $15, which is usually
included in the price of your plane ticket.
Mexico also imposes an exit tax of around
$18 on every foreigner leaving the country,
which again, is usually included in the price
of airline tickets.

Telephone/Fax

After a recent countrywide system change,
all telephone numbers in Mexico are now
seven digits plus a three-digit area code,
except for Mexico City, Guadalajara, and
Monterrey where local calls require that you
dial the last eight digits of the published
phone number. Many fax numbers are also
regular telephone numbers — you have to
ask whoever answers your call for the fax
tone. *("Me da tono de fax, por favor.")*
Cellular phones are very popular for small
businesses in resort areas and smaller com-
munities. To dial a cellular number inside the
same area code, dial 044 and then the
number — depending on the area, you may
need to dial the last seven digits or the
seven digits plus the three-digit area code.
To dial the cellular phone from anywhere
else in Mexico, first dial 01 and then the
ten-digit number, including the area code.

To dial any number inside Mexico from the
United States, just dial 011-52 plus the ten-
digit number.

The country code for Mexico is 52. To call
home from Mexico, dial 00 plus the country
code you're calling and then the area code
and phone number. To call the United States
and Canada, you need to dial 001 plus the
area code and the number. The country
code for the United Kingdom is 44; the
country code for New Zealand is 64, and the
country code for Australia 61. You can reach
an **AT&T** operator at ☎ 01-800-288-2872,
MCI at ☎ 01-800-021-8000, **Sprint** at ☎ 001-
800-877-8000, and **British Telecom** (BT) at
☎ 01-800-123-0244. Mexican pay phones
may sometimes require a coin deposit.

To call operator assistance for calls inside
Mexico, dial 020; for operator assistance for
international calls, dial 090. Both numbers
provide assistance for person-to-person and
collect calls.

Time Zone

Mexico's Yucatán peninsula falls within
Central Standard Time. Most of Mexico
observes Daylight Savings Time, but the time
change lasts for a shorter period of time
than it does in the rest of the world.

Tipping

Most service employees in Mexico count on tips for the majority of their income — especially true for bellboys and waiters. Bellboys should receive the equivalent of 50¢ to $1 U.S. per bag; waiters generally receive 10% to 20% depending on the level of service. In Mexico, it's not customary to tip taxi drivers, unless you hire them by the hour, or they provide guide or other special services. Don't use U.S. coins to tip.

Water

Most hotels have decanters or bottles of purified water in the rooms, and the better hotels have purified water from regular taps or special taps marked *agua purificada.* Some hotels charge for in-room bottled water. Virtually any hotel, restaurant, or bar will bring you purified water if you specifically request it, but they'll usually charge you. Bottled, purified water is sold widely at drugstores and grocery stores. Some popular brands are Santa María, Ciel, and Bonafont. Evian and other imported brands are also widely available.

Toll-Free Numbers and Web Sites

Airlines Serving Cancún Airport

Aeromexico
☎ 800-237-6639
www.aeromexico.com

Alaska Airlines
☎ 800-426-0333
www.alaskaair.com

American Airlines
☎ 800-433-7300
www.im.aa.com

American Trans Air
☎ 800-225-2995
www.ata.com

British Airways
☎ 800-247-9297
☎ 0845-77-333-77 in Britain
www.british-airways.com

Continental Airlines
☎ 800-525-0280
www.continental.com

Delta Air Lines
☎ 800-221-1212
www.delta.com

Mexicana
☎ 800-531-7921
www.mexicana.com

Northwest Airlines
☎ 800-225-2525
www.nwa.com

US Airways
☎ 800-428-4322
www.usairways.com

Major Car-Rental Agencies

Advantage
☎ 800-777-5500
www.advantagerentacar.com

Alamo
☎ 800-327-9633
www.goalamo.com

Auto Europe
☎ 800-223-5555
www.autoeurope.com

Avis
☎ 800-331-1212 in the continental
United States.
☎ 800-TRY-AVIS in Canada
www.avis.com

Budget
☎ 800-527-0700
www.budgetrentacar.com

Dollar
☎ 800-800-4000
www.dollar.com

Hertz
☎ 800-654-3131
www.hertz.com

National
☎ 800-CAR-RENT
www.nationalcar.com

Payless
☎ 800-PAYLESS
www.paylesscarrental.com

Thrifty
☎ 800-367-2277
www.thrifty.com

Major Local Hotel and Motel Chains

Best Western
☎ 800-528-1234
www.bestwestern.com

Blue Bay Getaway
☎ 800-BLUE-BAY
www.bluebayresorts.com

Camino Real
☎ 800-722-6466
www.caminoreal.com

Days Inn
☎ 800-325-2525
www.daysinn.com

Fiesta Americana
☎ 800-FIESTA-1
www.fiestaamericana.com

Hilton Hotels
☎ 800-HILTONS
www.hilton.com

Holiday Inn
☎ 800-HOLIDAY
www.basshotels.com

Hyatt Hotels and Resorts
☎ 800-228-9000
www.hyatt.com

Inter-Continental Hotels and Resorts
☎ 888-567-8725
www.interconti.com

Le Méridien Hotel
☎ 800-543-4300
www.lemeridien-hotels.com

Marriott Hotels (and JW Marriott)
☎ 800-228-9290
www.marriott.com

Plaza Las Glorias
☎ 800-342-AMIGO

Quinta Real
☎ 888-561-2817
www.quintareal.com

Ritz-Carlton Hotel
☎ 800-241-3333
www.ritzcarlton.com

Sheraton Hotels and Resorts
☎ 800-325-3535
www.sheraton.com

Westin Hotels and Resorts
☎ 800-937-8461
www.westin.com

Where to Get More Information

The following tourist boards and embassies provide valuable information regarding traveling in Mexico, including information on entry requirements and customs allowances.

The **Mexico Tourism Board** (Internet: www.visitmexico.com) has offices in several major North American cities, in addition to the main office in Mexico City (☎ 55-5203-1103). The toll-free information number is ☎ 800-44-MEXICO in the United States. and Canada. U.S. offices are in Chicago, IL (300 N. Michigan, 4th Floor, Chicago, IL, 60601; ☎ 312-606-9252); Houston, TX (4507 San Jacinto, Suite 308, Houston, TX, 77074; ☎ 713-772-2581, ext.105); Los Angeles, CA (2401 W. 6th St., Los Angeles, CA, 90057; ☎ 213-351-2069; Fax: 213-351-2074); Miami, FL (1200 NW 78th St., Miami, FL, 33126; ☎ 305-718-4095), and New York, NY (21 E. 63rd St., 2nd Floor, New York, NY, 10021; ☎ 212-821-0304). In addition, the Mexican Embassy Tourism Delegate is in Washington, D.C. (1911 Pennsylvania Ave., Washington, DC 20005; ☎ 202-728-1750). Locations in Canada include Montreal (1 Place Ville-Marie, Suite 1931, Montreal, QUEB, H3B 2C3; ☎ 514-871-1052); Toronto (2 Floor St. W., Suite 1502, Toronto, ON, M4W 3E2; ☎ 416-925-0704); and Vancouver (999 W. Hastings, Suite 1110, Vancouver, BC, V6C 2W2; ☎ 604-669-2845). The Mexican Embassy office is at 1500-45 O'Connor St., Ottawa, ON, K1P 1A4 (☎ 613-233-8988; Fax: 613-235-9123).

The **U.S. State Department** and the Overseas Citizens Services division (☎ 202-647-5225) offer a consular information sheet on Mexico that contains a compilation of safety, medical, driving, and general travel information gleaned from reports by official U.S. State Department offices in Mexico. In addition to calling, you can request the consular information sheet by fax at ☎ 202-647-3000. The State Department is also on the Internet: Check out http://travel.state.gov/mexico.html for the consular information sheet on Mexico; http://travel.state.gov/travel_warnings.html for other consular information sheets and travel warnings; and http://travel.state.gov/tips_mexico.html for the State Department's *Tips for Travelers to Mexico*.

For a **24-hour Tourist Help Line,** dial ☎ 800-903-9200 toll-free inside Mexico, and you can get information from English-speaking operators as to where to go for medical assistance and other types of assistance. It's also a great source for general tourism information. You can always find helpful operators who will try to get the information that you need. To call this office from the United States, dial ☎ 800-482-9832.

Health information

The **Centers for Disease Control** Hotline (Internet: www.cdc.gov/
travel) is an excellent source for medical information for travelers to
Mexico and elsewhere. The main Centers for Disease Control (CDC)
Web site (www.cdc.gov/) provides detailed information on health
issues for specific countries; otherwise, you can call the CDC directly
at ☎ 800-311-3435 or 404-639-3534. For travelers to Mexico and Central
America, the number with recorded messages about specific health
issues related to this region is ☎ 877-FYI-TRIP. The toll-free fax number
for requesting information is ☎ 888-232-3299.

Embassies and consulates provide valuable lists of doctors and
lawyers, as well as regulations concerning travel in Mexico (see
"Embassies and Consulates," earlier in this chapter).

Local sources of information

Local **tourist information offices** offer all kinds of information to travelers, including brochures, maps, and destination-specific magazines
and posters. If you want them to mail information to you, allow four to
six weeks for the mail to reach you. Try these offices:

- ✔ **Cancún Convention and Visitors Bureau** (Ave. COBA Esq. Ave.
  Nader S.M.5, Cancún, Quintana Roo, Mexico 77500; ☎ 998-884-
  8073, 998-884-6531, 998-884-3438; Internet: www.gocancun.com).
  Calling their U.S. toll-free number, ☎ 800-CANCUN-8, is the easiest
  and quickest way to get a free Cancún vacation planner.

- ✔ **Isla Mujeres Tourism Office** (Av. Rueda Medina 130, Isla Mujeres,
  Quintano Roo, Mexico, C.P. 77400) across from the main pier
  between Immigration and Customs; ☎ 998-877-0767; e-mail:
  infoisla@prodigy.net.mx).

Mexico on the Web

Following is a list of several Web sites where you can find updated
information about Mexico's most popular beach resorts. But keep in
mind that most of the companies that these Web sites recommend
received this lofty status by paying some sort of advertising fee.

The **Mexico Tourism Promotion Council** developed another official
site (www.visitmexico.com) with more current information on the
different destinations in Mexico. The pages are slow to load, but the
navigation is a lot easier. The site features sections for travelers
divided by region; a good search engine usually takes you to the information you're looking for.

For low-impact travel planning, visit the **Eco Travels in Mexico** section of the award-winning Web site www.planeta.com. You can find up-to-date information on reliable eco-tour operators in Mexico. This site, updated monthly, is also an excellent source for banks and telephone services.

The electronic version of *Connect Magazine* (www.mexconnect.com) is the ideal site to begin a more in-depth, online exploration about when and where to visit Mexico. The site offers an index where you can find everything from out-of-the-way adventures to Mexico's history to recommended accommodations.

Cancún South (www.cancunsouth.com) is a great site for independent travelers looking to explore the Riviera Maya. The site is easy to navigate and offers a wealth of information specific to the area.

Cozumel.net (www.cozumel.net) provides detailed information about the island's life. In my opinion, this site has the most reliable information about Cozumel — it even lists ferry schedules in the "About Cozumel" section.

Other Internet travel resources

Following is a selection of Web sites that can help you with the important stuff related to your Yucatán vacation — figuring out where to get cash, how to ask for a cold beer, where to go to send an e-mail to your friends back home, how to find really great deals, and so on.

At **Foreign Languages for Travelers** (www.travlang.com), you can learn basic terms in more than 70 languages and click on any underlined phrase to hear what it sounds like. *Note:* Free audio software and speakers are required.

Intellicast (www.intellicast.com) has weather forecasts for all 50 United States and cities around the world. *Note:* Temperatures are in Celsius for many international destinations.

The **Universal Currency Converter** (ww.xe.net/ucc/) lets you see what your dollar or pound is worth in more than 100 other countries.

With **Visa ATM Locator** (www.visa.com) or **MasterCard ATM Locator** (www.mastercard.com), you can find ATMs in hundreds of cities in the United States and around the world.

Travel Secrets (www.travelsecrets.com) is one of the best travel sites around. The site offers advice and tips on how to find the lowest prices for airlines, hotels, and cruises, and it also provides a listing of links for airfare deals, airlines, booking engines, discount travel, resources, hotels, and travel magazines.

Appendix B

Glossary of Spanish Words and Phrases

* *

Most Mexicans are very patient with foreigners who try to speak their language. And your trip can be much easier and more enjoyable if you know a few basic Spanish phrases.

In this glossary, I list some simple words and phrases for expressing basic needs. I also include common menu items and a description for each to take some of the guesswork out of ordering meals on your vacation.

English-Spanish Phrases

English	Spanish	Pronunciation
Good day (Good morning)	**Buenos días**	*bway*-nohss *dee*-ahss
Good evening/afternoon	**Buenas tardes**	*bway*-nahss *tar*-days
Good night	**Buenas noches**	*bway*-nahss *noh*-chase
How are you?	**¿Cómo está?**	*koh*-moh ess-*tah*?
Very well	**Muy bien**	mwee byen
Thank you	**Gracias**	*grah*-see-ahss
You're welcome	**De nada**	day *nah*-dah
Good-bye	**Adiós**	ah-*dee-ohss*
Please	**Por favor**	pohr fah-*vohr*
Yes	**Sí**	see
No	**No**	noh
Excuse me	**Disculpe**	dees-*kool*-peh
Give me	**Déme**	*day*-may
Where is . . .?	**¿Dónde está . . .?**	*dohn*-day ess-*tah*?

(continued)

English-Spanish Phrases *(continued)*

English	*Spanish*	*Pronunciation*
the station	**la estación**	lah ess-tah-*seown*
a hotel	**un hotel**	oon oh-*tel*
a gas station	**una gasolinera**	*oon*-ah gah-so-lee-*nay*-rah
a restaurant	**un restaurante**	oon res-tow-*rahn*-tay
the toilet	**el baño**	el *bahn*-yoh
a good doctor	**un buen médico**	oon bwayn *may*-dee-co
the road to . . .	**el camino . . .**	el cah-*mee*-noh ah/
To the right	**A la derecha**	ah lah day-*reh*-chuh
To the left	**A la izquierda**	ah lah ees-kee-*ehr*-thah
Straight ahead	**Derecho**	day-*reh*-cho
I would like	**Quisiera**	key-see-*ehr*-ah
I want	**Quiero**	*kyehr*-oh
to eat	**comer**	ko-*mayr*
a room	**una habitación**	*oon*-nuh ha-bee-tah-*seeown*
Do you have . . .?	**¿Tiene usted . . .?**	tyah-nay oos-*ted*?
a book	**un libro**	oon *lee*-bro
a dictionary	**un diccionario**	oon deek-see-on-*ar*-ee-oh
How much is it?	**¿Cuánto cuesta?**	*kwahn*-to *kwess*-tah?
When?	**¿Cuándo?**	*kwahn*-doh?
What?	**¿Qué?**	kay?
There is (Is there . . .?)	**¿Hay?**	eye?
What is there?	**¿Qué hay?**	kay eye?
Yesterday	**Ayer**	ah-*yer*
Today	**Hoy**	oy
Tomorrow	**Mañana**	mahn-*yahn*-ah
Good	**Bueno**	*bway*-no
Bad	**Malo**	*mah*-lo
Better (best)	**Mejor**	meh-*hor*

English	Spanish	Pronunciation
More	**Más**	mahs
Less	**Menos**	*may*-noss
No smoking	**Se prohibe fumar**	say pro-*ee*-bay foo-*mahr*
Postcard	**Tarjeta postal**	tar-*heh*-ta pohs-*tahl*
Insect repellent	**Repelente contra insectos**	reh-peh-*lehn*-te *cohn*-trah een-*sehk*-tos

More Useful Phrases

English	Spanish	Pronunciation
Do you speak English?	**¿Habla usted inglés?**	*ah*-blah oo-*sted* een-*glays*?
Is there anyone here who speaks English?	**¿Hay alguien aquí que hable inglés?**	eye *ahl*-gyen ah-*key* kay ah-blay een-*glays*?
I speak a little Spanish.	**Hablo un poco de español.**	*ah*-blow oon *poh*-koh day ess-pah-*nyol*
I don't understand Spanish very well.	**No entiendo español muy bien.**	noh ehn-tee-*ehn*-do ess-pah-*nyol* moo-ee bee-ayn
The meal is good.	**Me gusta la comida.**	may *goo*-sta lah koh-*mee*-dah
What time is it?	**¿Qué hora es?**	kay *oar*-ah ess?
May I see your menu?	**¿Puedo ver el menu?**	*puay*-tho veyr el may-*noo*?
The check, please.	**La cuenta, por favor.**	lah *quayn*-tah pohr fa-*vorh*
What do I owe you?	**¿Cuánto le debo?**	*kwahn*-toh leh *day*-boh?
What did you say?	**¿Mande?** (formal)	*mahn*-day?
	¿Cómo dijo? (informal)	*koh*-moh dee-ho?
I want (to see)	**Quiero (ver)**	key-*yehr*-oh vehr
a room	**un cuarto** or **una habitación**	oon *kwar*-toh *or* oon-nah ah-bee-tah-*see-on*
for two persons	**para dos personas**	*pahr*-ah doss pehr-*sohn*-as
with (without) bathroom	**con (sin) baño**	kohn (seen) *bah*-nyoh
We are staying here only.	**Nos quedamos aquí solamente.**	nohs kay-*dahm*-ohss ah-*key* sohl-ah-*mayn*-tay

(continued)

More Useful Phrases *(continued)*

English	Spanish	Pronunciation
one night	**una noche**	oon-ah *noh*-chay
one week	**una semana**	oon-ah say-*mahn*-ah
We are leaving	**Partimos or Salimos**	pahr-*tee*-mohss; sah-*lee*-mohss
tomorrow	**mañana**	mahn-*nyan*-ah
Do you accept . . .?	**¿Acepta usted . . .?**	ah-*sayp*-tah oo-*sted*
. . . traveler's checks?	**. . . cheques de viajero?**	*chay* kays day bee-ah-*hehr*-oh
...credit cards	**...tarjetas de crédito**	tar-*hay*-tahs day *kray*-dee-toh
Is there a Laundromat?	**¿Hay una lavandería?**	eye *oon*-ah lah-*vahn*-day-ree-ah
Is . . . near here?	**Es . . . cerca de aquí?**	Ace *sehr*-ka day ah-*key*
Please send these clothes to the laundry.	**Hágame el favor de mandar esta ropa a la lavandería.**	*ah*-ga-may el fah-*vhor* day mahn-*dahr* ays-tah *rho*-pah a lah lah-*vahn*-day-ree-ah

Numbers

1	**uno** (*ooh*-noh)	17	**diecisiete** (de-*ess*-ee-*syeh*-tay)
2	**dos** (dohs)	18	**dieciocho** (dee-*ess*-ee-*oh*-choh)
3	**tres** (trayss)	19	**diecinueve** (dee-*ess*-ee-*nway*-bay)
4	**cuatro** (*kwah*-troh)	20	**veinte** (*bayn*-tay)
5	**cinco** (*seen*-koh)	30	**treinta** (*trayn*-tah)
6	**seis** (sayss)	40	**cuarenta** (kwah-*ren*-tah)
7	**siete** (*syeh*-tay)	50	**cincuenta** (seen-*kwen*-tah)
8	**ocho** (*oh*-choh)	60	**sesenta** (say-*sen*-tah)
9	**nueve** (*nway*-bay)	70	**setenta** (say-*ten*-tah)
10	**diez** (dee-ess)	80	**ochenta** (oh-*chen*-tah)
11	**once** (*ohn*-say)	90	**noventa** (noh-*ben*-tah)
12	**doce** (*doh*-say)	100	**cien** (see-*en*)

Numbers

13	**trece** (*tray*-say)		200	**doscientos** (*dos*-se-en-tos)
14	**catorce** (kah-*tor*-say)		500	**quinientos** (keen-ee-*ehn*-tos)
15	**quince** (*keen*-say)		1,000	**mil** (meal)
16	**dieciseis** (de-*ess*-ee-sayss)			

Transportation Terms

English	Spanish	Pronunciation
Airport	**Aeropuerto**	ah-ay-row-*pooh*-air-tow
Arrival gates	**Llegadas**	yay-*gah*-dahs
Departure gate	**Puerto de embarque**	*pwer*-tow day em-*bark*-kay
Baggage	**Equipajes**	eh-key-*pah*-hays
Baggage-claim area	**Recibo de equipajes**	ray-see-boh day eh-key-*pah*-hay
First class	**Primera**	pree-*mehr*-oh
Second class	**Segunda**	say-*goon*-dah
Flight	**Vuelo**	bw*ay*-low
Nonstop	**Directo**	dee-*reck*-toh
	Sin escala	seen ess-*kah*-lah
Rental car	**Arrendadora de autos**	ah-rain-da-dow-rah day autos
Bus	**Autobús**	ow-toh-*boos*
Bus or truck	**Camión**	ka-mee-*ohn*
Intercity	**Foraneo**	fohr-ah-*nay*-oh
Lane	**Carril**	kah-*rreal*
Luggage storage area	**Guarda equipaje**	gwar-dah eh-key-*pah*-hay
Originates at this station	**Local**	loh-*kahl*
Originates elsewhere	**De paso**	day *pah*-soh

(continued)

Transportation Terms *(continued)*		
English	*Spanish*	*Pronunciation*
Stops if seats available	**Para si hay lugares**	*pah-rah-see-aye-loo-gahr-ays*
Waiting room	**Sala de espera**	*saw*-lah day ess-*pehr*-ah
Ticket window	**Taquilla**	tah-*key*-lah
Toilets	**Sanitarios**	sahn-ee-tahr-*ee*-oss

Glossary of Spanish Menu Terms

Achiote: Small, red seed of the *annatto* tree.

Agua fresca: Fruit-flavored water, usually watermelon or cantaloupe where ingredients such as lemon and hibiscus flower are added.

Antojito: Typical Mexican supper foods, usually made with *masa* or tortillas and contain a filling or topping such as sausage, cheese, beans, and onions; includes such things as *tacos*, *tostadas*, *sopes*, and *garnachas* (thick tortillas).

Atole: A thick, lightly sweet, hot drink made with finely ground corn and usually flavored with vanilla, pecan, or chocolate.

Botana: An appetizer.

Buñuelos: Round, thin, deep-fried, crispy fritters dipped in sugar.

Carnitas: Pork that's been deep-cooked (not fried) in lard, simmered, and then served with corn tortillas for tacos.

Ceviche: Fresh, raw seafood marinated in fresh lime juice, garnished with chopped tomatoes, onions, chilies, and sometimes cilantro, and served with crispy, fried, whole-corn tortillas or crackers.

Chayote: A type of spiny pear-shaped squash boiled and served as an accompaniment to meat dishes.

Chiles en nogada: Poblano peppers stuffed with a mixture of ground pork and chicken, spices, fruits, raisins, and almonds, fried in a light batter, and covered in a walnut-and-cream sauce.

Chiles rellenos: Usually poblano peppers stuffed with cheese or spicy ground meat with raisins, rolled in a batter, and fried.

Churro: Tube-shaped, bread-like fritter, dipped in sugar and sometimes filled with *cajeta* (caramel) or chocolate.

Enchilada: A tortilla dipped in a sauce and usually filled with chicken or white cheese; sometimes topped with mole sauce *(enchiladas rojas or de mole)*, tomato sauce and sour cream (*enchiladas suizas*: Swiss enchiladas), a green sauce *(enchiladas verdes),* or onions, sour cream, and guacamole *(enchiladas potosinas).*

Escabeche: A lightly pickled sauce used in Yucatecán chicken stew.

Frijoles charros: Beans flavored with beer; a northern Mexican specialty.

Frijoles refritos: Pinto beans mashed and cooked with lard.

Gorditas: Thickish fried-corn tortillas, slit and stuffed with choice of cheese, beans, beef, and chicken; served with or without lettuce, tomato, and onion garnish.

Gusanos de maguey: Maguey worms, considered a delicacy; delicious when deep-fried to a crisp and served with corn tortillas for tacos.

Horchata: Lightly sweetened, refreshing drink made of ground rice or melon seeds, and ground almonds. Also know as *agua de arroz* in certain destinations on the Pacific Coast, such as Puerto Vallarta and Ixtapa.

Huevos Mexicanos: Scrambled eggs with chopped onions, hot peppers, and tomatoes.

Huevos rancheros: Fried eggs on top of a fried corn tortilla covered in a spicy or mild tomato sauce.

Huitlacoche: Sometimes spelled "cuitlacoche." A mushroom-flavored black fungus that appears on corn in the rainy season; considered a delicacy.

Machaca: Shredded, dried beef scrambled with eggs or in a mild red sauce; a specialty of northern Mexico.

Masa: Ground corn soaked in lime used as the basis for tamales, corn tortillas, and soups.

Menudo: Stew made with the lining of the cow's stomach. Served in a red or white broth. A traditional hangover cure.

Pan dulce: Lightly sweetened bread in many configurations, usually served at breakfast or bought in any bakery.

Pibil: Pit-baked pork or chicken in a sauce of tomato, onion, mild red pepper, cilantro, and vinegar.

Pipián: A sauce made with ground pumpkin seeds, nuts, and mild peppers.

Poc chuc: Slices of pork with onion marinated in a tangy, sour, orange sauce and charcoal-broiled; a Yucatecán specialty.

Pozole: Pork or chicken broth with hominy and shredded pork or chicken. The traditional recipe calls for the pork's head, but now it's commonly prepared with chicken or pork loin. Pozole is served red in Jalisco and white in Guerrero. Thursdays are the traditional day to eat pozole in Acapulco and Ixtapa.

Quesadilla: Corn or flour tortillas stuffed with melted white cheese and lightly fried.

Queso relleno: "Stuffed cheese;" a mild yellow cheese stuffed with minced meat and spices; a Yucatecán specialty.

Rompope: Delicious Mexican eggnog, invented in Puebla, made with eggs, vanilla, sugar, and rum.

Salsa verde: A cooked sauce using the green tomatillo puréed with spicy or mild hot peppers, onions, garlic, and cilantro; on tables countrywide.

Sopa de lima: A tangy soup made with chicken broth and accented with fresh lime; popular in Yucatán.

Sopa de Tortilla: A traditional chicken broth-based soup, seasoned with chilies, tomatoes, onion, and garlic, with crispy fried strips of corn tortillas.

Sope: Pronounced "*soh*-pay;" an *antojito* similar to a *garnacha* (a thick tortilla), except spread with refried beans and topped with crumbled cheese and onions.

Tacos al pastor: Thin slices of flavored pork roasted on a revolving cylinder dripping with onion slices and the juice of fresh pineapple slices. Served in small corn tortillas, topped with chopped onion and cilantro.

Tamal: Incorrectly called a "tamale" (*tamal* singular; *tamales* plural). A meat or sweet filling rolled with fresh *masa,* wrapped in a corn husk or banana leaf, and then steamed; many varieties and sizes throughout the country.

Torta: A sandwich, usually on *bolillo* bread, typically comprising sliced avocado, onions, and tomatoes with a choice of meat and often cheese.

Tostadas: Crispy, fried corn tortillas topped with meat, onions, lettuce, tomatoes, cheese, avocados, and sometimes sour cream.

Making Dollars and Sense of It

Expense	Daily cost	x	Number of days	=	Total
Airfare					
Local transportation					
Car rental					
Lodging (with tax)					
Parking					
Breakfast					
Lunch					
Dinner					
Snacks					
Entertainment					
Babysitting					
Attractions					
Gifts & souvenirs					
Tips					
Other					
Grand Total					

Fare Game: Choosing an Airline

When looking for the best airfare, you should cover all your bases — 1) consult a trusted travel agent; 2) contact the airline directly, via the airline's toll-free number and/or Web site; 3) check out one of the travel-planning Web sites, such as www.frommers.com.

Travel Agency _____ Phone _____
    Agent's Name _____ Quoted fare _____

Airline 1 _____ Quoted fare _____
    Toll-free number/Internet _____

Airline 2 _____ Quoted fare _____
    Toll-free number/Internet _____

Web site 1 _____ Quoted fare _____

Web site 2 _____ Quoted fare _____

Departure Schedule & Flight Information

Airline _____ Flight # _____ Confirmation # _____

Departs _____ Date _____ Time _____ a.m./p.m.

Arrives _____ Date _____ Time _____ a.m./p.m.

Connecting Flight (if any)

Amount of time between flights _____ hours/mins

Airline _____ Flight # _____ Confirmation # _____

Departs _____ Date _____ Time _____ a.m./p.m.

Arrives _____ Date _____ Time _____ a.m./p.m.

Return Trip Schedule & Flight Information

Airline _____ Flight # _____ Confirmation # _____

Departs _____ Date _____ Time _____ a.m./p.m.

Arrives _____ Date _____ Time _____ a.m./p.m.

Connecting Flight (if any)

Amount of time between flights _____ hours/mins

Airline _____ Flight # _____ Confirmation # _____

Departs _____ Date _____ Time _____ a.m./p.m.

Arrives _____ Date _____ Time _____ a.m./p.m.

Sweet Dreams: Choosing Your Hotel

Make a list of all the hotels where you'd like to stay and then check online and call the local and toll-free numbers to get the best price. You should also check with a travel agent, who may be able to get you a better rate.

Hotel & page	Location	Internet	Tel. (local)	Tel. (Toll-free)	Quoted rate

Hotel Checklist

Here's a checklist of things to inquire about when booking your room, depending on your needs and preferences.

- ☐ Smoking/smoke-free room
- ☐ Noise (if you prefer a quiet room, ask about proximity to elevator, bar/restaurant, pool, meeting facilities, renovations, and street)
- ☐ View
- ☐ Facilities for children (crib, roll-away cot, babysitting services)
- ☐ Facilities for travelers with disabilities
- ☐ Number and size of bed(s) (king, queen, double/full-size)
- ☐ Is breakfast included? (buffet, continental, or sit-down?)
- ☐ In-room amenities (hair dryer, iron/board, minibar, etc.)
- ☐ Other_____

Places to Go, People to See, Things to Do

Enter the attractions you would most like to see and decide how they'll fit into your schedule. Next, use the "Going My Way" worksheets that follow to sketch out your itinerary.

Attraction/activity	Page	Amount of time you expect to spend there	Best day and time to go

Going "My" Way

Day 1
Hotel _____ Tel. _____

Morning _____

_____

Lunch _____ Tel. _____

Afternoon _____

_____

Dinner _____ Tel. _____

Evening _____

_____

Day 2
Hotel _____ Tel. _____

Morning _____

_____

Lunch _____ Tel. _____

Afternoon _____

_____

Dinner _____ Tel. _____

Evening _____

_____

Day 3
Hotel _____ Tel. _____

Morning _____

_____

Lunch _____ Tel. _____

Afternoon _____

_____

Dinner _____ Tel. _____

Evening _____

_____

Going "My" Way

Day 4

Hotel_____ Tel._____

Morning_____

_____

Lunch_____ Tel._____

Afternoon_____

_____

Dinner_____ Tel._____

Evening_____

_____

Day 5

Hotel_____ Tel._____

Morning_____

_____

Lunch_____ Tel._____

Afternoon_____

_____

Dinner_____ Tel._____

Evening_____

_____

Day 6

Hotel_____ Tel._____

Morning_____

_____

Lunch_____ Tel._____

Afternoon_____

_____

Dinner_____ Tel._____

Evening_____

_____

Going "My" Way

Day 7
Hotel_____ Tel._____
Morning_____
_____
Lunch_____ Tel._____
Afternoon_____
_____
Dinner_____ Tel._____
Evening_____
_____

Day 8
Hotel_____ Tel._____
Morning_____
_____
Lunch_____ Tel._____
Afternoon_____
_____
Dinner_____ Tel._____
Evening_____
_____

Day 9
Hotel_____ Tel._____
Morning_____
_____
Lunch_____ Tel._____
Afternoon_____
_____
Dinner_____ Tel._____
Evening_____
_____

Notes

Index

• B •

• *Q* •

• T •

• W •

• X •

• Y •

• Z •

Notes

FOR DUMMIES®

Helping you expand your horizons and realize your potential

PERSONAL FINANCE & BUSINESS

0-7645-2431-3 **0-7645-5331-3** **0-7645-5307-0**

Also available:

Accounting For Dummies
(0-7645-5314-3)

Business Plans Kit For
Dummies
(0-7645-5365-8)

Managing For Dummies
(1-5688-4858-7)

Mutual Funds For
Dummies
(0-7645-5329-1)

QuickBooks All-in-One
Desk Reference For
Dummies
(0-7645-1963-8)

Resumes For Dummies
(0-7645-5471-9)

Small Business Kit For
Dummies
(0-7645-5093-4)

Starting an eBay Business
For Dummies
(0-7645-1547-0)

Taxes For Dummies 2003
(0-7645-5475-1)

HOME, GARDEN, FOOD & WINE

0-7645-5295-3 **0-7645-5130-2** **0-7645-5250-3**

Also available:

Bartending For Dummies
(0-7645-5051-9)

Christmas Cooking For
Dummies
(0-7645-5407-7)

Cookies For Dummies
(0-7645-5390-9)

Diabetes Cookbook For
Dummies
(0-7645-5230-9)

Grilling For Dummies
(0-7645-5076-4)

Home Maintenance For
Dummies
(0-7645-5215-5)

Slow Cookers For
Dummies
(0-7645-5240-6)

Wine For Dummies
(0-7645-5114-0)

FITNESS, SPORTS, HOBBIES & PETS

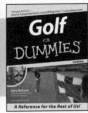

0-7645-5167-1 **0-7645-5146-9** **0-7645-5106-X**

Also available:

Cats For Dummies
(0-7645-5275-9)

Chess For Dummies
(0-7645-5003-9)

Dog Training For
Dummies
(0-7645-5286-4)

Labrador Retrievers For
Dummies
(0-7645-5281-3)

Martial Arts For Dummies
(0-7645-5358-5)

Piano For Dummies
(0-7645-5105-1)

Pilates For Dummies
(0-7645-5397-6)

Power Yoga For Dummies
(0-7645-5342-9)

Puppies For Dummies
(0-7645-5255-4)

Quilting For Dummies
(0-7645-5118-3)

Rock Guitar For Dummies
(0-7645-5356-9)

Weight Training For
Dummies
(0-7645-5168-X)

Available wherever books are sold.
Go to www.dummies.com or call 1-877-762-2974 to order direct

FOR DUMMIES®

A world of resources to help you grow

TRAVEL

0-7645-5453-0

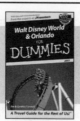

0-7645-5438-7

0-7645-5444-1

Also available:

America's National Parks For Dummies
(0-7645-6204-5)

Caribbean For Dummies
(0-7645-5445-X)

Cruise Vacations For Dummies 2003
(0-7645-5459-X)

Europe For Dummies
(0-7645-5456-5)

Ireland For Dummies
(0-7645-6199-5)

France For Dummies
(0-7645-6292-4)

Las Vegas For Dummies
(0-7645-5448-4)

London For Dummies
(0-7645-5416-6)

Mexico's Beach Resorts For Dummies
(0-7645-6262-2)

Paris For Dummies
(0-7645-5494-8)

RV Vacations For Dummies
(0-7645-5443-3)

EDUCATION & TEST PREPARATION

0-7645-5194-9

0-7645-5325-9

0-7645-5249-X

Also available:

The ACT For Dummies
(0-7645-5210-4)

Chemistry For Dummies
(0-7645-5430-1)

English Grammar For Dummies
(0-7645-5322-4)

French For Dummies
(0-7645-5193-0)

GMAT For Dummies
(0-7645-5251-1)

Inglés Para Dummies
(0-7645-5427-1)

Italian For Dummies
(0-7645-5196-5)

Research Papers For Dummies
(0-7645-5426-3)

SAT I For Dummies
(0-7645-5472-7)

U.S. History For Dummies
(0-7645-5249-X)

World History For Dummies
(0-7645-5242-2)

HEALTH, SELF-HELP & SPIRITUALITY

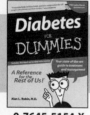

0-7645-5154-X

0-7645-5302-X

0-7645-5418-2

Also available:

The Bible For Dummies
(0-7645-5296-1)

Controlling Cholesterol For Dummies
(0-7645-5440-9)

Dating For Dummies
(0-7645-5072-1)

Dieting For Dummies
(0-7645-5126-4)

High Blood Pressure For Dummies
(0-7645-5424-7)

Judaism For Dummies
(0-7645-5299-6)

Menopause For Dummies
(0-7645-5458-1)

Nutrition For Dummies
(0-7645-5180-9)

Potty Training For Dummies
(0-7645-5417-4)

Pregnancy For Dummies
(0-7645-5074-8)

Rekindling Romance For Dummies
(0-7645-5303-8)

Religion For Dummies
(0-7645-5264-3)

Available wherever books are sold. Go to www.dummies.com or call 1-877-762-2974 to order direct

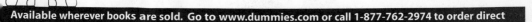

Helping you expand your horizons and realize your potential

GRAPHICS & WEB SITE DEVELOPMENT

Photo...

DUM...

A Reference
for the
Rest of Us!

Deke McClelland
Barbara Obermeier

0-7645...

Also available:

...DF

...ies

HTML 4 For Dummies
(0-7645-0723-0)

Illustrator 10 For Dummies
(0-7645-3636-2)

PowerPoint 2002 For Dummies
(0-7645-0817-2)

Web Design For Dummies
(0-7645-0823-7)

PROGRA...

C...

DUM...

A Reference
for the
Rest of Us!

Stephen Randy Davis

0-7645...

...ming

...r

...mies

JavaScript For Dummies
(0-7645-0633-1)

Oracle9i For Dummies
(0-7645-0880-6)

Perl For Dummies
(0-7645-0776-1)

PHP and MySQL For Dummies
(0-7645-1650-7)

SQL For Dummies
(0-7645-0737-0)

Visual Basic .NET For Dummies
(0-7645-0867-9)

LINUX, ...

Red Hat...

DUM...

A Reference
for the
Rest of Us!

Paul G. Sery

0-764...

...mies

Firewalls For Dummies
(0-7645-0884-9)

Home Networking For Dummies
(0-7645-0857-1)

Red Hat Linux All-in-One Desk Reference For Dummies
(0-7645-2442-9)

UNIX For Dummies
(0-7645-0419-3)

Dummies
(0-7645-1635-3)

Available wherever books are sold.
Go to www.dummies.com or call 1-877-762-2974 to order direct

 WILEY